HICKMAN POWELL

Ninety Times Guilty

HARCOURT, BRACE AND COMPANY, NEW YORK

Typography by Robert Josephy

PRINTED IN THE UNITED STATES OF AMERICA
BY QUINN & BODEN COMPANY, INC., RAHWAY, N. J.

CONTENTS

PREFACE   vii

i. MISS PRESSER GOES TO TOWN   3

ii. GIRL MEETS BOY   19

iii. THE PUBLIC GETS A MOUTHPIECE   35

iv. THE GANGSTERS   52

v. LUCKY   68

vi. A RACKET DISCOVERED   89

vii. THE GREAT GRAB   99

viii. DAVE MILLER'S STORY   108

ix. THELMA   143

x. THE GIRLS   164

xi. MILDRED   186

xii. ARREST   211

xiii. TALES OF THE WALDORF   219

xiv. TENSION BEFORE TRIAL   228

xv. THE RUN-OUT   240

xvi. COKEY FLO   248

xvii. THE POINTING FINGER   270

xviii. COUNTERATTACK   280

xix. DEFENSE   290

xx. THE JURY'S ANSWER   305

xxi. SENTENCE   311

xxii. INNOCENTS ABROAD   316

xxiii. WESTWARD, HO!   324

xxiv. APPEAL   334

PREFACE

In virtually every American city of more than middling size there is a criminal underworld, a community outside the law and ordinarily immune to the penalties which fall upon accidental and free lance criminals. It has survived and grown powerful because it is useful to large and influential bodies of citizens, in politics, in business, and in the providing of forbidden pleasures. It is a community in which brute force and money talk the language, and secrecy is the dominant law.

The underworld is well organized. Its strong men rise to dictatorial proportions. They are well entrenched in politics, in business, and are substantial factors in the lives of their localities, ruling with feudal power over those realms where the ordinary forms of social control cannot or will not function. Their characteristic gift to American life has been that form of extortion, or economic control, known as the racket. Often they are the strongest when they are the least talked about. Outlaws who are preyed upon do not complain to the authorities. Business men who take orders from unseen forces of violence, who pay vast sums of tribute for peace, do not go around talking about the men they fear.

Attention has thus been diverted to more spectacular and open, though less fundamental, forms of crime—the raids of desperados, the exploits of kidnappers. But even these are rooted in the substantial underworld. J. Edgar Hoover and

his Federal Bureau of Investigation have done effective work
in smashing itinerant bands of criminals, but their powers
apply only to certain crimes which cross state lines, and they
have been baffled by the local situations without which the
Dillingers, the Karpises, the Pretty Boy Floyds could not
exist. The rover needs his safe harbors, his protection; the
bank robber must have a place where he can dispose of stolen
bonds. These are provided by the local criminals who have
put down strong roots.

The underworld has been with us a long time. Its social
patterns developed in the street gangs of the great cities
during the Nineteenth Century. The gangs were tolerated,
even encouraged, because they were useful on election days to
the political bosses who held democracy in leash and bent it
to the purposes of practical men. As time went on the gangs
were useful to business men who found it inconvenient to
have purely democratic rule in the growing trades unions.
Then came Prohibition, and the gangs were tolerated by
everyone who was thirsty.

The twenty years after the war saw a mushroom growth
of the underworld, and the public has become more and more
conscious of its hidden power. Prohibition was the hotbed
which multiplied it overnight. Thousands of honest speakeasy proprietors and peddlers of bathtub gin discovered,
upon throwing off the restraints of law, that they had also
surrendered their freedom. They had become part of a world
in which there were no courts to fix, no penalties to evade.
The statutes were six-shooters, the constitution a machine
gun. The gangsters had moved in.

The gangster discovered, overnight, that he was no longer
a tolerated neighborhood thug, but a big business man. No
longer despised by all except his own kind, he found himself

regarded as a public benefactor. His interests spread over whole cities, states, and interlocked into a great confraternity with ramifications throughout the entire nation. For rum running was not a local industry.

Millions of dollars rolled in, plenty to buy lawyers, policemen, politicians, judges, with a big surplus left for other investments. The gangster was no longer a mere stooge for the political boss. Often he became the real boss himself, though he stayed in the background. He usually tried to stay out of the limelight, for those exceptions who got themselves talked about nearly always landed in jail or in a coffin. The outstanding exception was Al Capone. He was an exhibitionist; he flaunted his dominance over Chicago; he was not strong enough to rule without bloodshed; that is why he went to Alcatraz Prison for such a long time. Because he was a notorious gang leader, he received a much longer sentence than the usual tax evader. There were plenty of other big shots who were more discreet. They did not expect their tame judges to associate with them publicly or to attend underworld funerals, so long as they did their work satisfactorily in court. There were, and are, plenty of big shots the general public never heard of.

No big shot was ever more mysterious or more powerful than Charles Luciano, known to the knowing in the underworld as Charlie Lucky. In 1931 he became head of the Unione Siciliana in New York and in alliance with other big gangsters established a sway over the underworld in cities throughout the nation.

Considering the underworld's importance in our national life, considering the amount that has been said and published about it, surprisingly little is really known about its affairs. The newspapers have been unable to publish, or even to ob-

tain, a complete picture. They are bound by the laws of libel
and of demonstrable fact; and even so the partial facts come
to the surface only now and then, like brief glimpses of a sea
monster too fabulous for belief. The most complete presen-
tation of the underworld has come through the motion pictures; the gangster films, against carping opposition, have
done more than any other influence to awaken the nation to
the facts of life. But even Hollywood has had to trim the
edges. Considerations of censorship have made it necessary
to portray mobsters as reasonably nice people. A truly real-
istic film of the underworld would knock the Legion of Decency speechless.

During the last few years we have begun to learn something about the underworld, largely through the excavations
of Thomas E. Dewey, the special prosecutor of rackets in
Manhattan, who has now become District Attorney of New
York County.

Dewey made himself a big reputation by accomplishing
what was apparently impossible. He convicted racketeers of
racketeering; he smashed whole mobs. But for our present
purpose, it is more important that he discovered facts, let in
the light on hitherto unexplored regions of human society. It
is no longer necessary to guess, surmise, romance, and to sift
out the most credible bits from a conflicting mass of gossip.
We know what happened, from the lips of the participants.

Dewey's ultimate purpose was accomplished on February
25, 1939, when James J. Hines, Tammany district leader,
was convicted as the protector of the Dutch Schultz mob,
thereby clearly demonstrating to the satisfaction of a jury
the corrupt alliance of organized crime and politics.

Until then his most striking achievement was the conviction of Luciano, sentenced to serve from thirty to fifty

years in prison for the crime of compulsory prostitution. True, the vice racket was a small thing, so far as Luciano's enterprises went, but it was a racket. True, the sentence he got was proportionate more to the manner of his operations than to the specific crime of which he was convicted. But up to now the income tax laws had been the only effective weapon against the racketeer. This conviction was something new. Luciano became the first top rank American racketeer ever to go to prison for a crime involving moral turpitude. And the shock, the impact of this prosecution gave Dewey's drive the momentum that made it successful.

The Luciano case was not complete until the New York State Court of Appeals upheld the conviction in April, 1938, and the United States Supreme Court, in October, 1938, refused to review it. Up to that time the story had to be confined to the printed record. Now the case is closed. It is possible to tell, coherently, the detailed story of America's most spectacular criminal prosecution.

The facts about sex and prostitution used to be the exclusive domain of the preacher. All of us who ever went to a revival meeting can remember, I am sure, the evangelist's lush, fragrant visions of the plush-covered path of sin. That was hot stuff and it packed them in; and the Lord only knows how many millions of young men believed the ballyhoo and found the actuality disappointing.

Matters are different today. It is no longer necessary to be either romantic or horrified. When magazines discuss the pros and cons of chastity, when *The Ladies' Home Journal* takes a straw vote on matters of sex, when syphilis and gonorrhea are called by their right names in the front page headlines of the newspapers, then the old bars are down. Unsanctified folk may muscle in on the preacher's territory.

The Luciano case, involving a modern racket which preyed on the ancient institution of vice, constitutes a pictorial cross-section of American organized crime. As such, it is far more illuminating than any crime statistics, social theories, or fragmentary police reports. Even more, it is a story, the saga of Nancy Presser and Gashouse Lil, Jennie the Factory and Cokey Flo, Ralph the Pimp and Crazy Moe, Little Davie and Tommy Bull [1]—and towering over them all, misty, shadowy, foreboding, the figure of Luciano, like—

I was about to say like an evil genius, but I hope I shall not use the word "evil" in this tale. If the reader does not know the distinction between good and evil, it will do no good, I am sure, for me to tell him. The moralist, the reformer, the preacher, the student of criminology, sociology, or public affairs, each will find in these pages plentiful raw material for his trade.

For the story-teller it is enough that these people live—now, today—and that these events happened.

H. P.

February, 1939

---

[1] Underworld people are almost never known by their right names and people in the low life have a talent for assuming picturesque and rhythmic appellations. As the Dewey men combed through the underworld, they kept finding people with such names as Silver-tongued Elsie, Sadie the Chink, Abie the Rabbi. Many of them were turned up only momentarily and were turned loose when it seemed they had no importance to the investigation. Among these was a pimp known to all and·sundry as Jimmy Douchebag. Jimmy exists, I am convinced of that, and he may well be still operating in New York; but research fails to reveal any more about him and his highly original name.

CAST OF CHARACTERS

CHARLES LUCIANO, alias CHARLIE LUCKY, Number One racketeer of New York.

THOMAS E. DEWEY, Special Prosecutor of rackets in New York County (subsequently District Attorney).

NANCY PRESSER, racketeers' playmate, gun moll and prostitute.

RALPH LIGUORI, hold-up man, dope runner, and Nancy's boy friend.

GASHOUSE LIL, jilted by Liguori.

THELMA JORDAN, a prostitute from the Middle West.

BENNIE SPILLER, a loan shark, Thelma's boy friend.

JENNIE THE FACTORY, an old-time madam.

DAVE MILLER, booking agent for a string of prostitutes.

AL WEINER, a booker, who took over the prostitution business of his father, Cockeyed Louis, when Louis went to prison.

JACK ELLER, a booker, who took over Nick Montana's prostitution business when Montana went to prison.

PETE HARRIS, booker of the best-looking string of prostitutes in town.

MILDRED HARRIS, Pete's wife, a former madam.

FRISCO JEAN ERWIN, one of Pete Harris's sweethearts.

CRAZY MOE, a male madam and underworld go-between.

LITTLE DAVIE BETILLO, a ferocious gunman of the Capone and Luciano mobs, active head of the prostitution racket.

THOMAS PENNOCHIO, alias TOMMY BULL, old-time thug and dope-runner.

LITTLE ABIE WAHRMAN, head of Davie Betillo's strong-arm squad.

JIMMY FREDERICKS, front-man for the vice ring.

JESSE JACOBS
MEYER BERKMAN } bondsmen for the prostitution racket.

COKEY FLO BROWN, the smartest madam in town, sweetheart of Jimmy Fredericks.

GOOD-TIME CHARLIE, a pimp.

JO JO WEINTRAUB, lobbygow of Pete Harris.

JEANETTE LEWIS, Jo Jo's girl friend.

JOE BENDIX, a hotel sneak thief.

MOLLY BROWN, a Waldorf-Astoria bathmaid.

SOL GELB
FRANK HOGAN
HAROLD M. COLE
EUNICE CARTER } Dewey Assistants
BARENT TEN EYCK
CHARLES P. GRIMES

MOSES POLAKOFF, Luciano's lawyer.

GEORGE MORTON LEVY, Luciano's trial lawyer.

CAESAR BARRA, counsel to Betillo and Pennochio.

DAVID P. SIEGEL, Wahrman's lawyer.

SAMUEL J. SIEGEL, Fredericks's lawyer.

Various prostitutes, madams, pimps, gunmen, dope peddlers, racketeers, and lawyers.

Scene: Manhattan Island—its brothels, hotels, all-night restaurants, side-streets and courtrooms.

Time: 1933 to 1936.

NINETY TIMES GUILTY

I. MISS PRESSER GOES
TO TOWN

LEARNING A TRADE

If a girl wants to go places, see things, and meet people you read about in the newspapers, she can have no more effective equipment than natural blonde hair, pretty face, slim figure, high spirits, and low morals. Along that line Nancy Presser had just about everything. Before she quit school and got her working papers, Nancy waited until the lawful age of fourteen; but nobody ever told her about the age of consent.

While other girls of her age were still waiting to be kissed, Nancy left her home in Auburn, N. Y., got a job as a waitress in Albany, and discovered that a Senator who grudgingly tipped her a dime at lunch was eager, twelve hours later, to be far more generous. Nancy took this economic discovery on to Manhattan. At sixteen she wore orchids, went to the most expensive night clubs, saw the "Scandals" three times in a season, and got paid for it all.

Things happened rapidly in those days, which were 1928. Men stampeded in droves after common stocks and preferred blondes, and Nancy, like everything else, was going big. There were big sugar daddies galore, big butter and egg men, big brokers, big bootleggers; and Nancy, who rated as a big blonde, had her telephone number ready for all.

It is appalling to think of the years of prison eligibility

that were incurred by the big friends of willing young Nancy, for the statutory crime of rape upon a child.

She gave no warning that she was jail bait. Nancy had the dancing freshness of youth, but already there was a deep-breasted maturity about her, and a voluptuous fire that she got from a Polish mother. From her father came a well-thewed, big-boned Nordic body, fit for heavy duty. With it all she had breathtaking beauty. Men liked to be seen with Nancy. She was such a gorgeous animal, she dressed so beautifully, and she looked respectable, but not too respectable.

She wasn't really a professional yet. On arriving in New York, Nancy first got work as an artist's model and then as a model for hats and dresses. Her education progressed apace. Other girls taught her that her Albany wardrobe, of which she had been so proud, was practically rustic; and soon Nancy, except for her complexion, was a picture of utter urban sophistication.

She started going to parties, and there were plenty of parties in those days. The Arrival of Buyers department in the *Times* was Nancy's social and business index. It ran for columns every morning, and all the customers had to be entertained. Nancy had never had any idea, in the days when her girl friends were going to work in factories, that making money could be so easy, or so much fun.

For one reason Nancy was so popular was the youthful zest and enthusiasm she put into her work. That was before one of the older girls took her in hand and told her she would burn her life out that way, instructed her in ways and means to avoid a mixture of pleasure with business. Nancy took the warning seriously and began reserving her ardors for purely social occasions. It was then, I suppose, that she really became a prostitute. The men never knew the difference. She was too good an actress for that. She always took pride in her professional skill.

GETTING ON IN THE WORLD

Nancy's pay as a model soon amounted to nothing more than pin money, and it was really a bore to have to get up in the morning and go to the shop. She kept at it because of the contacts it gave her, but gradually she grew to think less and less of millinery buyers and cloak-and-suiters. Miss Presser had moved far beyond the social sphere she had known in Auburn and her clientele was of the sort to build up her ego. She had two steel executives from Youngstown who called up when they came to the city, and a toolmaker from Cleveland. She had gray-haired gentlemen who would pay her $75 to go to the theatre with them, and who then, having cut a dashing figure in public, would bid her a chaste good night. To go to dinner with a man, Nancy's price was $20. The big night of her whole career was an occasion when she was invited to the hotel room of an old dodo from the West. She stayed late, told him dirty stories, kissed the bald spot on top his head, and drank champagne with him until they both fell asleep in separate twin beds. He gave her a $1,000 bill.

By now Nancy was a busy high-class call girl, but for all the men she saw, she did not have any boy friend. She had not met any pimps yet and from what she heard of them she did not want to. She did have some girl friends whom she had met here and there at parties. One of them was a call girl named Betty Cook and it was through her that Nancy had her first inevitable meeting with the underworld. Betty Cook had a man named Charles Luciano.

This Luciano was good-looking for an underworld man. True, his legs were a bit short for his body, but he had a sharp-cut profile and crisp, wavy, black hair. He was, as Betty said, on the George Raft type. Betty regarded him with a mixture of infatuation and black fear.

Luciano was a hard character along Broadway. He was in the dope business, had some kind of tie-up with Arnold Rothstein and Legs Diamond. The relationship between Luciano and Betty is not entirely clear even now, and it is something we cannot find out about definitely. Betty long ago quit being a call girl and is married now (happily, I hope) to a policeman outside the state of New York; and she has never been available for any further inquiry, which is just as well.

Nancy saw all that she wanted of their love affair. She was eating with Betty one evening at the Tip Toe Inn at Eighty-sixth Street and Broadway when Charlie came in and joined them. Right away he and Betty got in an argument.

As Nancy sat and listened, anger boiled up in her. She had never heard a man talk to a girl like that, and there was nothing shrinking about Nancy. Managing men was her business and she had never stood in awe of them. She spoke up sharply to Luciano. She told him to quit talking to Betty that way. That was no way to treat a girl.

Luciano turned to her slowly, stared at her steadily, coolly for a while without speaking. She will never forget the icy black anger in his eyes. His eyes held hers as if by force. Now she knew why Betty Cook feared him like death. This man Luciano was full of pent-up force, and serpentine malevolence seemed to strike from his stone-like face.

Nancy got out of there as soon as she could. She said she was sorry, she had to be getting along. She forgot to take her change from the cashier, and she dashed down into the Eighty-sixth Street subway entrance and hurried aboard a train. After the train door was closed, she looked back, out the window. That was silly, for she knew no one had followed her.

Now and then after that Nancy saw Luciano on the street, or in restaurants. He hung out around Dave's Blue Room, an all-night restaurant in Seventh Avenue above Fifty-first Street, and on the sidewalk in front of Moe Ducore's drug store at Forty-ninth—that segment of the Broadway neighborhood which was to become celebrated in Damon Runyon's short stories. Luciano nodded casually when he saw her. She always smiled and spoke to him very nicely, but did not stop to talk. Neither of them had any notion of what important roles they were to play in each other's life.

THE MOB RELAXES

Nancy's contacts with the underworld were made in other directions. She quit her job as a model after she had been set up in an apartment by a fellow named Joe. He was a married man and Nancy has forgotten his surname, but he had a flower shop on Broadway, or at least that was his front. Nancy did not stay with him very long. Being a kept woman cramped her style, and Joe quit paying the rent when he discovered that she was having regular weekly meetings with two other men, one of whom greatly improved her wardrobe, "being as he was in the dress business." Though Nancy sometimes says she was a good girl until she met Joe, his only real importance in this story is that he took her on a trip to Hot Springs, Arkansas, and there she met Willie Weber, Chink Sherman, and other members of Waxey Gordon's mob, who were there for a holiday.

Waxey Gordon was probably the biggest bootlegger in the eastern states. An experienced member of Dopey Benny Fein's old east side gang,[1] Waxey was ready for action when Prohibition came along, and soon had a rum running syndicate with fleets of fast boats going to Rum Row, private radio stations, secret codes, and all the trappings of bootlegging romance. Later he went in mostly for breweries, and also invested his money in various legitimate enterprises. He owned at least three hotels in the Times Square sector of New York. Waxey was the bankroll for "Strike Me Pink," a musical show starring Jimmy Durante; and one night, with a gesture truly baronial, he took the chorus of the show in a private car up to Great Meadow Prison for the entertainment of the felons there confined. The warden is said to have been mightily pleased at this generosity and concern for the comfort of his charges. Nancy Presser went along on the trip, and had the time of her life.

Steel company executives were all right, but as spenders they were not in the class with Nancy's bootlegger friends. When she got in with the Waxey mob, she knew she was really in the big time. It was as fine a lot of mugs and killers as she could have tied up with anywhere. Mobsters were in need of entertainment, and Nancy was there to provide it.

There is widespread assumption, encouraged by a ditty of W. S. Gilbert's, that when a felon's not engaged in his employment his capacity for innocent enjoyment is as great as any other man's. The contrary is true. Nancy's friends were primitive, uncomplicated, untutored mugs, dripping with

[1] Dopey Benny was a pioneer specialist in the field of industrial gangsterism. There was hardly a strike for years in which Benny did not enlist his sluggers on one side or the other, sometimes on both at once. But he was a piker. He collected small money, and it never occurred to him that he might become the boss of those who hired him.

money, with very few ways in which to spend it. True, some of them were pigeon fanciers, followers of an engrossing but inexpensive sport always favored by gangsters. They could gamble. They could go to fights and, as some of them did, take over actual operations in the fight racket. They could loaf around in night clubs. But, while the normal man thinks of pleasure and relaxation almost synonymously with alcohol, the bootlegger had to be very careful of how he sampled his own wares.

The racket man lives under tension. Death may at any moment be behind his back. In such circumstances alcohol may easily become his master. And though criminals be tolerant in most matters, they will not long associate with a lush. Alcoholics lose their nerve. Drunkards talk too much. The drinking man becomes dangerous, and is likely to be disposed of with little ceremony, by means conveniently at hand. It is very easy to take a drunk for a ride.

Women, of course, were always there. But in them also the average man's pleasure was denied the racketeer, for he had too much of them. In sex matters, lacking a romantic attachment, the elements of uncertainty and pursuit are much of the pleasure. But these are absent when every girl is a push-over. When all a man's girls are as easy as Nancy, the joy of the chase just is not there. Add to this the racketeer's tradition, widely believed, that "a guy who won't go for a dame is yellow," and the gangster's sex life is hardly a happy one. The demands made upon him by his companions, if not by his own self-esteem, are almost superhuman. This combination of alcoholic abstinence and strenuous sex were the reasons why Nancy's friends went in so extensively for the smoking of opium.

Hitting the pipe, at least so the gangster told himself,

was not habit forming. If a man were careful, he could be a
"pleasure smoker" and use the pipe occasionally for an
opium jag without becoming a hopeless addict, as with heroin or morphine. A man was not charged up all the time. If
lodged for a day or so in jail he might crave the drug, but
he would not have the gnawing, crazy desire that would
make him become a squealer. But opium relieved tensions,
it made a man forget the dangers of life, it made him feel as
if he were walking on air. It built up his ego, made him feel
important. And it was aphrodisiac.

Waxey's mob were confirmed opium smokers and soon introduced Nancy Presser to the pastime. Nancy went to her
first opium smoking party when she was seventeen years old.
Being a beginner, she smoked only four or five pills, but
even that made her very sick. Not so deathly ill, however, as
the time she went opium smoking after drinking beer all evening. Nancy would try anything once, and has tried most of
them, but beer and opium smoke is a combination she would
not advise anyone to tackle. Alcohol and opium never mix
well anyhow.

The party was in one of Waxey's hotels, in West Forty-
sixth Street, and Nancy went with Willie Weber. Three
other couples were there, for the pipe was a sociable habit;
and when they all had arrived, the word was given downstairs
that the room was not to be disturbed. Then the door to the
corridor had its cracks all thoroughly stuffed with cotton
wadding, and taped also, so that fumes could not escape and
perhaps bring a crash raid by police. The windows were
taped too, as if for fumigation, and heavy blankets were
hung over the windows, to catch and hold the fumes and
keep the air heavily saturated. When the place was thor-

oughly airtight, the smoking began. Nancy thought it was really quite thrilling.

Chink Sherman prepared the pipe.[2] The opium was a gum-like substance which he had in a small can. In an alcohol lamp he would heat the end of a little metal rod, something like a crochet needle, and then work it around in the opium until a little pill of the gum had been formed on the end. This pill he would place on the bowl of the pipe. The pipe was a metal tube, about an inch in diameter and nearly three feet long; the bowl was a large, hollow pan-like protuberance near one end, with a tiny hole at the center. The smoker would place the bowl with its pill in the flame of the lamp, and, as the opium bubbled, would suck the fumes in through the bowl, slowly inhaling them. They all sat cross-legged at first, on mats on the floor, and took turns with the pipe, passing it around from one to the other.

After the first few pipes, the party really began to get going. Nancy was not shocked. She took everything in her stride, even in those days. But since on this evening she was more sick than doped, the proceedings appeared different to her than to the more active participants. Nancy, though she

[2] Dapper little Chink Sherman was the one who spread the notoriety of Dutch Schultz by shooting him one night in the Club Abbey, a racket hang-out in West Fifty-fourth Street. A Schultz man retaliated by cutting Chink seven times with a beer bottle, broken for the purpose.

Chink used to sit at a corner table in Dinty Moore's and speak with cloying politeness when he was passed by Police Commissioner Mulrooney, who would go on to his own table muttering his indignation. Chink infuriated the cops, especially one time when they knew he had killed two men in Los Angeles but found he apparently had been a conspicuous figure along Broadway through all that same week. They were convinced he had made a rapid airplane trip to California, but could not prove it.

The week after Schultz was murdered in 1935 (doubtless mere coincidence) a farmer noticed a trail of blood leading to a barn in the Catskill Mountains. A few turns with a shovel disclosed a fresh body in a grave of quicklime. It was Chink. He had been done in with a hatchet.

would not use such words in describing it, had never seen or imagined such slobbering, orgiastic promiscuity in all her life. Each man seemed to think he was Priapus himself, or a Casanova trying to live a whole autobiography in an evening. To Nancy, who was not without experience, and even though she dropped off to sleep rather early, it was amazing.

She was to learn later that opium smoking did not mean much to women, except to soothe jaded nerves. It made them feel lazy, sleepy, and acquiescent, that was all. But to a man, it seemed to swell and exalt the ego. It made him feel lord of all men and, more immediately, the unquenchable lord of all women. Whether it actually made him more powerful may be questioned; it made him think so, which served the purpose. To Nancy it always seemed that it magnified the effort and minimized the accomplishment, but whatever the men wanted was all right with her. Nancy, who later took to morphine, never cared much for the pipe. But she smoked often, for the social advantages. After all, it was not every girl who could be on such intimate terms with one of the toughest mobs in America. Nancy was even able to smoke sometimes with Waxey himself. He was a hard, flint-eyed man, but at such times he became almost human.

Nancy had practically made the grade, in one of the most inaccessible groups in New York Society. She was so appreciative of her luck that she operated in this sphere on practically an amateur basis. That is, her friends gave her presents instead of dealing on contracts. She was what was known in those days as a very nice dish. Her clothes came from the most expensive shops, and her furs were the best that could be stolen. Nancy lived at the Hotel Emerson, Seventy-fifth Street and Amsterdam Avenue. There were swankier addresses, but her social ambitions did not run toward the east

side, and it was a convenient business location. A fine retinue
of clients had her phone number, she was on good terms with
head waiters all over town, and had working arrangements
with bellboys in various places. In one evening she might be a
caller at a half dozen hotels and apartments, for a whacking
price at each. She could afford to take a night off now and
then to play with her boy friends.

Even so she would pile up a bankroll every now and then,
and would take a trip. On one of these in 1930 she had an
especially good time. She went to Hot Springs and stayed at
the Arlington Hotel and there, through some of Waxey's
crowd, she met Al Capone's brother Ralph and Machine-
Gun Jack McGurn, the gunner whose marksmanship made
the St. Valentine's Day massacre such a precise ministration
of death. She went back to Chicago with them and spent a
week playing around. They took her out sight-seeing one
night with a convoy of liquor trucks. As a visitor in Chicago,
she was sorry not to meet Al Capone himself, but he was win-
tering in Miami.

Back home, Nancy's contacts broadened. Two or three
times she went on parties at the penthouse of Joe Masseria,
known as Joe the Boss, atop a luxurious apartment building
in West Eighty-first Street, just off Central Park and across
the greensward from the American Museum of Natural History. Nancy didn't know much about Joe the Boss except
that his wife was away and he was a big shot in the Unione
Siciliana. She didn't know much about the Italian mob, except that everybody was afraid of it. She hardly realized
that she was treading the inner sanctum of underworld society.

Everybody in town knew about Waxey Gordon. He was
famous, a newspaper character. Hardly anyone had heard of

Joe Masseria. At one time Joe had been on the verge of no-toriety. During the summer of 1922 he was engaged in three pistol ambuscades on the crowded sidewalks of the city, one of them a sanguinary encounter within a block of Police Headquarters. The casualties of those fights were: wounded —thirteen men and women, mostly innocent bystanders, and one pony which was hitched to a lemonade cart; killed—one gangster, one bystander, one street cleaner, and one ten-year-old girl. Joe Masseria got two bullets through a new straw hat and two arrests on his police record. The arrests were no more effective than the bullets. Joe had a pistol permit.

After that summer of 1922 Joe Masseria had dropped into obscurity. Such a development, with a criminal, may mean that he has reformed or become unimportant. With Joe it meant that he had become too important to do his own dirty work any more. He was questioned after important murders, but the police had nothing on him, and the newspapers had nothing about him that they could print. He was Joe the Boss now, New York leader of the Unione Siciliana, a diver-sified criminal enterprise which stemmed from the deadly secrecy of the Sicilian Mafia, and which had its ramifications in all parts of America.

At the penthouse of Joe the Boss one night, Nancy found herself looking into a pair of eyes that had about them some-thing that was hauntingly familiar, and yet had a quality more sinister than ever they had in memory. The man was introduced to her as Charlie Lucky, and she realized she was talking to her acquaintance of two years ago, Charles Luci-ano. There was a scar on his face now, and a droop to his right eyelid which multiplied the somber ruthlessness of his expression.

Luciano may have been at the bottom of the social ladder when she first had met him, but he was mounting fast. Already he was Joe Masseria's right-hand man. The year before, in 1929, Luciano had been found unconscious one night on a lonely street in Staten Island, slumped down in a stolen car, his face slashed, his mouth taped, his head beaten. Straightway he met a degree of fame, as the gangster who had been taken for a ride, and who had lived to refuse to tell the tale to the grand jury. Men began calling him Lucky.

Luciano had not been taken for a ride in the usual way, but had been taken out and tortured by men who wanted to find out where the mob had a vast cache of narcotics. One version of the event has it that his captors were led by Legs Diamond, and that as part of the procedure Luciano had his forefingers forced into the barrels of a loaded shotgun. A version which seems closer to the truth is that the kidnapping was faked by officers of the law. At any rate, he met the test and refused to give up the secret. After that the men of his mob treated him with new respect. In such ways leaders are made.

Nancy was not abashed by his new eminence. She too had progressed in the world. But she treated him with new interest and regard. Here, obviously, was a young man who was rising in the world and marked for success; and Nancy specialized in those. She smiled in her prettiest way, talked her hottest line, and nothing was said of past unpleasantness.

NANCY INFLUENCES HISTORY

For the time being Nancy's big time contacts were mostly with the Waxey Gordon mob. She got pretty friendly with

Waxey himself. But that mob and the security of Nancy's social position were to disintegrate with the end of Prohibition and other devastating events of 1933.

When the federal government made beer legal again, in the spring of 1933, Waxey had either to go legitimate or go broke. He was loaded up heavily with breweries,[3] and they would be a loss to him unless he could operate them.

He went about the business of reorganization in an orthodox way. Obviously he would not need artillery to help sell legal 3.2 beer. So, the story goes, he notified his torpedo men their services would no longer be required. It was another case of technological unemployment. But the trigger men turned out to be less docile than other industrial workers who were thrown on the scrap heap in that springtime of depression and panic.

The headquarters of the Gordon beer syndicate was in an elaborate suite of rooms in the Elizabeth-Carteret Hotel in Elizabeth, N. J., and there was a visitation there on the afternoon of April 15, 1933, by a committee of unemployed. Gordon, whom they had expected to find there, was absent, so the deputation lodged its devastating protest with his two chief lieutenants, Abe Greenberg, who fronted for him in the hotel business, and Max Hassell, who ran the Pennsylvania end of the beer syndicate. Greenberg stopped five bullets with indiscriminate parts of his person, but a more delicate job was done on Hassell. He received one bullet through the heart, and one, neatly, through each ear.

Waxey dropped out of sight. He was so upset that he quit shaving. He was found several weeks later by federal agents,

---

[3] The blow of repeal to the alcohol and whisky men was not so severe. Taxes were fixed so high that there still remained an ample margin of bootleg profit on goods with counterfeit labels.

sound asleep in a secluded hunting lodge in the Catskill Mountains, while his bodyguard also snored. Waxey seemed glad to exchange this location for the greater security of a jail. In the interlude, federal men had wound up three years of investigation and indicted Gordon for violating the income tax laws.

It did not come out until long later how Waxey came to miss the committee which called upon him that springtime afternoon in the Elizabeth hotel. He escaped because he was in an adjoining room, in bed with a blonde. According to Nancy Presser, she was the blonde. She says she was never so startled in all her life.

Thus do trivial matters influence great events. The April impulse of a racketeer, at an inappropriate time of day, the incontinence of a convenient harlot, these changed the whole course of events in the underworld.

If Waxey had been killed that afternoon, it would have wiped out years of work by a young federal prosecutor in New York, Thomas E. Dewey. There would have been no trial six months later, and Waxey would not have been sent off to prison for ten years, as a sardonic exclamation point on the repeal of Prohibition. And if Dewey had not been the man who convicted Waxey Gordon, it is entirely unlikely that he would have been chosen, in the summer of 1935, as the special prosecutor to lead a crusade against the racketeering mobs whose march to power had ruffled even the blasé complacency of New York.

Big events often hang on such slender threads of chance. If that were all, this one would have been too trivial to mention. It might seem improbable that the stars of Tom Dewey and Nancy Presser should ever cross again, especially so that the two should ever meet. But life holds more improbable events than fiction.

It was to be told, years later, that Nancy Presser also was the girl who went to bed with Luciano, who had become the top man of the underworld.

II. GIRL MEETS BOY

SPRINGTIME IDYL

Prostitution is a lonely life. There are so many men who just come and go, impersonally. Even regular playmates do not take a girl very seriously. Nancy Presser needed a real boy friend, and in the spring of 1931 she got one.

It was probably some thwarted maternal instinct in Nancy which caused her to take up with Ralph Liguori. He was such a runt. Nancy was a trifle more than average size, and Ralph stood less than five feet two. But he was chunky and he was tough.

They went for each other the first moment they met, in a speakeasy one night in 1931. To him she was a glamour girl, friend of big racketeers. Ralph was flattered when she gave him the eye, like a freshman who has made the grade with a prom queen. Ralph was, he gave her to understand, a big shot holdup man, and he spent his money with a lavish masterful hand.

At first they had a date only now and then, just chippied a bit. Nancy was a busy girl most evenings, and Ralph was a roving free lance up and down Broadway. But gradually theirs got to be a steady relationship. Nancy for the first time had a real boy friend. Nature is a determined force, and when her major purposes are thwarted or perverted, they are likely to burst forth in strange ways with pent-up rushing force. Unsuspected springs of affection welled up in Nancy, and on Ralph she lavished them.

19

To other gangsters she had been merely a momentary plaything. But now she and Ralph seemed to belong to each other. He let her share his life. With Ralph, for the first time, Nancy became a real gun moll. His specialty was robbing houses of prostitution.

They took each other seriously. Ralph's family were respectable people over in Brooklyn, and his sister worked for $25 a week in an office in the Bronx, an hour's ride from home on the subway. The sister also took care of Ralph's little son, for he had a wife somewhere, and sometimes she gave Ralph money when he needed it. Ralph used to take Nancy home for Sunday dinner, introduce her as his girl friend, a cigarette girl in a night club. Nancy put on her most dazzling manners on those occasions; it gave her a little thrill to feel that she was bringing glamour into the drab lives of these home folks. Twice she took Ralph home with her to Auburn on vacations, and introduced him as her fiancé; and then did she hold her head high! Ralph had a big Cadillac car that he had bought second hand, several years old but still shiny, and they cut a dashing figure in the streets of Auburn.

GASHOUSE

But the course of love did not run entirely smooth. Ralph had another girl named Lillian Cardella, or Gordon, but commonly known in the profession as Gashouse Lil. Lil barged into Nancy's room one day and cut loose with such a stream of profanity that Miss Presser was quite breathless for a moment before she could recover her dignity and her voice. Then she laid Gashouse out.

"Just imagine," said Nancy to Ralph later. "Just imagine her talking to *me* that way. But I told her off. I ast her where she got off talking to *me* that way, and her nothing but a dirty two-dollar bag!'"

Gashouse was not a permanent obstruction. Ralph was getting fed up with her anyway. Madams didn't want to hire Gashouse any more because she had acquired a reputation, in the past, for working in a place and then putting the finger on it for Ralph to come around and clean it out with a holdup. It had got so Ralph had to get her jobs himself, go to the madams and tell them to hire Gashouse. They protested, but they knew Liguori or knew his reputation well enough so that they did what he wanted. But even when Gashouse Lil was working, the revenue wasn't as much as it should be. For she had got such a swelled head over having a tough gorilla for a boy friend that she was sassy with the customers, and wouldn't take the trouble to please them. You'd have thought she was doing them a favor, the way she acted. Of course that got around among the trade, and business fell off.

Eventually Gashouse got sick. She had to go to the hospital for an operation, one of those occupational hazards which a girl in the business encounters sooner or later. So she asked Ralph to cash in on a life insurance policy she had, to get the money for the hospital bill. He was glad to oblige, and he got Nancy to forge the endorsement on Lil's check when it came. He gave Gashouse $200 of the money, and used the rest to pay off on his car. He had traded in the Cadillac for a Cord. The new car was fancy, with all the shiny gadgets it could hold, and Ralph and Nancy could practically feel the envious eyes fixed upon them as they drove along Broadway. They didn't bother with Gashouse Lil after that. She was washed up anyway.

Liguori had the habit of sleeping around in various hotels, always under some other name than his own. For some time he spent part of the week in Lil's hotel, as Mr. Cardella, and part of the time in Nancy's hotel, as Mr. Presser. Gradually he took to spending most of his nights with Nancy. He was her pimp now, and regularly she gave him money.

GUN GIRL

Nancy also helped Ralph in his business. Even when he was not there, he kept his guns in Nancy's room, and before long, when he would go out on a holdup, he would have Nancy come along and carry the gun until he got ready to use it. Possession of a pistol without a license is a penal offense in New York, and Ralph did not want to take any more chances than necessary. But it made Nancy feel important to take the risks. It was thrilling.

The first time Nancy went on a holdup with Ralph was at Jean's Place in West Seventy-first Street. She took the guns from under the mattress in her room, and they got in Ralph's car and picked up his partner, a fellow named Johnnie. Nancy sat in the car and waited outside Jean's, while they went inside to do the robbery. There was not any great risk in that for Ralph because he knew no one from a house of prostitution was going to squawk to the police. That was a pretty smart racket, Nancy thought.

After the boys came out, Liguori headed the car downtown and they dropped Johnnie on Broadway.

"How much'd you get?" asked Nancy.

"About $200," said Ralph.

"Hey, hey, we'll go on a party tonight!" cried Nancy. This was easy money, this was swell.

"Nix, I don't get it all," said Ralph. "Got to report down

at the office. Here, take this but don't say nothin' about it."

He handed her a pretty little platinum wrist watch, set with small diamonds. It had Mary Lou engraved on the back of it. Nancy put it on and held up her hand for Ralph to admire. She kept it and treasured it always. It was one of the few presents Ralph ever gave her.

Liguori swung his car across town and down the east side, along Lafayette Street way down to Grand, then across past Police Headquarters and around the corner a couple of blocks into Mulberry Street. Nancy could not imagine what was the business at the place where they stopped. There was a dirty soft drink sign at the window, but nothing that made it look like a going establishment. Liguori went in, nodding to a group of hard-faced men who were hanging around the entrance. Nancy felt a vague uneasiness as she waited. Later she was to become well acquainted with the dives of this neighborhood, but never was to feel entirely at home. Ralph came out after a while, looking glum, not saying anything, and they drove away.

Gradually Nancy learned that, while Ralph was very proud to be tied up with "downtown," the connection was not entirely happy. To outsiders he might seem a big shot because he was in the Italian mob, but in reality he was merely a cheap jack of all work, an odd job man who was not even on the regular payroll, who was rewarded only with crumbs dropped by the bosses. Before he could go on a hold-up, he had to get the O.K. from bigger men. That was why he had depended on Gashouse, and now on Nancy, for money. The wages of crime, except for those who give the orders, are pitifully low. When a criminal organization is a going concern, it finds plenty of people ready to work for it

for chicken feed, just as youngsters working up in any legitimate business accept small wages for the prestige of the
connection and for the experience they are getting.

Protection, of course, was an advantage. Once Liguori got
arrested on one of his errands, and detectives beat the living
tar out of him trying to get a confession. Much as they deny
it, the police do that. One reason is that when they have their
hands on a crook, they want him to remember it; and the
chances are very good that the next day, in magistrate's
court, he will be sprung.

In this case a high police officer of the neighborhood had
a caller next day, a prominent politician of Tammany Hall,
who gave him and his command a thorough bawling out for
their treatment of Ralph. The police officer, who had not
realized Liguori was so well equipped with friends, was apologetic. The case later went out the window.

We have to slide rapidly and sketchily over this incident
because it deals with important people. To support the story
there are only Nancy's word and Ralph's word, and circumstances are such that they both would deny it now. Doubtless
the politician and other persons concerned would object to
having their names used with such insubstantial support.
Possibly the tale is exaggerated, for there is nothing that so
builds up the ego of people like Ralph and Nancy as the
knowledge that a cop is subservient or crooked. At any rate
the story goes that Ralph and the police officer became good
friends after that. They would drink together at a bar, and
it is said that once the policeman came to Nancy's room to
call on Liguori. After all, Ralph was a man with connections.

SMALL FRY IN THE MOB

After 1933 Ralph made fewer and fewer expeditions to hold up houses of prostitution, because the mob was protecting the joints, but there were many other adventures in which Nancy took part. Sometimes she went with Ralph and waited while he shook down restaurants on the upper east side. The downtown mob, it seems, had a restaurant racket which, though less tightly organized, was similar in many respects to that by which the Dutch Schultz mob terrorized the food industry in all the Times Square area. It had taken command over a waiters' union, which is no longer in existence, and like the Schultz mob put the squeeze on the employers by starting strikes. Liguori's part was to put the bite on the proprietors for $1,000, $2,000 or more to bring an end to their labor troubles. It was the riskiest role in the whole racket, so it was a small man's job, the same part that was played for the Schultz mob by Louis Beitcher, who collected hundreds of thousands of dollars shakedown money while working at a salary of $50 a week.

Two or three times Nancy went with Liguori and others to piers on the North River, where they got cans of opium that had been smuggled ashore from ships.[1] Nancy, got a tremendous thrill out of those nights, because they let her carry the opium, and told her to say it was hers in case the cops picked them up. They would take it over and leave it in a garage in Brooklyn.

Nancy had known all along, of course, that Liguori's mob were the big guns in the dope racket. Ralph always got her

[1] Along with Jerry Bruno, a big shot in the mob, and a drug smuggling ring including some night club owners from Texas, Ralph Liguori was convicted of drug running in a Federal Court trial in the spring of 1938.

morphine for her. She no longer smoked opium, but she was using quite a bit of morphine, a quarter of a cube three times a day. The first time had been one morning when she had a frightful hangover and couldn't sleep. Nancy's customers expected her to get drunk with them, and this time she had been fool enough to do it, in a big way. A girl friend gave her a morphine pill which put her to sleep and gave her a good rest. After that she used it every once in a while, and it became more and more frequent, for there were many hard nights in a playgirl life such as Nancy led. She found it soothed her nerves, and she was living on her nerve most of the time now. After a while she started taking it regularly as a hypodermic. She would take a small cube, cut it in quarters with a knife, and dissolve each quarter in water for a shot in the leg.

Nancy knew very soon, vaguely, that Charlie Lucky was the head man of Liguori's mob, that he had succeeded Joe the Boss. That is, she heard it vaguely. Ralph did not talk about Lucky at all, and she did not ask. But Nancy had plenty of people from whom she learned about the underworld. All during this period she was going out with her other friends, most of whom were much bigger than Ralph. Liguori, she had learned long since, was pretty small fry; but he was her man, and that was that. Once when she and Liguori went into a restaurant, Luciano was sitting there with some of his crowd, and while Ralph looked the other way, Lucky gave her the eye with a nod toward Ralph, as if to tell her he did not want them to stop at his table. Liguori, though he objected strenuously, was getting to be known around town as Ralph the Pimp.

Nobody talked much about Lucky. He was there. You saw him around, and he was treated like some sort of god, but if anybody mentioned his name he was likely to be told to shut up. Everybody in the underworld knew about Charlie Lucky, but they didn't know much that was specific about him, and they knew he was not to be gossiped about. He did not want it. Ownie Madden had got himself talked about, and the parole board had sent him back to prison. Al Capone and Waxey Gordon and Dutch Schultz had got themselves talked about, and were either in prison or on the lam. Lucky was content to be obscure.

MONEY TROUBLE

Nancy's friendship for other gangsters, big fellows, was one of the things that was to come between her and Ralph. For, sad to say, their boy and girl love affair was to turn to bitterness and a fierce struggle of wills for dominance.

First, there was the matter of money. After 1933 Ralph began demanding more and more of it from Nancy. When they first met, Liguori and two or three other fellows had had a prosperous little business of their own. Apart from his holdups, and the money he was drawing down from Gashouse, Ralph in those days had several joints that were paying him and his associates $25 every week for protection.

There were two basic ways of running a house of prostitution in those days. One was fly-by-night, hopping from place to place every few days to avoid detection by the hoodlums who would come to shake the joint down if they found it. The hoodlums would demand money, and if not paid they would take the joint apart. The hoodlums used only strong-arm methods of extortion; they would not threaten to report the joint to the police. That was considered unethical, and was done only by stool pigeons.

The other way of running a joint was to have a location

more or less permanent, and pay protection to a group such as Liguori's. Then if some hoodlum came around for a shake-down, the madam would stall for time and make an appoint-ment for next Thursday, say. Then on Thursday she would have her protectors there to meet the visitor. The inter-view ordinarily would be without rancor or unpleasantness. Liguori probably would know the hoodlum, and would merely tell him he was protecting this joint, and please lay off. Usually that was all. Unless he wanted to muscle in and start a war, the hoodlum would just take a powder. Of course, jurisdictional disputes often arose; and in that case the bosses downtown would be asked for a decision. Thus the system grew into a pyramid, with the bosses distributing territorial monopolies so everybody could make a living, like a political leader distributing patronage. Thus cohesive groups developed, with reserve strength for emergencies.

Nowadays everything was different for Liguori. The downtown combination had taken over the bonding of the houses, and the protection rights had gone to other fellows. Ralph was permitted to stick up a joint now only when it was not paying up properly, to put the arm on it for the combination. Even then he got only part of the dough. He had been crowded down to the point where he had small pick-ings. It was that way for almost everybody in the depression following Repeal. Some of the regular payroll men in the mobs, gunmen, got down as low as $25 a week.

But a guy like Liguori had to have plenty of money. He had to spend easy, like the others, or he would look like a crumb. Liguori liked to brag about the night he lost $38,000 at Saratoga, which everybody knew was a lie; but after that he could not lay a $2 bet on a horse, or Willie Spiller would think he was a joke. When a man was tied up with downtown, his bets had to run into real money. He had to pack a bankroll, even if it was the Philadelphia kind, of brown paper with a century note wrapped around the outside. Sometimes if Liguori ran short of money he would borrow from a shylock at the regular rate, six for five. That is, if he borrowed $100 from Bennie Spiller this week, he would owe $20 a week for six weeks; if you couldn't pay up promptly, that ran up into real money. If the ponies were running against a guy, the losses and the loan sharking drained off dough like nobody's business.

Ralph accused Nancy of holding out money on him, which of course she was doing, though she hardly dared give him less than $125 a week. Nancy was an independent wench, used to having money of her own, and the idea of handing it all over to a man never appealed to her, even if the man was Liguori. Ralph started to crab about the money she was spending for junk, which ran sometimes up to $50 a week when she was sniffing cocaine as well as taking her shots. He started buying her heroin instead of morphine, because it was cheaper, and told her to take it and like it.

THE GREEN-EYED MONSTER

Then Liguori started getting jealous. He bellyached about her running around with other men. When it was strictly business, that was one thing, but Nancy was a girl who played around. He bet she was chippying with a lot of those guys for nothing, he bet she was untrue to him. It was the old, old story of a career woman and her man. Nancy was far more successful in her work than Ralph in his. She could play around with guys so big they wouldn't even give Ralph a tumble. It burned him up.

Nancy, of course, was not making as much money as she

had been accustomed to. It was tough bucks in those days for everybody, and especially so for a luxury girl. Business men weren't throwing their money around the way they had, and many of her old friends had dropped out altogether. Prison, homicide, and Prohibition repeal had wrought great changes among her gangster friends. It seemed almost as if a century had come easier in the old days than a sawbuck now. Competition was keen too. A lot more girls were going into the business than there had been in prosperous times, and some of them were very young and pretty and were cutting prices.

By 1935 Nancy had got really afraid of Ralph. He was unreasonable. At those times when she couldn't work, Ralph said she was loafing. There was no satisfying the man.

Finally he said the thing for her to do was to go in a house, where he could watch her. He would get Pete Harris to book her. It would mean $2 from a customer, and half of that to the madam, instead of $10 or $20, but there would be more customers. She would have a steady income, for once, and it would keep her from running around with other men.

Nancy heard the words with dull chilling dread. For weeks, months, she had been fearing this.

"Nuts," she said. "I'm never going to do that."

Ralph dropped the subject for the time, but came back to it next day, when she told him she was nearly out of heroin.

"Lissen, baby," he said. "No more of that stuff for you until you do like I say."

"Oh, yeah?" said Nancy. "I got plenty places I can get that. You needn't think you're so smart."

One day Ralph smacked her and pushed her around, punched her in the ribs. She fought back.

"Say," she said. "You need your wagon fixed, and I know guys that can fix it."

Sure, she knew plenty of guys who could fix Ralph's wagon. They were tougher than he was. But down deep inside she knew, dully, that she never would ask them. Nancy had pride. She could not just imagine herself going to someone and saying that her man wanted to make her work in a $2 house, and please don't let him do it. She knew too it wouldn't do any good. She was Ralph's, and one man wouldn't interfere with another man's racket, unless he wanted to take it himself. And she knew no one but Ralph would want to take her for keeps.

Another day the battle grew hotter than usual. Ralph punched her, she scratched back, and he shoved her back on the bed. Then Nancy saw through horrified eyes that Ralph had drawn a shining sharp knife. She snatched at his wrist, and as they grappled, the blade cut an ugly red gash across her arm. It was weeks before it healed up decently at all. She still has the scar.

After that Nancy decided she might as well give Liguori's idea a try. Liguori saw Pete Harris about booking her, and though Harris was not eager to take her on, he yielded to urging. Nancy went to work at Jennie the Factory's place.

"So Liguori made you go to work in a $2 house!" exclaimed an interested lawyer long later.

"Yes, he did," said Nancy. "And he was mean and rotten about it too!"

A NEW ROUTINE

Nancy didn't like her new work. She had always considered herself an artist, but in this job she had no time for anything like that. It was routine.

Six calls had been a very busy night in the past, but this first week she took in 300 checks. A check was a dollar, and each customer was two checks. Nancy had a narrow blue card, and each time she turned over money to Jennie, the madam would punch the card once for each check. Some of the money was from $2 customers and some paid more. Nancy lost count of how many there were. It was all pretty much of a blur, and she could never have kept track without the blue card. It was like rushing the trade through a barber shop or, even more, like a shoe-shine parlor. Though she took in $300, at the end of the week after paying the madam's $150, Pete Harris's $15 commission, $35 board, and $5 to the doctor, she had $95 left for herself. She told Liguori as she gave it to him that she would never do it again.

He kept at her. One day he wrapped a wire coat hanger around her neck and choked her, and she doesn't know what might have happened if she hadn't managed to scream before it tightened. A passing bellhop banged on the door, and that stopped Liguori.

All through that year of 1935 the struggle waged between them. Nancy had her old clientele she did not want to neglect and lose; and that made it difficult when she was working in a joint all afternoon and evening. But some weeks Ralph was not able to get bookings for her, since the madams remembered Gashouse and hated Liguori. Sometimes Nancy was booked, but she just didn't go to work. Ralph dealt with the first problem as he had with Gashouse, by taking Nancy to the madam and demanding that she be given a job. As for Nancy's rebellion, he took her to work at noon every day and waited a while outside to be sure that she stayed. Even so, Nancy worked in joints only about a dozen weeks in all of 1935.

Toward the end of the year Ralph got worse and tougher.

He started complaining again about the money it cost for Nancy's dope, and one day he insisted she stay home and take the cure. Nancy was taken off heroin that week so rapidly that she collapsed, and had to be taken to a sanitarium in Connecticut for two weeks. Ralph was very mad about that. After she had been through that ordeal she was off dope, but in a weak condition, and much more pliable to Liguori's will.

But rebellion still was there. Nancy had figured out a way to hold out money on Liguori. Whatever the madam bargained for with the customer, Nancy had to turn over. But her tips she could keep for herself. So she worked for tips instead of just checks. The flat $2 fee didn't call for much; a girl didn't even undress. There were lots of ways in which Nancy could earn extra money. The madams stood for it, even though it cut down the week's gross, because the customers liked Nancy and she made good will for the house. Nancy liked it better too, apart from the money. It gave her some chance at self-expression, she felt less like an automaton, she regained some of the self-respect she had felt in her days as a free lance. But when Liguori got wind of it he was sore. He got so he would sit in the front parlor where Nancy was working and watch her. If she stayed out of the room more than fifteen minutes with a customer he would raise holy hell.

AN INTERLOPER

On the night of February 1, 1936, Liguori was sitting in the front parlor reading the racing form, at the place of Polack Frances in West Twenty-third Street, while Nancy proceeded with the activities of a busy night. She went in the back room with her eighth customer of the evening, and they had been there hardly more than a few minutes when there came a thunderous bang on the door. It swung open, and framed there stood a huge figure of a man. Nancy knew by just the looks of him that he was a cop.

"Put on your clothes," he said. "The joint is pinched."

Nancy moved slowly as her customer hurried out. Suddenly she felt very tired. Looking at her face in the mirror, she noticed that it was puffy.

Nancy Presser had done a lot of living in the last ten years. A small fortune had flowed through her fingers. She had known excitement, carried her head high, played with big shots.

Now she was twenty-four years old. She had a gnawing hunger for morphine. She did not know yet that she had a 4 plus Wassermann test, but there was a nagging ache in her side. She hopefully told herself that was not an abscess, but was where Liguori had punched her. Nancy was twenty-four years old, and she was an aging, diseased, two-dollar whore. In the hands of the law.

All this trouble, she told herself indignantly, on account of that damned Ralph Liguori!

Ralph was being pushed out the front door with the customers as Nancy came into the parlor. She had regained her composure now and walked defiantly. The policeman who had found her grinned.

"This is a good case, sergeant," he said. "Right in the act. Besides, I've seen her around a lot on Broadway. She's a well-known whore."

Nancy drew herself up into a picture of outraged dignity. She spoke sharply, imperiously, in the voice she reserved for house detectives and unpleasant head waiters.

"Sir!" she said. "Don't be so vulgar! The word is *prostitute*."

III. THE PUBLIC GETS A MOUTHPIECE

A DIFFERENT KIND OF GRAB

After her first few minutes of panic and high-pitched defiance, Nancy calmed down very quickly. She knew there was nothing to worry about. She would be out in bail within a few hours, and then the case would be taken care of. None of the girls in the bonded houses ever went to jail.

But this pinch was different from any that Nancy had ever heard about. They took her to the police station for only a few minutes, then put her in a van with two dozen other girls and took her way downtown and then high up in a skyscraper. There she and the other girl and the maid, who the cops thought was Polack Frances, were put in a large room furnished with flat tables and desks. A lot of other girls and madams were there already, many of them that Nancy knew, and more were arriving all the time. The cops must have jumped half the joints in town.

Everybody was being very stiff and formal, pretending not to know anybody else. Somebody said that this was the Dewey office, but that did not mean anything to Nancy. The only things she read in the paper were the horse race results and the pay-off numbers for the Italian lottery and policy.

The room was crowded now and there weren't enough places to sit. Nancy perched on a flat-top table, by herself, and looked about her. It struck her she had never seen so many girls and madams together all at once. It was like a convention. There must be sixty or seventy women in the room. Some of the girls had been given time to get into street dresses, but most of them, like Nancy, still had on their working clothes. They looked very wilted and smeary. Nancy took out her compact and went over her make-up.

Somebody whispered that Dave Marcus, Al Weiner, and Bennie Spiller were in the can too, and Pete Harris had been pinched over in Philadelphia. Some of the girls had been taken in for questioning and had heard about that. Nancy wished Ralph Liguori would hurry up and get her bailed out. But somebody said they had also arrested Little Davie and Tommy Bull, and even the bondsman, Jesse Jacobs. Maybe nobody would bail her out.

Nancy began to get the jitters. Something big, mysterious, and strange was happening. Nancy had acquired the gangster's hatred and contempt for cops and prosecutors, and cultivated an attitude of bravado. But even so she was upset. Suddenly she remembered forging that insurance check of Gashouse Lil's, running dope with Ralph. Other girls were being called for, taken out of the room somewhere else. She feared that. Yet she wished somebody would pay some attention to her.

"Take it easy, dearie," said old Jennie the Factory, out of the side of her mouth. "Everything's going to be all right. Just remember you don't know from nuttin."

Well, old Jennie could take it easy. One pinch more or less didn't mean much in her life. She'd been at it a long time. Since before Nancy was born.

Nancy suddenly felt exhausted, as though all the strength had wilted out of her. She was still weak from the morphine cure. She had most of the table to herself now, and she stretched out on it to lie down.

Jennie the Factory was sitting near by, comfortably tilted back in a swivel chair, snoring. There was a calm regularity, a solidity, a calm, lulling, reassuring quality about Jennie's snore. Nancy listened awhile, and then she also dozed.

Before she was disturbed, Nancy slept there for a long time. She made a slightly ridiculous appearance as she slumbered there in her working clothes, a plump blonde girl in a low-cut red evening dress and no underwear, with her heels turned up. Hardly an edifying sight. While she is sleeping it is just as well for us to turn our attention to other matters of more solid importance, such as the function of the grand jury in the Anglo-Saxon system of jurisprudence.

THE PEOPLE'S PROTECTION

In the old days of England, the grand jury was developed as a protection both to the community and those accused of crime, and as a positive instrument for hunting out acts of wrong-doing. At stated periods twenty-three substantial residents of the county would meet and consider the crimes which had been committed, or had come to light, since their last meeting. The peace officers would bring accusations before them, and the members themselves would report on those crimes they knew about. If the evidence before the grand jury were sufficient to warrant a conviction, unless disproved or explained away, an indictment would be voted and the accused would be brought to trial. To protect the unjustly accused, and to prevent alarming the unapprehended criminal, the proceedings were secret. Among its other strong powers, the grand jury had authority to subpoena witnesses and compel them to testify under oath, an authority which made it an even more effective investigating body than the ordinary law enforcement officers.

These same basic powers and functions reside in the grand jury today, but in the American states, with their vast routine of criminal prosecution, its deliberations have tended to become a mere formality. In some states the grand jury has been eliminated. In New York an indictment is necessary for any felony accusation, but the county grand juries usually do what the prosecutors suggest. Especially in a unit as large as New York County, Manhattan Island, with 5,000 felony cases a year, the grand jurors tend to become rubber stamps.

But in the New York County Grand Jurors Association was a group of substantial business men who resisted this tendency, among them a real estate executive named Lee Thompson Smith, who became foreman of the grand jury of March, 1935.[1] Just at this time the power and immunity of the underworld were flaunted with peculiarly brazen defiance.

J. Richard (Dixie) Davis, Dutch Schultz's lawyer and head of the legal departments of the policy and restaurant rackets, was called as a witness in an inquiry into bail bond

[1] A year earlier Mr. Smith had been foreman of a grand jury which took cognizance of various murders of policemen which had been blamed on alleged laxity in the state parole system. The grand jurors started under the impression assiduously fostered by J. Edgar Hoover and reactionary policemen, that parole is crooked and incompetent and habitually frees dangerous criminals. They were surprised to discover that the murders in question were not to be blamed on parole, and that the parole system was a valuable agency of public protection. In most states, parole continues to be merely a disguise for executive clemency, a means of emptying the prisons and keeping their budgets down. In other states, notably New York, the majority of prisoners continue to be released after a certain time, to live under rigid supervision and to be sent summarily back to prison if they don't behave. But when prisoners appear to be dangerous, the parole board uses its discretion to lengthen their sentences. Such judgments are necessarily fallible, and when the inevitable mistakes are made, the propagandists shout about the iniquities of parole.

abuses, conducted by Irving Ben Cooper,[2] special counsel to the Commissioner of Accounts under Mayor LaGuardia's reform administration.

Feeling secure in his political protection, Davis spent a brazen afternoon on the witness stand, and then he talked with reporters. Boastfully, and presumably to thumb his nose at Mayor LaGuardia and the police, he said the annual turnover of the policy game was $500,000,000 a year. The figure was as exaggerated as it was bold, but it had the effect of starting Mr. Smith's grand jury off on an investigation of its own.

Serious as it was, the career of the "runaway" grand jury was one of high comedy. It was soon at odds with District Attorney William Copeland Dodge and all his assistants, suspecting them of undue friendliness with Jimmy Hines, the district leader, who was commonly believed to be allied with Schultz. The grand jury excluded all the public prosecutors from its deliberations and set out on its own. As a legal advisor it got Samuel Marcus, counsel of the Society for the Suppression of Crime, an earnest reformer of the old-fashioned type, who soon found himself all snarled up in obstacles. He had a witness who he hoped would tell all about Schultz and Hines, but he couldn't get $20 from the District Attorney to pay the witness's expenses to the city. Finally Marcus withdrew in disgust.

Then there was Martin Mooney, a reporter for the New York *American*, who wrote a series of articles on the rackets, and was called before the grand jury, which demanded that he tell the inside sources of his information. As any honor-

---

[2] Mr. Cooper, now a city magistrate, was the young investigator who was responsible for a large number of the sensations in the Seabury investigations. As counsel for the Association of the Bar, he obtained the disbarment of Dixie Davis for his part in the policy racket.

able reporter would, Mooney refused to reveal them, which was a matter of some amusement to his colleagues who knew that nearly all of his sensations could be dug out of the clippings of a well-stocked newspaper morgue, or from the common knowledge of police reporters. But Mooney stood by the traditions of his craft, refused to tell, and went to jail for thirty days for contempt, which made him famous and got him a fat Hollywood contract.

VICE GETS THE PLAY

As usual at such times, the regular public authorities started stirring up a fuss about prostitution. The newspapers eagerly lumped that all in with the information about the runaway grand jury's doings, which was meager at best. The police raided the flat of Polly Adler, expensive call house operator, the best known madam in town. They found Polly and two beautiful girls watching a motion picture, of the blue variety, with two vice presidents of a nationally-known advertising agency. Reporters attending Polly's arraignment dutifully, and not without glee, wrote down the names of her customers. But all the newspapers refrained from publishing them, feeling it was bad taste to mention such prominent gentlemen in a matter of prostitution. So it all turned out happily for the advertising men, especially since the beautiful girls flunked their Wassermann test. Polly Adler had a little black book filled with customers' names; and, after studying it to determine whether there was any evidence of value in it, the magistrate destroyed the book. That will be good news to many of the city's men of property.

The cops dug up bigger fish than Polly Adler. They caught Cockeyed Louis Weiner and Nick Montana, thereby revealing that for years it had been the custom of New York bawdy houses to operate after the manner of vaudeville circuits, with a change of entertainers each week. Cockeyed Louis, a nearly blind old man, and sleek, sinister ex-convict Nick were bookers, competitors of Pete Harris, who booked Nancy Presser. They supplied girls to the houses and took a 10 per cent commission on their earnings, like any theatrical agent. Louis pleaded guilty, thereby quickly removing himself from the public eye. But Nick fought for freedom through two trials, before he went to prison for a long term, and thereby he became famous as the "vice czar." He was supposed to be the head of a great chain-store vice syndicate which had been broken up. He was the biggest of the bookers; but, as we shall see, he had been reduced to a mere $50-a-week cog in the system, and his place was immediately taken by his assistant, so that the business continued without interruption. However, that was not known until long later.

The runaway grand jury, meanwhile, was concerned with matters of much more serious import than prostitution. It became more and more convinced that there was an underworld empire, preying on the city, immune from the law. Influences of the underworld seemed to be everywhere. It was all-seeing. One day Foreman Smith decided a certain Tammany leader should be subpoenaed to be questioned about the Hines link with the District Attorney's office. The issuance of the subpoena was supposedly a close secret among Mr. Smith, the judge who signed it, his secretary, and a trusted process server. But within an hour after it was served, the subpoenaed Tammany leader received a letter warning him of dire consequences if he did not keep his "platter mouth" shut.

Plainly there was a link between organized crime and politics, though no one could prove it.

THE POLITICAL SETUP

New York County, Manhattan Island, is only one of the five counties in New York City, and not the most populous; but in power, prestige, and general importance it towers over all. Manhattan is the hub of a metropolitan area one hundred miles in diameter, it is the heart of the nation's finance and business. For generations it has been, normally, under the absolute rule of Tammany Hall; and by its prestige Tammany also has ruled the city.

Tammany Hall is neither better nor worse than the usual metropolitan political machine, but long experience and the immensity of its opportunities have made it smoother and less obvious than others. Tammany is basically a business organization and nowhere is there more thorough belief in the sacredness of the profit motive.

The leader of Tammany in these days was James J. Dooling, a decent enough young fellow without much power, an invalid during most of his regime, who held his post merely because the district leaders, real seat of power, could not agree upon a successor. The Hall had fallen upon evil days. It had emerged victorious in its own territory from the municipal election of 1933, but the other counties of the city had swept Mayor LaGuardia into power. Out of this situation, two leaders emerged as the Hall's strongest men, struggling against each other for power. They were Jimmy Hines and County Clerk Al Marinelli.

Jimmy Hines was an old-timer, long a guerilla leader within the Hall, who had fought the established powers until they bought him off with the concessions he wanted.

A hard-bitten ex-blacksmith with a firm handclasp and a direct eye, he had made himself master of the Eleventh Assembly District by helping the poor, giving their children a free outing in Central Park, and by cultivating the friendship of the neighborhood gangsters. His district comprised mostly the uptown lowland below Morningside Heights and the Cathedral of St. John the Divine, on the west fringe of Harlem. He also established his power over neighboring districts.

For years the first elementary principle of local politics was that Hines was the protector of organized crime, especially, as a jury has now found, the murderous Dutch Schultz mob. The second elementary principle was that nobody would ever prove anything on Hines. So great was his power and so secure his position that he became the acknowledged political representative and patronage dispenser of the New Deal in New York.

The other strong man in the Hall in 1935 was Al Marinelli, of the Second Assembly District, the old lower east side stronghold of Big Tim Sullivan and his clan. Marinelli's rise to power was almost simultaneous with that of Charlie Lucky, and was a part of the same resurgence of national spirit among the roughneck elements of the Italian community.

At the beginning of 1931, the year when Joe the Boss was killed, Marinelli was an unknown alderman from the Second, running errands and taking care of political contracts. Leader of the east half of the district was Representative Christopher Sullivan, and in the west half the boss was Sullivan's half brother, Harry C. Perry, chief clerk of the City Court. For many years they had relied, for election day sluggers, on the mobs of Mulberry Street, and the neighborhood toughs ran a gambling game in his clubhouse. But now in the spring of 1931, the Italian rough-neck element asserted themselves more strongly. Perry gave up his leadership and Marinelli stepped in. I don't know it to be true, but it has been published that armed men told Perry to get out. Perry has not said: Tammany men do not blow the whistle about such things. But a man close to Perry in that period has whispered to me that he was told to get out by Charlie Lucky.

Against the resistance of the old-line Tammany Irish, Marinelli extended his hegemony over other districts. He permitted Congressman Sullivan to keep his leadership in the Second, and in the summer of 1937 he had so increased his power that he made Sullivan leader of Tammany Hall. But everyone knew Sullivan was subject to Marinelli's whims.

At risk of getting ahead of our story, it is well here to consider certain happenings of the New York City political campaign of 1937. Running for District Attorney, Special Prosecutor Dewey concentrated his attack on Marinelli, whom he called the "pal" of Luciano and the "political ally of thieves, pickpockets, thugs, dope-peddlers, and big-shot racketeers," citing the police records of some dozens of Marinelli's county committeemen. Actually these thugs were pretty small fry, but the speech electrified the city; and after election Governor Lehman asked Dewey to prove it in removal proceedings against the County Clerk. The matter having become official, Dewey put his grand juries to work on it, and soon had evidence of the far more important fact that Marinelli had received privately, in conference at his political club, not only Charlie Lucky but also many others of the most important men of the underworld.

Dewey sent out subpoenas for Little Augie Pisano, Joe Adonis, Mike Miranda, and various other gentlemen of that stripe, who certainly had no desire for inquiry into their affairs. Within a few hours Marinelli had spared their feelings by resigning as County Clerk. But he continued to be a leader in Tammany Hall.

People wondered then why Dewey said nothing about Hines. The answer came six months later, when he indicted Hines as the protector of the Dutch Schultz policy racket. On February 25, 1939, after a trial in which it was shown that Hines had picked Dodge as District Attorney and elected him with gangster money, Hines was found guilty on thirteen counts.

All this was background of the picture the runaway grand jury suspected in the spring of 1935.

A NEW PROSECUTOR

By June, 1935, the runaway March grand jury had progressed far enough to know that it was barking up the right tree, but that its own efforts would never bring it closer than barking distance to the masters of organized crime and their political allies.

It decided to conclude its inquiry, and it appealed to Governor Lehman to appoint a skilled, independent special prosecutor to make a thorough investigation of organized crime in New York County. The Governor agreed, and called an extraordinary term of the Supreme Court, to be presided over by Justice Philip J. McCook.

Then there was the matter of a prosecutor. After some maneuvering, in which the District Attorney tried to appoint a man of his own, the grand jury recommended a number of prominent lawyers, headed by Dewey. The Governor offered the appointment to a number of older, more experienced men; but they refused to serve, and by common agreement told the Governor that Dewey was his man.

The Governor hesitated. Dewey was only thirty-three years old, and was relatively unknown to the public. Yet he had been United States Attorney and had successfully prosecuted Waxey Gordon. And he was recommended by the leaders of the bar. Finally the Governor appointed Dewey.

Tom Dewey had come to New York in 1923, a small town boy fresh from the University of Michigan, twenty-one years old, perfectly confident that he was going to have a great career as an opera singer. His home town was Owosso, Michigan. His father had been the publisher of a small weekly newspaper.

Dewey had won a state-wide singing contest while at the University and had placed third in a national contest. To tackle the big city he was equipped with a musical scholarship, a fine baritone voice, and a tenor's ego.

But even in those days he qualified his ego with discretion. He always liked to have an ace up his sleeve. While he studied voice and sang in a church choir to meet expenses, he also went to Columbia University and studied law. That was fortunate. Something went wrong with his vocal cords and ended his hopes of a musical career. Dewey merely shifted ambitions. Instead of being a star of the Metropolitan Opera, he would be a star of the metropolitan bar.

His musical studies had given him two things—he had married a mezzo-contralto schoolmate, Frances Hutt, from Sherman, Texas, who had made some success of her own as a singer in musical comedy. He had developed a speaking voice and diction which could coo and could roar. It could dramatically arrest attention to the farthest corner of a courtroom, and would be worth much more to him in court than it ever could have been on a stage.

Dewey's career as a student was not spectacular. In his first years at the bar he made no great mark for himself. He was just another junior in a big law office. He had indeed traits of personality which might have made him a failure. He was so sure of himself, so self-assertive, so insistently willing to take command of any situation in which he found himself, so over-brimming with energy, that he got in people's hair. Often he rubbed people the wrong way. Later, those same people were likely to turn out to be his greatest admirers and friends. It still works that way.

Early in the year 1931, Dewey had been working on the preparation of a case for trial, and his law firm retained George Z. Medalie, one of the town's leading jury lawyers, as trial counsel. After they had worked together for a month, Medalie was impressed with the thoroughness of Dewey's labors and the energy with which he worked without considering the hours, the pugnacity with which he went out and got whatever he wanted for his case.

On the last day of the trial, Medalie received an appointment from President Hoover as United States Attorney for the Southern District of New York, the biggest Federal prosecuting office in the country. He took Dewey with him as his chief assistant.

Dewey was twenty-nine years old and was to be in executive charge of dozens of men older and more experienced than himself. He had never tried a criminal case. He had tried very few cases of any kind. But he put on a bold front and made the grade.

The Medalie office made a brilliant success. This was at the time when Samuel Seabury was stirring up scandals about the magistrates' courts, Mayor Walker, and Tammany Hall, when the town was excited about racketeering, and when the County District Attorney's office was doing practically nothing about it. Dewey's first criminal prosecution was an income tax case against a vice cop whose nefarious doings had been exposed in the early Seabury investigations. He was one of the few characters turned up by Seabury who went to jail.

Medalie put Dewey in active charge of preparing cases; and the office went out after racketeers with energy that no local prosecutor had previously shown. After long investigation, Dewey obtained income tax indictments in 1933 against Dutch Schultz and Waxey Gordon.

When Medalie retired from office late in 1933, Dewey carried on temporarily, designated as United States Attorney by the Federal Judges to complete the successful prosecution of Waxey Gordon.

At the age of thirty-two, Dewey set up his own office and hung out a shingle as a former United States Attorney. In the summer of 1935 he was doing all right. He had an office in the Equitable Building, a reasonable number of paying clients. Summer Sundays he sailed in the races at fashionable Tuxedo Lake. In winter evenings he played indoor tennis two or three times a week or went to committee meetings of the Bar Association and told the big guns of the bar what was wrong with the criminal law.

As special counsel to the Bar Association, he had forced a judge from the bench, and as Special Assistant Attorney General, he was helping the United States Government collect income taxes from Charles E. Mitchell and others.

Now, at the insistence of older men, he had been given the special job of breaking the rackets of New York.

THE DEWEY APPROACH

Dewey had a definite theory and plan about attacking the racketeers. It would doubtless take years to do the real job. It had taken three years for the Federal Government to make its cases against Al Capone, Gordon, Schultz.

He knew that he would have to do something to show he was active, maintain public confidence in the expense of his investigation. But he expected also, he said, that his first prosecutions would not really be the important ones.

Dewey approached his job with a cool, calculated willingness to bargain with criminals. It was his notion that the small fry in crime were not especially important. Prosecutors for years had been going along handling police cases against small policy gamblers, for instance. There were thousands of cases every year against little people who were found possessing slips in the policy lottery. They were sent to jail, and it did no good at all.

Meanwhile, everybody knew that Dutch Schultz was running the policy racket. Everybody knew that the racket had corrupted the processes of law enforcement. While the gambling on the policy racket might not be serious, merely an example of eternal human nature, corruption of justice was important. Everybody who knew anything about it suspected that Jimmy Hines was the corrupting factor. The runaway grand jury had been very much excited about that. Everybody in town who knew anything about politics knew about Jimmy Hines. But nobody had been able to do anything about him. Seabury, with all his success, had investigated Jimmy Hines and failed to get anywhere.

Dewey's method of procedure was, first, to make cases against small people, even to make cases against apparently respectable people who refused to tell the truth about their contact with racketeers. Thereby he would force them to tell the truth. He was perfectly willing to turn loose a small-fry law violator if he could persuade that little fellow to open up and tell him what was going on.

Now he was following, indeed he was glorifying, the only method of police work that has ever been effective—the toleration of little people who can give information.

He had to be practical about what he undertook to do also. For instance, he knew that Charlie Lucky was probably the biggest of the big shots. But Lucky's rackets were almost exclusively the rackets that dealt with and preyed upon criminals themselves. There was almost no place where one could hope to break quickly through the protective silence of the underworld. A real member of the Unione Siciliana would let himself be cut to pieces before he would talk. And Dewey, of course, was determined that nobody during his investigation should be physically tortured, not even smacked around, as had been the old police custom.

As a practical matter, he had to strike at those big shots who were clearly the most vulnerable. It would be tough enough to get them. He charted his course especially to knock off Dutch Schultz, and Lepke and Gurrah, who had made themselves conspicuous.

Dewey's attitude was that he was ready always to let the small fry off easy, or even set them free, if they would testify or give information against a master criminal. In every such case, Dewey knew the witnesses would be terrible. They would be bad characters, subject to the usual attacks by defense counsel. But if the job were done thoroughly enough, if the facts were piled up sufficiently, if they all built together, interlocked, and dovetailed with facts proved through respectable witnesses, then a case could be proved beyond a doubt of any reasonable man.

It was a tough, courageous assignment for any man to take for himself. Any experienced lawyer knows that the defense to such a case, built up from such witnesses, especially if it is a good case, is likely to be an attack on the character of the prosecutor as well as on the character of his witnesses.

Coldly and insistently Dewey went ahead on that basis. He gathered about him the best staff he could find. Then he tried to make it clear to the public what he was undertaking to do.

He made it clear he intended to work methodically, quietly, secretly, over a long period, toward the exposure and conviction of the big men of organized crime. He patiently undertook to disabuse the newspapers and the public of the notion that this was another vice investigation.

"Hell," Dewey said, "I didn't quit a good law practice to chase after prostitutes."

IV. THE GANGSTERS

THE OLD GANGS DIED

A little bit north of the Brooklyn Bridge, a hundred yards from Chinatown, lies Mulberry Park, a tree-shaded square which the city has recently equipped with swings, wading pools and showers for the children in the summer. On this ground a century ago lay the confluence of streets known as Five Points. Off to the west, surrounded by marsh, then stretched a stinking, garbage-strewn pond called the Collect; the filling of the Collect was New York's first great civic improvement, a work relief project undertaken to quiet the mobs of starving sailors in the winter of 1807-08.

At the Five Points stood the Old Brewery, which became a tenement after it had outlived its original purpose; in its dark airless cells, from 1837 to 1852, dwelt swarms of Negroes and whites, in the utmost degradation of poverty and bestiality. Seventy-five men, women, and children were once found living in one small room of the Old Brewery.[1] There were children who lived for years in one room without going out, for the corridors were dangerous. Murder was as unremarkable and daily a commonplace in the Old Brewery as hunger, vermin, incest, and prostitution. The hardy young males who ventured forth into the streets met others of their

[1] These matters are well dealt with in Herbert Asbury's excellent history, "The Gangs of New York" (Knopf). It is still in print and is valuable, as well as amusing, background for anyone who would gain perspective on the crime problems of today.

kind in the green grocery speakeasies of those environs, and there formed the first gangs of New York.

Associations cling to neighborhoods. Throughout the Nineteenth Century the stretch from Mulberry Bend through Chatham Square and up the Bowery remained the center of the sin industries of the metropolis. Amid it all the gangs flourished. They were purposeless, hand-to-mouth aggregations of hoodlums, a brass knuckle and lead pipe crew of ear-biters and eye-gougers. They caroused and fought and pimped and held up stuss games, shook down the neighborhood store keepers, and made everybody buy tickets for affairs they held in Tammany Hall, called rackets. If fortunate enough to be offered the job, they would poison a horse or shoot a man in the leg for $25, kill a man for $100, or often for less. But generally they were feudists and rowdies, committing murder and mayhem out of group and individual rivalries, out of jealousies over women, out of plain general cussedness.

In the early days of the Twentieth Century, all of Manhattan was cut up into territories with rigid frontiers. In each of them a gang dominated the streets. The gang territory on the lower east side was divided by the Bowery. East of the Bowery, below Fourteenth Street, the streets were ruled by thousands of hoodlums, led by Monk Eastman, bullet-scarred thug, killer, pimp, opium smuggler, cat lover and pigeon fancier, later to be a World War hero, sentimentally recalled as "the prince of gangsters." West of the Bowery, other gangs ruled, chief of them the Five Pointers. The Eastmans and Five Pointers fought many a bloody battle over their boundary line around Chatham Square and Chinatown, for that neighborhood yielded rich pickings.

The old gangs had fallen apart, had fought their last wars just before the coming of Prohibition. But while the gangs died, the gangsters lived on. Enriched by bootlegging, they moved uptown. Crime began to become big business, and soon the outer characteristics of underworld life had changed.

The underworld is a fluid society. A high homicide rate keeps it always young, and there are no courts to preserve the status quo. We are still fighting in courts and legislatures about the modern trend toward consolidation and specialization and monopoly, the breakdown of local and sectional units in business and politics. All that happened much more quickly in the underworld. Crime has become as cold, inhuman, and efficient as industry; murder has become a matter purely of policy, discipline, or profit. The mug of today is not out to die for the dear old gang; he is a professional, in it for the dough. The crime leader is a business man, sobered and weighted by responsibilities. He is a big shot. Just as the old-fashioned neighborhood grocer is disappearing, giving way to the A & P chain and the General Foods Corporation, so the old-fashioned gangs and gangsters have vanished, to be replaced by well-articulated confederations of mobs working on an industrial rather than a local basis. The gangster of today is no longer a grotesque tough guy hanging out in the dives of the Bowery and Hell's Kitchen, but is a well-tailored, soft-spoken man of money who hangs out in the fanciest night clubs and lives in the best hotels. But the same sort of people, often the same people, are in the business. They have the same naive, amoral approach to life. And they come from the same roots.

THE PAST FADES

Long ago the Mulberry Bend district faded into a seeming innocence. The shining new limestone of the courts and public office buildings crowded Mulberry Park from the west. Papa Moneta's little restaurant was just below the Bend, through all the dry years one of the best places in town to eat, where judges from the courts would lunch on scallopine, white wine, and black coffee percolated over an alcohol flame. Almost any Saturday afternoon you could see a dozen or more small Chinese boys in clean shirts and neatly knotted neckties, under the supervision of a solemn young man, playing some decorous game on the broad empty sidewalk by the county courthouse; they were just like the supervised play groups in Central Park, only cleaner and better behaved.

Even the remnants and reminders of the old day were passing. Jack Sirocco was the last leader of the Five Pointers, but long ago had retired to more prosaic life. But for long years his place, Pearl Hall, was a landmark in Pearl Street, just through the alley from the corner where Cardinal Hayes was born. On the ground floor was Jack's bar, behind a locked door; upstairs lived his mother, overlooking a backyard garden of ailanthus trees; and the higher floors were a rookery of dark cubicles where dwelt a musty collection of Park Row wraiths and has-beens, who paid rent to Jack if and when they could. Pearl Hall has had its face lifted now, and is a valuable property, for the federal government built its new courthouse next door and Jack has sold out and retired to Coney Island.

As years went on Chinatown became as much a tourist commonplace as Grant's Tomb. The Chinatown bus stood every night in Times Square with two old ladies sitting in it, shills to calm the doubts of prospective slummers. The rubberneck wagon took its loads down to the Chinese Theater in little twisted Doyers Street and barkers told about the tong wars and the hatchet slaying and the days when the pavement of the Bloody Angle ran red. The Chinese Theater had long been a rescue mission, conducted by an ex-convict named Tom Noonan, God rest his soul, who had discovered that godliness is profitable.

With all the old gangs dead, with most of the old gangsters of the neighborhood turning into honest speakeasy proprietors, it seemed as though all the old criminal malevolence and general demoralization of Chinatown and Mulberry Bend had faded away. But that was before we realized that in the cafés of Mulberry and Kenmare Streets, just above the Bend, dark, violent plans were being laid.

ENTER THE BLACK HAND

Though the old gangs were dying, during the early part of this century there was a new growth of purposeful, calculated malevolence in the Italian segment of the underworld which had been made important by heavy immigration from Sicily. This was personified in no way more clearly than in the career of Lupo the Wolf.

Ignazio Saietta, known as Lupo the Wolf, killed a man in Palermo, Sicily, in 1899, and thereupon hastened to emigrate to New York. He settled in East Harlem and there struck up partnership with Giuseppe Morello, who with his several brothers formed the core of one of the fiercest gangs that hung around the famous Murder Stable in East 125th Street, a rendezvous for horse-thieves which was celebrated for having more murders than any other spot in town except the Bloody Angle of Doyers Street. Lupo married a sister of the Morellos, and together they formed a combination which was to hold power for many years.

Linking the past with the present, a younger brother of the Morello clan, who used the name Ciro Terranova, was to become the most famous of New York's Italian racketeers thirty years later, known as the Artichoke King.

With the Morellos and another kindred spirit known as Petto the Ox, Lupo the Wolf set up in New York an American branch of the Sicilian Mafia. With old Black Hand methods, this group preyed upon the members of the growing Italian community, and they were as murderous and ruthless a gang as the underworld had ever known. It was they who started the fashion, popular in that period, of putting the bodies of murder victims in barrels and trunks and shipping them away on the railroads. William J. Flynn, chief of the United States Secret Service, attributed no less than sixty murders to Lupo's mob, including that of Lieutenant Joseph Petrosino of the New York police, who had fought the gang relentlessly for years and was slain when he went to Sicily to look up the records of some of its members. In addition to attending to its own business, Lupo's gang hired out as expert executioners for other criminals. Lupo's name was one of terror not only because of his bloodthirstiness, but also because he was commonly supposed to possess the Evil Eye. The stilettos, revolvers, and bombs of his followers were feared no more among their countrymen than was their witchcraft, against which there was no defense.

Lupo the Wolf finally got in trouble through branching out into an unfamiliar line of endeavor. He promoted a real estate enterprise, and then tried to improve on his profits by paying dividends in counterfeit money. Federal agents found his counterfeiting plant at Highland, in the Catskills, and in 1909 Lupo was sent to federal prison, with a maximum sentence of thirty years.

After ten years of good behavior, Lupo the Wolf came out in due course, on parole; but he found the restrictions of parole irksome, especially since he wanted to make a trip to Italy. So President Harding gave him a conditional pardon and Lupo sailed back to Sicily. Doubtless with great exaggeration, it was commonly reported in the newspapers that he had gone to salt away there a sum of $3,000,000 which he had accumulated through the years. In a few months Lupo was back again, and was detained by the immigration officials at Ellis Island. They thought it clear he was an undesirable alien, and were surprised when they received orders to admit him again to the country. Lupo came ashore and disappeared into the shadows of Brooklyn.

One night in the summer of 1936, Lupo the Wolf was startled to be seized by federal agents, put aboard a train, and hurried back to Atlanta Prison. He was there almost before he knew what had happened; and then it was announced that, on application of District Attorney Geoghan of Brooklyn and Governor Lehman of New York, President Roosevelt had revoked the conditional pardon granted so many years before. He had been informed that Lupo was up to his old tricks, intimidating Brooklyn bakery owners and extorting money from them. Lupo spent his time after that suing out writs of habeas corpus. He and his lawyers felt he was a victim of unAmerican, arbitrary, and dictatorial power, but the courts held otherwise and Lupo remained in the can.

UNIONE SICILIANA

The new type of Italian gang typified by Lupo the Wolf's was gaining in strength and numbers during the early years of Prohibition. It no longer worked only in the Italian community but branched out to other fields, sometimes fought wars with the Irish and Jewish mobs which had grown up out of the remnants of the old gangs.[2]

The Italian mobs' chief contribution to underworld life was a dark and fearful secrecy. The city's old gangs had been a recognized part of community life, an adjunct of politics, and their leaders had been figures of public importance. In the old days the police and, to an extent, the public had known what was going on in the underworld, even though they could not prove it. But the Italians presented a blank wall of mystery. Outsiders did not know what was going on; and when an Italian was killed, the cops could not even get the time of day.

The word Mafia originally meant the general unwillingness of the population in Sicily to give information about outlaws to the authorities, and thus it came to be applied to the secret bands of Blackhanders who terrorized the people of that island. The secrecy of the criminals themselves was a thing awful to imagine, and it was this that was transplanted to America. Giuseppe Morello's own eighteen-year-old stepson was tortured and murdered because he was suspected of talking too much about the Lupo gang. Murder victims were found with their tongues slit. From time to time an Italian was found with his breast punctured a dozen or more times with the stiletto. The gang had formed itself

[2] The underworld commonly classifies the mobs as "Irish," "Jewish," and "Italian," usually in accordance with the national origins of their leaders. The membership of any one mob, however, is likely to be a racial mixture.

into a council of execution, and each member had struck a knife blow upon a faithless one.

It is this secrecy which makes the Unione Siciliana such a mysterious and terrifying thing. The authorities would have a hard time actually to prove the existence of that far-flung confraternity of crime.[3] The only way it could be proved would be for a member to talk, and a member of the Unione would be cut to pieces before he would open up. But the Unione is believed in by the underworld, and accepted as an ever-present fearful fact of life, with national and international ramifications.

In 1935, according to a man who was for years associated in racketeering with members of the Unione, the Unione Siciliana had 1,800 members in New York City, of whom 200 bore the technical designation "soldiers." Their function was to be ready for murder at a mere nod.

The Unione Siciliana is not identical with the Italian mobs, but rather an inner, secret clique of leaders which dominates them, and holds them in a sort of loose confederation with co-operating units everywhere. Its members are not all gorillas, but include men of high position in the business world. It came to public attention first in Chicago where it was spoken of as the guild of alcohol cookers, but New York was its seat of power.

[3] The name of this nebulous secret society is sometimes spelled Unione Sicilione or Siciliano. The common underworld pronunciation is Unioan Sicilian, the accents being on the final syllables. This is not the proper Italian pronunciation.

L'Unione Siciliana in Garibaldi's day was a patriotic organization devoted to the freedom of Italy, and the phrase has become somewhat a generic term referring to various organizations. The underworld secret society is not to be confused with the respectable organizations of Sicilians which may use the name openly in some cities.

The Chicago Unione Siciliana, which figured extensively in the Capone wars, is the best known; that in New York operates much more secretly.

The Italian underworld was strong in the East but it made its first bid for dominance over other gangs in Chicago. There the Italian groups, symbolized by the Neapolitan Capone, sought to dominate the whole show. The center of population was small enough there so that this was possible, and it was so new and brash that graft was open; the alliance between politics and the underworld was as unabashed as it had been in New York a generation before. It was all dramatic. Capone was big enough so that in the public mind he personified the whole Italian group, a single overpowering villain. Yet his opposition was still so strong that he had to fight a war, a bloody continual conflict through many years. If Capone had not had to fight so hard, he would not have seemed so powerful.

PEACEFUL PLUNDER

The growing power of the Italian mobs was not just a Chicago phenomenon. Capone and his mentor, John Torrio, both came from New York, and throughout the wars of Chicago the shock troops came from the mobs of Mulberry Street and Brooklyn. The New York underworld had a large share in the Chicago rackets.

The situation along the eastern seaboard was different from that in Chicago. In the first place, the territory was incredibly richer. There were more people, living closer together, and they had more money. There was enough business to keep several mobs from going hungry and minimize the temptation for them to fight over the spoils. Secondly, the old Irish and Jewish mobs were well rooted, with established political connections, and were ready and able to fight to retain their power. Thirdly, the cities were ruled by old, sophisticated political machines: each had an efficient one-party system of government and, as a result of reform movements a generation ago, the processes of graft had been so refined and surrounded with legal hocus-pocus that they seemed almost legitimate.[4]

In New York, Tammany Hall operated on the principle that what the public did not know would not hurt it, and especially would not hurt Tammany Hall. The police often did not know much about racket crime and when they did they were smart enough not to talk about it. Since the police are the chief source of crime news for the papers, the public did not learn much.

The Italian mobs had a large piece of the profits during Prohibition, but through all the early part of that period no Italian in New York attained real notoriety as a racket power. People spoke about the "Mulberry Street boys" but as individuals these were shadowy, obscure or totally unknown. Frank Yale, though he had a cigar named for him, did not become really famous until he was machine-gunned in the summer of 1928 as he drove along a Brooklyn street; he made good copy for the papers because he was supposed to be the man who had handled some important murders for Capone in Chicago, and because it appeared Capone had similarly accommodated the New York underworld by sending men east to kill Yale. A year later Frank Marlow, another Italian who had been high in the Unione Siciliana, also became notorious by being murdered. He made news-

---

[4] As Comptroller Morris Tremaine of New York State remarked to me in 1932, when Seabury was revealing the surprising wealth of Tammany leaders, a politician can make a lot of money with relatively little dishonesty in New York City, but one had to be very crooked to do it in a small town. Mr. Tremaine had just required a group of contractors to refund several hundred thousand dollars to the upstate town of Irondequoit, a sum equivalent to two-thirds of the town budget. A proportionate refund in New York City would have been $400,000,000.

paper copy because he was a well-known figure in the world of night clubs, prizefights, and race tracks, because there was a girl in the mystery known as Micky of the Rendezvous, and because the Police Commissioner at the time was publicity-loving Grover A. Whalen.

For a while police blamed the Marlow murder on Ciro Terranova, whom we have previously identified as the younger brother-in-law (some say nephew) of Lupo the Wolf.

Terranova, along with Lupo and other elders, formed a ruling council among the Sicilians, backing the leadership of Joe the Boss, Nancy Presser's old acquaintance. But all these things were so mysterious and so little known that they did not make Ciro important in the public eye. Ciro became famous while he was alive because someone dubbed him the Artichoke King, after the small pickling artichokes for Italian antipasto which were an important item in his produce rackets. That identified Ciro for the public and made him memorable, and he also had a $52,000 pink stucco villa on Peace Street, Pelham Manor, for the press to photograph and discuss. Such is fame.

Later police said that Marlow's death had been ordered by "the head of an Italian secret society" which had recently "disrobed" him. That obviously meant Joe the Boss; but some weeks later, when Joe dropped in to see the cops, they merely questioned him for a while and let him go. They had nothing on Joe except rumor and underworld information; and, since nobody had thought to nickname Joe after a vegetable, he did not attract much attention.

Ciro Terranova, the Artichoke King, however, was to attain a legitimate place in history. In the autumn of 1929, he was the patron of a political club's dinner and entertainment, and was sitting in a box with Magistrate Albert Vitale when gunmen entered, held up the party, and seized the personal effects of various guests, including the pistol of Detective Johnson of the New York police. There seemed to be something screwy about that holdup, because an hour later Detective Johnson's revolver was returned to him by none other than Judge Vitale.

Police Commissioner Whalen charged that Terranova had engineered the holdup in order to obtain a paper in the possession of a Chicago gangster who was present. The paper, said Whalen, was a signed contract in which Terranova agreed to pay $20,000 for the murders of Yale and Marlow. That story never rang true, and the matter still remains a mystery.

But the Terranova dinner started an important chain of events. It caused the investigation and removal of Magistrate Vitale from office, which led to a general investigation of the magistrates' courts, then the Seabury inquiry into the whole city government, the fall of Mayor James J. Walker, and the election of Mayor Fiorello H. LaGuardia— an Italian who represented everything antithetical to what Terranova, Luciano, and all their crowd stood for. Out of that series of events, almost a grand climax, grew the onslaught on the underworld.

THE HUNDRED PERCENTERS

In May, 1929, Al Capone went to a peace conference in Atlantic City. For years he had been warring with the old Irish and Jewish mobs of Chicago, warring also on occasion with the Unione Siciliana of which he was not a member. The last year had been bloody. There had been the killing of Frank Yale in Brooklyn, the St. Valentine's Day massacre in Chicago, and various minor killings. Frankie Costello, the slot machine man, who has never been one to encourage violence, arranged the meeting and spent $25,000 of his own money on it. Various gang chieftains were entertained for several days at the Hotel President.

The aim of the Atlantic City conference was to establish peaceful co-operation in the underworld instead of warfare. One disturbing element had been a group commonly called "greasers" who were very influential in the Unione Siciliana —old-line, unassimilated Italian leaders and recent immigrants. Out of that conference grew the movement to modernize the underworld or, as some expressed the idea, to Americanize the mobs.

The day after the Atlantic City peace conference, Capone was arrested in Philadelphia for having a pistol in his pocket, and was sentenced to serve a year in jail. He was locked up until March, 1930, and real developments were considerably delayed. It was not until March, 1931, a full year later, that the Americanization of the underworld really got started. The men responsible had been laying their plans, making their preparations, and gathering their gunmen.

Late one night in March, 1931, Joe the Boss, leader of the Unione Siciliana, was leaving an apartment house in the Bronx. From a clump of shrubbery came an outburst of bullets. Joe's luck stood by him as it had in those old gun fights in the streets in 1922. This time his two bodyguards were killed, but not a bullet struck Joe.

A month later, on April 15, 1931, Joe went out in his armored car to a slick new spaghetti joint which Gerardo Scarpato had opened in a shabby street of Coney Island. How he came to go there, we do not know. He was playing

cards at a table in the restaurant when a band of executioners entered and fired twenty shots. Five of them hit Joe
the Boss.

Joe was there alone when the cops arrived, dead, with
the ace of diamonds clutched in his right hand. Plainly his
bodyguards had departed in a hurry without joining in the
hostilities. Their brand new fedoras still hung on the hat-
rack, and their two .38 revolvers had been thrown away in
the alley behind the restaurant. They had not been fired.

The news of Joe's death was the first his neighbors around
Central Park West knew that they had such a distinguished
man among them; and West Eighty-first Street was so
crowded with children, and nursemaids, and women in smart
spring outfits that it took fifty policemen to keep the way
clear for the funeral. Joe's obsequies were expensive. He
had a $15,000 coffin, and forty Cadillacs were in his funeral
procession, sixteen of them loaded with flowers—crosses of
lilies, ten feet high, great clocks of lilies and roses, with the
hands pointing to 3:20, the hour at which Joe had been
knocked off. But as the cortege moved to the Church of
Mary Help of Christians for the requiem mass, and then
on to the family vault in a Queens cemetery, ten of the cars
were empty. The honorary pallbearers, the men of the underworld, had stayed away.

The murder of Joe the Boss did not make much of a
sensation. The newspapers knew he was big, and said so,
but they did not know enough about his business or personal affairs to write much about him, and what the police
knew they did not tell. The murder remained a mystery.
During the next few weeks, there were several other mysterious Italian murders. Scarpato, in whose restaurant Joe
died, told the cops he had been out for a walk when the

shooting occurred; and shortly after this he abandoned his business and went to Sicily. Probably he knew something. When he returned to New York a year later, he was quietly strangled.

With the passing of Joe the Boss, a new era had dawned in the underworld.

V. LUCKY

SUCCESSOR

The murder of Joe the Boss remained a mystery but it soon became clear that the chief beneficiary was Charlie Lucky, Charles Luciano, Joe's erstwhile bodyguard and right-hand man. Charlie had been absent the night of the shooting in the Bronx when Joe's bodyguards were shot down. On the afternoon when Joe was killed in Coney Island, it is said, Charlie had gone to the washroom just before the shooting began. From then on he mounted in power. He was a very lucky fellow. He also had foresight.

A bodyguard should not have too much brains, and Joe the Boss made a mistake when he picked Lucky. For years Charlie had been more than a bodyguard—more and more a privy councilor firmly located at the seat of power. Charlie had not confined his friendships to the Italian mobsters but had strong contacts outside the Unione Siciliana. I have been told that he was present at the Al Capone peace conference in Atlantic City. Whether that is actually true, I do not know. It is clear, however, that in later years he was close to Capone and closer still to others who were rising to succeed Capone in racket power. For leader of the Italian gangs, Lucky was the candidate of those who were out to "Americanize" the underworld.

STREET GAMIN

Lucky's real name was Salvatore Lucania. He was born in Sicily and brought to New York in 1907, when he was nine years old. He lived with his parents, two brothers, and a sister, on First Avenue just south of Fourteenth Street, enrolled in public school, and played truant with regularity. At fourteen he quit school and went to work at $5 a week as a shipping clerk in a hat factory, but soon found it more pleasant and profitable to hang around crap games.

He grew up on the rim of the lower east side, a black-eyed gamin ranging the streets of as fabulous a slum as the world has ever known. Never, I am sure, has there been such a city, such a conglomeration of vice, of virtue, of plain human energy, as that huddled mass of stinking tenements, that maze of crowded streets, roaring with elevated trains, jammed with pushcarts, bedraggled with washing on the line. We say very easily that the congested areas breed criminals. They also breed strong men to conquer, idealists to preach. From Lucky's school came reformers and judges, artists and musicians, pickpockets and racketeers.

What immediate set of circumstances caused him to pick his set of ideals and associates, instead of others, we do not know. He might easily have wandered two blocks westward to Union Square and joined in with the Socialist movement which was so active there in his youth. The youngster very soon observed the people around his neighborhood. They did not look to him like downtrodden masses. They looked like crumbs.

They worked hard, for small money, when they could get work. They skimped and saved, but even then the wolf was near the door. Their only social security was the Tammany leader, who provided a basket of food when necessary, kept their children out of jail, and on election day collected their votes. But there were fellows hanging around the street corner and the pool room who were not crumbs. They wore flashy clothes, had money to spend, called the Tammany captain by his first name, and never did any work.

"I never wanted to be a crumb," said the unregenerate Lucky in later years, when he had occasion to expound his philosophy of life. "If I had to be a crumb, I'd rather be dead."

TO MULBERRY STREET

The neighborhood where young Lucky lived was in the territory which had been ruled by Monk Eastman. But it was at the other end of the Bowery, down around Mulberry Bend where the Five Points gang hung out, that the youngster found kindred spirits. He started wandering down there before he was wearing long pants. The leader of the Five Points gang in those days was Paul Kelly, an Italian, the first one ever to rise to real leadership in the gang world of New York.[1] Among the tough boys of Mulberry Street he soon found ways of living without work.

Distinctions of race and nationality are necessary in any objective discussion of cosmopolitan New York life, for the city is organized along racial lines, in business, in politics, and also in the underworld. When the early English settlers came to America, they brought plenty of London riffraff with them who formed the early criminal class. It was

[1] Italian gangsters and prizefighters have long had a custom of adopting Irish names. Why, I do not know. Perhaps it was because in the early days of the gangs around Mulberry Bend, the Italians were only a slight sprinkling among many Irish, and the adoption of Irish names was an attempt to compensate the numerical inferiority of their race.

poverty-stricken Irish, breeding in the unspeakable slums of the Old Brewery and Cow Bay, whose sons banded into the first rowdy, brawling street gangs of New York. Later the wave of Jewish immigration brought its own criminals, and so also the Italian. The most criminal class in the United States are the "native" Americans. Stemming from the old feudists and cattle rustlers, they predominate in the prisons. The most notorious desperado bands of recent years, such as those of Dillinger, the Barkers, the Barrows, came from the good old American stock of the western hills and plains. But the American of predatory disposition, if he has executive ability and dominating personality, is likely to end up in Wall Street. With the same qualifications, your son of more recent immigration, bred in the streets and educated in a reformatory, turns up as a racket man. This story happens to deal with an Italian.

Through outside alliances, young Lucania was to become the greatest leader of the Italian underworld. Like Mussolini, he was to cut the Italians in on rackets they had never touched before, and bring the Italian mobs to new stature among gangs led by men of other races.

THE RISE OF LUCKY

Charlie Luciano never was a crumb after his first few weeks as a shipping clerk. From then on he was an apprentice in crime. He was first arrested when he was eighteen, after he had started peddling dope for Big Nose Charlie. He went to the reformatory for six months, and after that he was a certified, confirmed criminal. As he marched on toward the top in the underworld, he was frequently arrested, but it never amounted to more than a few days' detention.

There are only occasional glimpses of him in his early years. He acquired a taste for silk underwear, heavy gambling, and fine cars. He got a ticket several times a year for passing a red light or for other traffic violations. Every two or three years he would be picked up on some charge involving narcotics or a gun. In 1923 he made the mistake of selling morphine to a federal stool pigeon and was arrested, but he avoided prosecution by informing the narcotic agents of a trunk full of opium which was hidden on Mulberry Street. The men who owned that opium did not learn, until twelve years later, how it was they were detected. He always gave his name to the cops as Charles Lucania, but they knew him as Luciano.

Lucky's specialties were narcotics and gambling. He was a gunman himself and, as he accumulated a bankroll, he gathered followers around him. He had qualities of leadership. He was of phlegmatic disposition, calm and firm in times of danger, never emotional or flighty as were so many of his Latin confreres. He spoke slowly and always thought before he spoke. Ruthless with his enemies, he was, like any good politician, one who would go down the line for his friends. He was never stingy with his money, but cultivated the free and easy generosity of the gambler. That made him popular.

ROMANCE

As an up and coming young man in the Unione Siciliana, Lucky had a piece of the war in Chicago. And that is said to be what really put him up among the top men. Whether he actually went to Chicago and took part personally in the hostilities, I do not know. But New York City was a reservoir of trigger men and supplied them for the Chicago fighting.

One of the trigger men who went to Chicago was a youngster known as Little Davie Betillo, whom Lucky had known as a kid along Mulberry Street. This Little Davie had been first arrested in 1919 when at the age of eleven he stole a handbag containing $1,500 worth of jewelry from a store. Two years later he had been picked up trundling four bottles of liquor along the street in a pushcart. After that he had developed into a pickpocket, gambler, and gunman.

Little Davie spent four years in Chicago and came back to New York just before the murder of Joe the Boss, to cash in on a reputation of having been one of Al Capone's most desperate torpedoes. He was an egocentric, vicious little fellow, though mild enough in appearance, and he spread fear wherever he went. People told Lucky that Little Davie ought to be knocked off, but Little Davie was useful and Lucky liked him.

Another of Lucky's tie-ups with Chicago was a kinsman who was a boss out there; and the reason we know about that is through the matrimonial troubles of an Italian gunman named Tommy Ryan. Ryan was out fighting in the Chicago war and while there he secretly married the daughter of Lucky's kinsman. But almost immediately thereafter he was ordered to go back East as the town was getting hot. Back home he forgot all about his war bride and settled down for the time being to a comparatively peaceful life. But the Chicago girl had not forgotten, and she rose to haunt him just about the time he was going to marry another girl in New York. Ryan was now one of the leaders of a small mob protecting houses of prostitution and other joints, and much to the dismay of his partners he got to taking mysterious airplane trips to Chicago. Frequently they had to call him up on the telephone and hurry him back to New York when there was trouble to be taken care of, and they got fed up with that. Finally, he confessed that he had been in Chicago getting married again. Lucky himself had reminded him of his old liaison and informed him that one of two things was going to happen to the Chicago wife. She either was going to be a real bride, with veil, flowers, cake, priest, and a bridegroom in a dress suit, or she was going to be a widow. Ryan was allowed to take his pick and had accepted the obvious alternative. He never regretted it, for he got in with influential people and now is said to be one of the bosses in Boston.

NIGHT LIFE

After the mysterious murder of Joe the Boss, life went on as usual in the speakeasies, the horse pool rooms, the clip joints, the crap games, and the race tracks. But in the cafés of Mulberry Street and the inner circles of the gambling, bootlegging world, word was passed that Lucky was the new boss.

Not much was said about it. The new boss was even more secretive than the old. In the past Lucky had always lived with one woman or another, but now he just took his girls where he found them though he did often have a show-girl that he was making a play for.

As a matter of fact, Charlie Lucky knew a lot of show-girls. The days of his eminence were the heyday of the gangster in the life of Broadway, for the depression had banished the big-spending business man who had been meat for gold-diggers. During the boom days it had been the custom for the more glorified show-girls to go out on parties every night with lavish spenders who liked to be seen with them. A girl might be paid $50, $100, or more, merely for the pleasure of her company in an expensive night club. No physical intimacy was necessarily involved in the transaction, if the girl knew her way around, and it made a very nice racket. After the stock market crash there were fewer stockbrokers who could afford this sort of display, and then the mobsters had their innings. They were the best pickings to be had.

Lucky often gave parties, by proxy. He would send liquor to a girl's apartment and have her entertain a lot of visitors from out of town; or he would have one of his men rent a hotel suite and throw a party there. Show-girls would be invited, and would expect a large money present for "taxi-fare." I have been told about these things by a girl who knew many gangsters. She tells me she knew Lucky well, and I believe her.

This girl did not like to tell me details of the gangsters' parties, because she said they were not nice parties. Sometimes embarrassing things would happen. For instance, a girl who did not know the ropes might take a $100 bill from the wrong man, some visitor from the Middle West who did not know the proper inhibitions of Broadway. Then there would be misunderstanding in the bedroom. Usually no one interfered on such an occasion. Gunmen do not like to meddle in each other's personal affairs; they prefer to let live and live. As for the girls, well—a girl has to take care of herself; she expects others to do the same.

My friend did tell me about one of Lucky's parties, though, which he threw for members of the Purple Gang of Detroit. Overwhelmed by the charms of some of Broadway's most glamorous girls, certain of the mugs from Michigan were impetuously intent upon retiring to the bedrooms. It was getting pretty bad when Lucky spoke up.

"Listen," he said, "these girls are show-girls. They work for a living."

But Lucky could not fail in hospitality, so he had a couple of girls sent over from Polly Adler's, to take care of the bedroom end of the entertainment. As the Adler girls mingled in the party (more beautiful than any of the show-girls, according to my friend) a strange thing happened. When one of them would put down her empty highball glass, a gangster would pick it up and throw it in the fireplace, so no one else could drink out of it. Don't expect me to explain why a girl should be more poisonous while drinking highballs than while in a bedroom. I'm just telling it as it was told to me. The fireplace was filled with shattered glass.

Moralities and taboos are strange things, which appear in different forms in all levels of society. As we shall see later, racketeers scorn the pimps upon whom they are perfectly willing to prey. The combined chivalry and hospitality of Charlie Lucky on that night have sharp significance, in the light of things which were to be said about him later.

Girls liked Charlie. He had a flashing white smile, and a debonair manner, with a steely showing of harsh cruelty underneath. He was filled with a vitality, a joy in life. He liked to unbutton his vest, loosen his belt, and eat large plates of spaghetti, with red wine.

"You wouldn't like me if you knew who I was," he told a new girl once. She didn't know who he was, but she sensed it. She knew he was underworld, and she saw that strong men, bad men, jumped to obey his slightest word.

Lucky kept his life in compartments. If he was playing

with a girl, she wouldn't even know where to call him on the telephone. He would call her, tell her to come where he was, or would drop in at her apartment late at night.

In a sense he was almost a recluse. He moved from one hotel to another where only his intimate vassals could find him. On outings at Hot Springs or Miami, he lived under his own name, and sometimes he was pointed out by insiders at race tracks and night clubs as Charlie Lucky. But back home in New York, he was Mr. Charles Lane of the Barbizon Plaza, Mr. Charles Ross of the Waldorf-Astoria; he was always under an assumed name in his hotel. The general public knew him not at all.

Charlie's daily life was the routine of the sporting man. He represented himself to be a gambler, as indeed he was. At times he ran gambling clubs in Miami and Saratoga. His joint at Saratoga was The Chicago Club, a popular resort which had every gambling device from a bird cage to roulette, and was equipped with an armored machine gun nest over the front door. He had a piece of Fred Bachman's big horse room syndicate. His followers and supporters controlled territories and had a finger in gambling and alcohol everywhere.

You would never have thought that Charlie was a man of affairs. He slept until noon or later, had conferences with lieutenants in his hotel room, then went to the race track. There he would often meet other big shots and presumably transact business with them between races. Evenings were spent in restaurants and night clubs. Often Lucky hung out in the Villanova Restaurant on Forty-sixth Street, or Celano's Garden on Kenmare Street, down near Mulberry Bend. The hot spots would see him at night, and often he would wind up before bedtime at Dave's Blue Room.

A similar, sleek, well-tailored, sporting existence seems to have been routine for all the big racket men except Dutch Schultz. The Dutchman had a frugal personality all his own. He always kept close track of his money; indeed he died while studying a detailed accounting sheet of the policy racket. He was always rushing around, stirring up his executives and nosing into the details of the racket business. The Dutchman paid $35 for his suits and they looked it. But Lucky and most of the others, got theirs from the same Fifth Avenue tailor at $190 apiece.

Lucky usually had someone staying with him. One of his roommates was a stupid fellow called Chappie Brescia, who strutted around the hotel in riding breeches. Chappie did not know the first thing about the beer business, but he was president of a beer distributing company and could prove it. He had a pistol permit.

Lucky was not going to repeat Capone's mistakes. He did not need a conspicuous bodyguard. He passed the word that he was not to be talked about. People in the underworld said he could pick up a telephone and get quick action anywhere in America. But the talk was in whispers.

A night club doorman, taking his ease in a bar one evening in 1932, started to tell an anecdote about Charlie Lucky. Suddenly he was interrupted by a dark, hard man who broke into the conversation.

"Pipe down," said the dark man. "That name isn't talked about."

And that night club doorman quit talking in the middle of a sentence.

Little things showed the change in Lucky's status. Instead of being part of a retinue at the race track, he now had his own sleekly-tailored retinue. In June, 1932, when Tammany Hall went to Chicago for its last stand fight against the nomination of Roosevelt for President, Lucky went along with Albert Marinelli, leader of the downtown Italian district, the new rising power in Tammany. He neglected to register at the Drake Hotel, or if he did so it was under a phoney name. But he was there, around Marinelli's suite, with seemingly inexhaustible supplies of liquor at his command. Some of the delegates had neglected to supply themselves with sufficient to drink, but Lucky took care of them.

Lucky's police record shows his rise as plainly as anything. Before Joe's murder Lucky was being arrested every now and then on charges of felonious assault, robbery, and various matters involving guns. Only a month or so before Joe's murder, Lucky was accused of participating in a vulgar street brawl, beating up two Jersey City policemen who had ventured across the river into Manhattan. In the five years after Joe's death, Lucky was picked up in Cleveland for investigation, in Chicago for investigation, and in Miami he registered voluntarily with the police, in accordance with the law. But in New York City he was not arrested at all.

THE POWER OF THE BOSS

Lucky had plenty of money, but that did not mean that he was the proprietor of all the various enterprises over which he held sway. He was partners with others in various things, but as a big shot his status was less that of an owner than that of a feudal ruler, a man whose leadership was accepted by other barons of the underworld and who represented his own Italian element in the councils with leaders of other mobs.

The rigidity of the control maintained by the top men is astonishing to contemplate. For instance, everybody who goes into an enterprise in the racket world is supposed to have the O.K. from the right people, and if the matter is sufficiently important, the O.K. has to come from the top. A few years ago, there was a boss around Mulberry Bend known as Don Cheech. Cheech had a small mob working for him, shaking people down, protecting houses of prostitution and that sort of thing; and he stood in well with the bosses. That is why he was called Don, meaning lieutenant. One day it was discovered that Don Cheech had been running a joint in Westchester, a roadhouse which was also a house of prostitution, without having an O.K. for it. This was a bad offense for a member of the organization. The ordinary penalty would have been death but Cheech stood in well with his bosses and they merely chased him. He went into exile, back to Italy. The mobsters who were working for him bade him a merry good-by and never knew until later that he had been kicked out of the country. Don Cheech's offense was a mild one. If he had killed anybody without getting the O.K., there would have been no forgiveness. That is one thing people in mobs have to remember— unless you are a big shot, you have got to get the O.K. before you kill.

As a leader and a ruler, Charlie Lucky discouraged bloodshed. He was a peacemaker and that was one reason why he was so popular. Take, for instance, the case of Ciro Terranova, the Artichoke King. In his later years, Terranova seemed an obstacle to the ambitions of younger men. He was also greedy and they thought he took too much of the profits for himself. Terranova was a partner with Dutch Schultz and he also had the monopoly in the policy game in Westchester. One day a number of the young bucks got together with Trigger Mike Copolla and decided that Trigger Mike should take over. So they went to see Charlie Lucky and get the O.K. Lucky told them to lay off, that he would handle the matter himself.

Lucky called in Ciro and told him he was through; it was time for him to get out of the racket. He thereby made two friends—one by gratifying Trigger Mike's ambition, another by saving Terranova's life.

Trigger Mike took over. Later, after the death of Dutch Schultz, he was to take over the Schultz enterprises.

The Artichoke King lived to distinguish himself in yet another way. In 1937, with the Schultz mob broken up and Lucky gone, Terranova could not meet the payments on his oil burner. Creditors moved in and took away his pink stucco villa on Peace Street and everything with it. But Terranova lived to the ripe age of forty-nine and died in February, 1938, of natural causes, in bed, practically penniless.

THE COMBINATION

As has been indicated, the rise of Lucky as the leader of those who wanted to "Americanize" the underworld was not a purely individual accomplishment. He had not only his strong backing in the Unione Siciliana but was allied with powerful and desperate mobs outside. Through the Artichoke King, he had strong diplomatic relations with Dutch Schultz, racket overlord of the Bronx and upper Manhattan. Personally, he tied up with the great industrial racket team of Lepke and Gurrah.

When Herbert Asbury wrote his excellent history, "The Gangs of New York," he wound it up with the murder in 1927 of Jacob Orgen, Little Augie, whom he called the last of the gangsters. But he wrote the obituary of the gangster a bit too soon. Little Augie had been at that time the chief exponent of strong-arming in labor disputes, successor to the tradition of Kid Dropper and of Dopey Benny Fein. Augie's successors were to be bigger than he.

Suspected and arrested for murdering Augie were a loft burglar named Louis Buchalter and a tough gorilla named Jacob Shapiro who, as soon as they were released, proceeded to take over and develop his power. These men were to become known as Lepke and Gurrah, a terror to industry in New York. In the succeeding eight years, they established hegemony over the painter's union, bakery and flour trucking, fur industry and garment trades. The time came when their terror was so great that a gorilla no longer needed to mention their names when he went on an errand. All he needed to say was he came from "the boys" and his word was law. Lepke and Gurrah had developed the industrial racket to unprecedented power over business.

Up until this period, the Italian mobs had never taken any part in the bigger industrial racketeering in New York. From now on Charlie Lucky had his hand in all of it through Lepke. Lepke was an ally of Lucky's, supported by Lucky's military strength, and for years he never did anything of importance without consultation with the Italian boss.

Also allied with Charlie Lucky was a mob of quick shooters organized by the team of Bug Siegel and Meyer Lansky, which was to become known everywhere as the Bug and Meyer mob. Bug Siegel was a young terror; Meyer, as he is generally known in the underworld, is a quiet, brainy fellow, an advocate of peace for which the mob gets a good price. While Dutch Schultz was obtaining notoriety by taking over the policy racket in Harlem, the Bug and Meyer mob was quietly establishing contacts and dominations over mobs in other cities and getting control of the policy rackets and other rackets everywhere.

Allied also with these men was Abe "Longie" Zwillman of Newark, New Jersey, dominant boss of the industrial region west of the Hudson. His chief interests were centered in the heavy construction industries.

After Charlie Lucky had been convicted, after Lepke and Gurrah had fled from the law, Longie Zwillman and Bug and Meyer remained powerful in the vast, rich territories beyond the confines of Manhattan Island. Philadelphia, Cleveland, Detroit, Chicago, New Orleans and Los Angeles are localities in point.

A great change had come over the underworld. Where once there had been small and isolated neighborhood gangs, now the major interests of the underworld were really all one mob. Underworld people began to talk about the Combination.

Now, every mob is a combination or every racket is a combination, and the word is commonly used by men in the gangster business. It has been our habit to talk of this big gangster and that big gangster as the ruler of vast underworld enterprises. But actually every important mob is an alliance of diverse elements who work together because that pays better than fighting. Gradually, out of all the small combinations there now had evolved one big Combination which, for a time at least, laid down the law for the underworld.

From several sources, underworld sources, comes the story of a meeting held late in 1931 or early in 1932, in a Brooklyn hotel, at which these various big underworld leaders formed the Combination. Doubtless many meetings occurred. These men saw a great deal of each other, socially as well as in a business way. Whether any single, outstanding meeting actually took place, I have not been able to determine. But it is clear that the big shots had got together. The power of Charlie Lucky had a lot to do with that. Through the underworld he and his allies spread the Pax Siciliano.

EXTERMINATION

The value of such alliances in the movement to "Americanize" and modernize the underworld became apparent soon after the rise of Charlie Lucky to leadership in the Unione Siciliana, for his election was not unanimous. The "greasers" were fighting men, cold, hard, Sicilian gunmen. They would not give up without a struggle. In July, 1931, their leaders got together at Coney Island and elected their own chief, one Salvatore Maranzano.

Maranzano was a newcomer in the country. He had been here a couple of years, become a naturalized citizen almost immediately,[2] done a bit of bootlegging, and set out to recruit for himself an army of trigger men from abroad through a system of alien smuggling.

There were plenty of recruits. In Italy, the Mafia was hard pressed by Mussolini. To obtain a plentiful supply of death-defying gunmen, it was necessary only to get them

[2] Two days after Maranzano's death, it was discovered that all the papers relating to his naturalization had been stolen from the files of the Federal Immigration office in New York, and where the data concerning him had been written in books, the pages had been cut out with a knife.

past the United States Immigration authorities. They were
a strange type. Bred in the tradition of secrecy and assassination—small, swart men with stupid eyes—they did not
know the language, they did not know much of anything.
But if you put the right man on the spot and gave the nod,
they would drill him without batting an eyelash. Very good
men for mob purposes.

Maranzano had his headquarters for alien smuggling in
a luxurious office high in the gilded tower of the New York
Central Building, 230 Park Avenue, Manhattan.

Maranzano set about challenging the power of the Combination. One incident that we know about involved an effort
by certain union leaders in the garment industry to get out
from under the pressure of Lepke and Gurrah. They went
to Charlie Lucky, and he turned a deaf ear. They went to
Maranzano and he was glad to cut himself into the industrial racket business.

Soon after this, on September 10, 1931, Maranzano was
having a busy day in the office at the New York Central
Building. There were twelve other men in the office with him.
Suddenly three men entered with drawn guns and ordered
them all to face the wall. All obeyed, whereupon Maranzano alone was thoroughly riddled with bullets and stabbed
with a knife until dead. The others were spared.

The leader of this assassination crew was Bo Weinberg,
an ugly thug who was Dutch Schultz's right-hand man. Bo
was one of the town's most accomplished murderers. Often
Bo would kill a man, mutilating him in strange fashion, then
plant the body in the precinct of a police captain that he
did not like. Bo was not entirely a heartless fellow, however.
Among the dozen in Maranzano's office that day was a friend
of his named Tommy Brown whom he was also supposed to

kill. Bo let him off and got bawled out for it when he arrived back to report. But since he had done the main job, he was not seriously blamed.

Getting out of the New York Central Building was not easy after that murder. Bo got separated from his companions and spent an uncomfortable hour before he made his escape. He would run up and down stairs, meet people on the stairway, and turn around and run away again. Part of the time he hid in the women's toilet, which he happened to find unlocked. He kept his gun because it looked for a while as though he might have to shoot his way to freedom. And when he finally emerged he still had the incriminating weapon concealed in his right-hand coat pocket. He boasted later of the way in which he got rid of the gun. Elbowing his way through a thick crowd, he quietly dropped the pistol into the coat pocket of an unsuspecting stranger and quickly made his escape.

Nothing illustrates better than Bo's activities that day the spirit of peaceful co-operation which the major mobs of the underworld had undertaken to establish. They were all helping each other now and they no longer had to commit their own murders.

There were plenty more gunmen abroad that day. Maranzano was only one of the victims marked for slaughter. I get the story from two men, one of whom was associated with Lepke in these years, and another of whom was an intimate of Bo Weinberg's. The more conservative version is that thirty of Maranzano's followers were murdered within the next few days. The other one, probably nearer the truth, is that ninety of Maranzano's recruits and old-line "greaser" leaders were wiped out in cities all over the country, most of them within the same hour as that in which Maranzano was killed. It would take a great deal of research to check up on this precisely but the truth probably lies somewhere between the two versions. At any rate, the Maranzano minority was exterminated. It was a purge. The underworld had been "Americanized."

PUBLICITY

During these years while Lucky had been building his secret power and keeping himself out of the newspapers,[3] the best known of New York City's racketeers had been Dutch Schultz. He had won public attention first by getting shot by Chink Sherman in a brawl early in 1931 at the Club Abbey; later by fighting a war of extermination with his former lieutenant, Vincent Coll; then through the misfortune of being prosecuted by the federal government on income tax charges.

In the autumn of 1935, having finally won an acquittal after two income tax trials, the Dutchman took refuge in New Jersey where he fought the attempts of the federal authorities to continue prosecuting him in New York. But the Dutchman's number was up. His own mob was sick of him. His own men were sore because of all the publicity he had been getting; because he had ordered the death of his old pal, Bo Weinberg; and the big shots generally had de-

[3] Printed references to Luciano were extremely rare. The New York *Times* report of Maranzano's murder in 1931 noted briefly that he was reported to be a rival of Lucky's for leadership of the Unione Siciliana. Stanley Walker, in "The Night Club Era," in 1933, mentioned Luciano briefly. John O'Donnell, star reporter of the New York *Daily News*, ran across Lucky's name and printed it a couple of times. This had a significant sequel; O'Donnell relates that about January, 1933, he was invited to a betting commissioner's office, where it was proposed that he might, without risk, win a large bet on a fixed hockey game, if he would just forget about Lucky and give him no more publicity. Naturally he refused and resolved to find out more about Lucky; but shortly after he was transferred to Washington and had no further occasion to write about the mobs. The incident shows that there were positive efforts to keep Luciano's name quiet.

cided he was no longer an asset to the underworld. The Dutchman had been out of his mind, practically crazy, for several months, and had killed too many people for anyone to like him very much.

One night in October, as the Dutchman and three of his henchmen were sitting in the backroom of a Newark saloon studying a balance sheet of the policy racket, gunners entered and shot them all down. At almost the same instant two other Schultz lieutenants were shot down in a barber shop in Times Square, New York.

Remnants of the Schultz mob carried on his enterprises for a while, but eventually all were taken over by the Italians.

The Schultz murder is important in this tale because for the first time it brought to the general knowledge of the public a group of men whom the police listed as the Big Six. These included Lepke and Gurrah, Bug and Meyer, Longie Zwillman and Charlie Lucky, who was called the biggest of them all. The police wanted these men for questioning and there were hints in the papers of a secret syndicate of crime, a set-up so fabulous that it was hard for anyone to believe in it.

For twenty-four hours before the Schultz murder and five days thereafter, Charlie Lucky did not stir from the Waldorf-Astoria Tower where he occupied an apartment on the thirty-ninth floor under the name of Charles Ross. On the fifth day after the murder, Lucky gave up his apartment and quietly left town.

He had given the slip to the police but he was not happy. For more than four years he had been the secret boss. Now for the first time he had been unmasked. He was front page news. That is bad news for any big gangster.

VI. A RACKET DISCOVERED

A WOMAN ON THE SCENT

While Nancy Presser had been waiting there for someone to pay attention to her, she did not realize that she was about to meet a very special group of young men. Thousands of New York City's lawyers had applied for jobs on Dewey's staff, for it was a big opportunity. Dewey chose his key men from among those who had worked with him in the Federal Prosecutor's office. Others he drafted from law offices and combed with care from the thousands of applicants. Of the twenty chosen, one was a woman, Eunice Carter, a Negro.

Mrs. Carter was a girl who knew her way around town, knew how to make things happen. During the previous winter there had been riots in Harlem, violence growing largely out of the abject economic condition of the community and its frightful housing; and Mrs. Carter was secretary of the Mayor's committee which investigated those distressing occurrences. Just before the adjournment of the Legislature, when Albany was in its usual tail-end uproar and hardly anybody knew what was happening, Mrs. Carter appeared at the Capitol with seven bills proposed by the committee. They embodied long over-due housing reforms which had been blocked for years by the powerful tenement house lobby. She was a stranger, but she went around quietly buttonholing the right people, and three days later four of her seven bills had passed both houses of the Legislature. That is the kind of girl Eunice Carter is.

She was soon recognized as an able member of the staff. Her cubicle was far down at the end of the corridor, next to the room where the cops hung out. Her nearest neighbors among the assistants were Harold M. Cole and Charles P. Grimes, two gentlemen of distinguished qualities. Charlie Grimes had formerly held a job of importance with the NRA and practiced corporation law; Cole too had been drafted out of a corporation law office, largely because he had taken an amateur's interest in the underworld and could talk to mugs in their own language. If these two had not been married, either of them would seem to be tailor-made for a hero in slick-paper magazine fiction. Both were large, dark-haired, handsome, independently wealthy. Grimes, proud possessor of a membership card in the boilermaker's union, was a figure in the smoothest society; Cole played squash at the Union League and sailed his own two-masted schooner out of the American Yacht Club. But they were practical fellows too. When Cole began prosecuting felony cases in 1938, he hung up such a formidable score of convictions that his colleagues said facetiously it must be because there were women on the juries now. Grimes specialized on the Harlem policy racket and plugged away for three years without making much noise about himself, then turned up with the indictment against Jimmy Hines. These two and Mrs. Carter were kindred spirits, and together with a few picked detectives, they soon had a combination all their own, a secret combine against crime.

It was Mrs. Carter who first got wind of the fact that there was a racket in prostitution. During that springtime fuss over Nick Montana and Polly Adler, the vice squad had worked overtime, and the load at Women's Court had been so heavy that Mrs. Carter had been called in as a volunteer assistant to the magistrates. Someone had remarked, while she was there, on the strange fact that a certain lawyer appeared never to lose a case. Either he was a genius, which he obviously was not, or something was wrong. She remembered that when she became an investigator.

Making discreet inquiries, as she proceeded with more urgent subjects, she became convinced that there was some centralized force in the prostitution business, something that went beyond the bookers like Nick Montana and Cockeyed Louis, with their business of booking girls into chains of houses. There were vague reports of a racket. With Murray I. Gurfein, one of Dewey's chief assistants, she went and laid the matter before the boss.

Dewey was not enthusiastic. He had a specific job, an attack on the big shots in the rackets, and he was finding it a much tougher job than he had expected. The suppression of prostitution was the job of the regular law officers, not Dewey's. He was not a reformer, in the old-fashioned sense at least, and anyone who called him a reformer had better smile when he said it. He felt no demanding call to reform the sexual conduct of the community or any of its parts, and did not think he could do so even if he wanted to. A vice prosecution would be just more of the same old stuff, just what he had been educating the public not to expect from him. Besides, from every aspect and for everybody, prostitution was a hot stove. It did not pay to touch it.

However, if it appeared that gangsters had taken control, if there appeared to be a large-scale criminal operation, then the situation might be different.

Something of that sort, said Mrs. Carter and Gurfein,

was just what they thought they had turned up. It was a racket.

All right, said Dewey, go to it.

DEWEY'S JOB

The word "racket" is commonly used in the American language for any method of making money without too much work. More specifically it designates any large-scale criminal enterprise.

But for the purpose of his drive on organized crime, Dewey had a still more specific definition—the organized extortion of money, often with the apparent willingness of the victims, by the use of threats, force, or violence. He had in mind especially the industrial rackets, preying on business, which were his major objective. But the essential ingredient was the violence, the tactic of the gangster. An additional essential was the existence of the big-shot gangster, or racketeer, who directed operations from remote safety. He had been immune to the law, because he performed no open criminal acts himself, because he confided only in a few trusted associates, and because his victims were ordinarily outside the protection of the law.

In the Dewey sense, bootlegging is not inherently a racket. The dope traffic is not a racket; prostitution is not a racket, even though it involve large-scale trade in women; gambling, betting, and the comprising of lotteries are not rackets. Violation of the anti-trust laws is not racketeering. These crimes become rackets only when the gangsters move in and assume control, usually monopolistic control.

When our local and national governments prohibited prostitution, gambling, the sale of alcohol, the traffic in narcotics, and combinations in restraint of trade, they did not abolish any of these forms of economic activity. What actually happened was that government expressed its disapproval, and abdicated the function, surrendered the right, of regulating such matters. Then the mobs moved in and exploited the criminals.

Roughly there are two kinds of rackets, the rackets relating to illegal pleasures, such as the control of bootlegging, and the industrial rackets. The basic pattern of the industrial racket is control of a combination in restraint of trade, violating the anti-trust laws. This is done by controlling a labor union, a trade association, or both. In those industries subject to cut-throat competition, the racket often is welcomed by many business men, for the same reasons that they welcomed the NRA. Its combination freezes prices and otherwise reduces the hazards of competition. But in the racket the governmental function of regulation is performed, not by an ineffectual board of compliance, but by the gangsters. Their edicts are promptly enforced by bombing, acid-throwing, and murder.

The industrial racket is, of course, all mixed up with labor union racketeering. Labor strife is a natural field for the gangster, for despite all the legislation and court decisions, it remains largely outside the law. The struggle over labor's share of profits is warfare, whether tacit or open, and neither side bothers much about legality, except to complain that the opposition is violating the law. Originally the gangsters were called in by both sides as mercenaries; they found the field a fertile one and decided to stay. Labor racketeering has many special aspects, but basically it also conforms to the pattern. The corrupt union leader, fattening on bribes or extortion money, is basically more a grafting politician than a racketeer. But as a criminal he is easy prey for the gangster army. He becomes the slave and partner of the muscle men, just as the bootlegger and speakeasy owner became the vassals and the enforced customers of the mob monopolies during Prohibition.

Generalizations are dangerous, and should not be too fine-spun. The racketeer is no more confined by definitions than by the law, and is interested in making money and acquiring power, not in any theory of method. That is why it is so difficult to define a racket. The best definition, probably, would be any criminal organization which is dominated by a boss of gangsters.

Dewey's job was not to fight crime generally. Crime is a phenomenon almost as vast as society itself, growing out of an environmental complex in which law enforcement agencies are only one factor, and not too important a factor at that.

Dewey's job was not to fight criminals generally. That was the job of the regular law officers.

As special prosecutor, it was his job to go after the big criminals who had attained unprecedented power. The job was paradoxical, and Dewey recognized the paradox. The primary victims of the racketeers were the small criminals, the rag-tail and bob-end of the underworld.

As special prosecutor, Dewey was to be the knight champion and defender of the downtrodden vassals, the payers of tribute, the victims of monopoly, in the underworld of crime.

STALKING THE QUARRIES

With the cops and the aid of other assistants, Mrs. Carter set to work tracing the prostitution racket, first verifying its existence, then identifying the participants. This was a stalking job, done very much on the quiet, to avoid alarming the quarry. It was mostly police work.

Gradually the facts were developed, partly through discreet inquiries from informers, but not so much; for too much curiosity would spread alarm. Mostly it was by wire tapping.

Wire tapping has been much under public discussion lately, and it is with some difficulty that I refrain from entering into a lengthy dissertation on the subject. It is not a pretty method, but crime detection is not in any respect a pretty business. For many years, where complex and hidden crimes were concerned, most of the effective police work done in this country has relied on wire tapping. It is one of the important reasons why the police of our large cities have been able so unerringly to name the big criminals and tell what their rackets are, although unable to prosecute them. For the wires are better at producing information than at gathering legal evidence.

At any rate, information about the vice racket was gradually developed. It was at this time that it evolved that the incarceration of the two bookers, Cockeyed Louis and Nick Montana, had interfered with the operations of the business not at all. Louis's young son, Al Weiner, had taken over the business of his father and had continued without interruption, while Nick's assistant, Jack Eller, had succeeded him.

There were two other important bookers providing girls to houses in Manhattan and Brooklyn, Pete Harris and Dave Miller. As the picture developed, the bookers seemed to have a relatively minor role in the general scheme of things. There was a system called "bonding," which appeared to be directed by one James Frederico, a squat, dark ex-convict and ex-pimp, commonly known as Jimmy Fredericks, and by an unlicensed bondsman at Women's Court, Jesse Jacobs. Clearly important as executives also were Bennie Spiller, a loan shark who operated from a bar and grill in West Fifty-fourth Street, and two mugs from Mulberry Street, Thomas Pennocchio, known as Tommy Bull, and Little Davie Betillo, gangsters whose records showed them to have been interested in narcotics.

Center of communications was a room in a midtown hotel, occupied only by a little fellow known as Bingie.[1] He would be notified when a joint was grabbed, and would put the legal department into action to get the girls out of jail.

But the one central fact which stood out about the whole prostitution set-up was that, in addition to her booker's ten per cent commission, and the madam's half, each girl had to pay $10 a week to the bonding syndicate.

In January the investigation was still incomplete. Though there was enough evidence to make arrests, there was not enough to get convictions. But there were signs and warnings that speed was now imperative. For one thing, a girl who had been gypped by a madam went squawking to the cops about it. Her booker, Pete Harris, blew out of town to Philadelphia—followed by a Dewey detective, and was kept under surveillance, for now was not the time to make a grab. There were other signs of restlessness.

---

[1] This Little Bingie, meeting failure as a preliminary boxer and needing to make a living, got a job as doortender in a house of prostitution, but soon better opportunity came his way and he became telephone boy at $5 a week for Jimmy Fredericks, then booking women from headquarters in the office of a doctor in West Thirtieth Street. By 1936 Bingie had become telephone man for the whole syndicate, on the job from noon to midnight in a hotel room where he kept, screwed behind the panel of an electric light switch, a list of houses which were in good standing. For this he was paid $15 a week. Criminals hire their help cheap.

As a matter of fact, Bennie Spiller had a hunch, and on the night of January 30 he gave expression to it in a night club known as the Bal Musette. This Bal Musette was a new spot, with a lot of fancy decorations and a fag show (for female impersonators were then popular) and it had a big opening on January 6. Little Davie and Tommy Bull had a piece of the place, and the whole crowd was using it for a hangout. There was one big table reserved for the mob, the vice combination, the racket men—Tommy, Davie, Little Abie, Vito, Jerry the Lug, and all them. There was another table for the prostitution people. Bennie sat mostly with the prostitution people, though he was a member of the combination. His social position was compromised because he ran a joint. The racket men would not be too chummy socially with a prostitution man. They would lose face.

On this Thursday night Bennie had a vague worried feeling, and he went over to Tommy Bull's table to talk to him and Little Davie.

"I got a hunch," Bennie said. "I don't feel right. Maybe this guy Dewey is getting on to us. Maybe we ought to take a powder. Maybe we ought to lay low for a while."

"Nuts," said Tommy Bull. "I was just telling Mildred Harris to tell Pete to come home from Philadelphia. I told her to tell Pete to come home, his case is all squared up."

"I don't feel right," said Bennie.

"Forget it," said Tommy Bull. "If they do start something they won't get nobody more'n a couple bookers anyway."

But Dewey was already in action. He was issuing his orders.

A REAL RACKET

This was a real racket, a mob of gangsters forcibly taking over an industry. The industry was disreputable, it was criminal—the age-old business of prostitution. But it was the gangsters Dewey was after, the gangsters who were levying tribute of $10 a week from every girl who worked the town's joints. Dewey had promised himself and promised the men with him that they were not going out after prostitutes, but this was different. They were up against real criminals. He gathered his staff around him and issued secret instructions.

Let there be a raid. Let it be a Dewey raid. Let it be the most secret, the most sudden, the most sweeping, the most terrifying raid this town has ever seen. And the gaudiest and the bawdiest, if necessary.

The idea was to go out softly, quietly, and to grab the gangsters first, then to grab the bookers. Then with all those in custody, the plan was to strike simultaneously at joints all through the town, grabbing the madams, the pimps, and the girls. Dewey told his men to make cases on the girls and bring them in. They would threaten the girls, bully them, gentle them, coddle them, cajole them, kid them along. Anything within reason to make them talk.

Dewey sent out one of his men to order coffee and sandwiches to be sent up that night to make his prisoners comfortable.

"And I'll be damned," said Dewey, "if we sent a single one of the babes to jail."

VII. THE GREAT GRAB

PICK-UPS

A bit after midnight, early Saturday morning, February 1, 1936, Thelma Jordan received a telephone call from Jeanette Lewis, sweetheart of Jo Jo Weintraub, Pete Harris's assistant. Jeanette wanted to borrow a traveling bag. The town felt too hot. She and Jo Jo were going to blow and meet Pete in Philadelphia.

Thelma took her bag up to Pete's apartment at 106th Street and said good-by to Jeanette. As she left the place and turned up the street, a detective stepped out of the shadows and took her into custody. Then the cops went up to the apartment and found Jeanette just about to start for the station with Jo Jo, a small man in a form-fitting suit with a large nose and bald head like a billiard ball.

Detectives had their eyes on the racketeers all over town, and were waiting for opportunities to grab them without the knowledge of their friends, to avoid spreading the alarm. Jack Eller was picked up on Riverside Drive, Jimmy Fredericks on Broadway. Bennie Spiller, Tommy Bull, and Little Davie were grabbed all together at Sixteenth Street and Seventh Avenue, as they drove away from the apartment house where Davie lived.

Dave Miller, a booker, was picked up as he stopped at a red light in Brooklyn, driving with his wife and three children. Pete Harris was arrested in Philadelphia.

The prisoners were salted away at the Greenwich Street

police station, near the Woolworth Building, and held in-communicado. Meanwhile work went on as usual at the Dewey office until afternoon, when staff members were called in and told to expect a hard night's work.

In the early evening one hundred and fifty plainclothes policemen were assembled at various police stations for an unspecified purpose. They were mixed up so that they were not with their usual partners, and were sent out in teams to various posts, with sealed orders, and with firm instructions not to open the orders until 8:55 o'clock. Each envelope contained detailed instructions for a raid, and promptly at 9:00 o'clock forty houses of prostitution were raided simul-taneously. Little Bingie was grabbed too. The police had done a superlative job.

WAITING FOR BAIL

The Woolworth Building never before and probably never again will experience such a night as this one. Soon prisoners were pouring in by the vanload—a collection of wenches, doxies, hustlers, tarts, raw-boned madams with horn-rimmed spectacles, tough gangsters' molls and slick, pansy-handed pimps. In the room ordinarily occupied by Dewey's assist-ants, ninety-nine harlots now were gathered, sullen, defiant, waiting for bail. The bail would come surely. They all knew the law was nothing to fear. The combination's girls never stayed in jail.

The room was misty with smoke and reeking with the stench of mixed perfumes. Most of the girls were still in their working clothes, bright silks and satins with shoes to match. They worked their powder puffs and looked in their vanity cases and used their lipsticks. But still there was a blowsy appearance over all.

The girls were parceled out to the individual assistants for interrogation. The cops had done a splendid job but soon it began to appear as though the Dewey end of the coup might be a terrible bust. The girls simply would not talk.

A few months before this, the Dewey office had executed its first public job with a somewhat similar raid in which were captured a large number of the shylocks, or loan sharks, who made small loans throughout the city, charged extortionate rates of interest, and exacted their payments with threats and physical violence. Victims of the loan sharks had willingly identified them, once they saw their tormentors under arrest. It had been expected that something of the sort would happen with the prostitutes this night. But it had been a false hope.

Unlike the loan shark victims, these were underworld people. An arrest was a routine matter, and they were ready for it. The first thing each girl did on a Monday when she reported for work, even before she had her doctor's examination, was to give the madam her professional false name, and then still another phoney name, which she would use in case of arrest. Each girl had a whole repertoire of stories commonly used in the business, on those rare occasions when girls took the witness stand in Women's Court, to explain away embarrassing circumstances. On the night of the Dewey raid, the whole repertoire was worked and overworked and worn threadbare. The girls would not believe this was not just another pinch. They expected to be bailed out soon.

As dawn picked out the stately spire of the Woolworth Building on Sunday morning, the questioning still went on, high in the Dewey offices. The chimes of Trinity and St.

Paul's called out for early communion in the empty echoing canyons of the downtown streets, and again they called their flocks to morning prayer. Still the blowsy girls in evening gowns insisted they were respectable working girls; still the Dewey men battered at the sealed lips of the underworld.

DEFIANCE

Some of the prosecutors were resting a bit in the corridor talking with Sol Gelb, one of the senior assistants. Little Sol, unassuming as his name, was older and more experienced than the rest. They leaned on him. Dewey leaned on him too, as a matter of fact. He was to take over the whole management of the Luciano prosecution. Years later, he was to handle much of the Jimmy Hines case.

"Where are we getting, Sol?" the youngsters asked. "Where are we at?"

"It doesn't look so good," said Sol, "but don't worry, fellows. I know one thing. Somehow the boss will salvage something out of all this wreckage. Once some of them start telling the truth the others will do it too."

Through the ground glass panels of a near-by cubicle, they could hear a voice, growing louder now, almost shouting, impatiently. Mannie Robbins, a bright boy from the previous year's Harvard class, was in there trying his luck. Everybody had been drafted into this questioning job, $1-a-year law clerks and everybody else. The door opened and Mannie came out. He was not exactly a fat youngster, but was very wide, and now he was droopy, looked as if he had lost about ten pounds.

"How'd it go, Mannie?"

"Hell, I walked out on her. She says she's a virgin."

Now down the corridor came Dewey, all full of vim and

vinegar, stirring things up, and with him was the chief of his detectives, Inspector John Lyons, tall, gray-haired, dignified. An intellectual cop, the man whose brainwork, I am sure, was as much responsible as anything else for the capture of Bruno Hauptmann.

Here came Dewey, looking as though he had just stepped out of a barber's chair. It could be irritating at times like this; Dewey is a man who never gets rumpled. His thick, dark hair is of the crinkly sort that never gets mussed. His profile is of the sharply-defined sort which always seems to focus itself for the cameras. His clothes never get wrinkled. His linen never seems to get soiled. Here he was, looking as though he had just had a good breakfast, as indeed he had, and stirring things up.

Suddenly the door to Mannie's cubicle flew open, and there, with face pale and eyes flaming, standing up to her full height in terrible defiance, stood that dizzy blonde Nancy Presser. She was in an ugly mood.

Nancy looked at Dewey, up and down, appraisingly.

"So you're Dewey," she said. "So you're the big shot they talk about around here." Nancy seemed to be looking down at him, for Dewey is not a tall man. "Well—run along, boy scout, and peddle your papers!"

"And as for you, mister—"

Nancy's voice was brazen. She jabbed her right fist against her hip, and swayed toward Inspector Lyons.

"Mister, you're just a great big platinum blond to me!"

BOLD STROKE

Dewey was in his inside office, preparing new action. Save something out of the wreckage? Certainly not. He would deliver another blow and increase the wreckage.

He telephoned to Justice Philip J. McCook, of the Supreme Court, who had been designated by the Governor to supervise the rackets investigation, and asked him to come downtown. He was needed for the arraignment of a hundred-odd people who were in custody. The Judge came down on Sunday afternoon, to hold court in the Dewey office.

Justice McCook is a man of stature in New York. An able, fair, experienced judge and—rare article in Manhattan—a Republican judge; a man of mettle, moreover, known as Fighting Phil to his men in the World War. When the Governor decided to hold the rackets investigation, McCook was appointed immediately to preside. He was the obvious choice. Then after some delay, the Governor had named Dewey as prosecutor, and Dewey had moved in to take command, like a gust of something or other. McCook did not know quite what to make of it at first, this self-assertive, self-confident—hmmpf! whippersnapper! But before long he was watching with admiration. Well, the years pass. Other days, other men. "And what a man this Dewey is!" said McCook.

Dewey explained the situation to Judge McCook. He had about a dozen prisoners who would be arraigned on Monday. They were dangerous criminals, vicious men, who had been running an unspeakably degraded racket, and he would ask that they be held in high bail.

In the meantime, he had about a hundred prostitutes and madams. He had cases on them and could arrest them and convict them, but he did not want to do that. He wanted to hold them as material witnesses and make them testify against the big criminals. The bail should not be small, for this was a bail-bonding racket, and the underworld had vast sums of money with which to protect itself. It would not hesitate to tamper with witnesses. Right now its fear held these girls. They had been offered their freedom, but everyone was lying, not one of them had talked. Of course, the bail should not be unreasonable. It seemed to Dewey a moderate figure would be $10,000 apiece. He suggested that figure; indeed, he urged it.

McCook looked the young man up and down. The usual bail for a prostitute was $300. The courts had not infrequently turned holdup men loose on the streets in $10,000 bond. Dewey was very much in earnest, looked very self-confident. O.K., said the Judge finally.

The girls all stood in line waiting to see the Judge. They made a queue which stretched down the whole length of the Dewey office through the corridor—a tawdry, bleary-eyed crew looking like something that had been swept up after a New Year's party. One by one they stepped up before the Judge.

"Not guilty, Your Honor," they would say. They still had the idea they had been arrested as prostitutes, could not get it out of their heads.

"Held as a material witness, in $10,000 bail," said the Judge.

And the girls went out to the House of Detention, with the figure ringing in their ears.

Ten grand! It would take a million dollars to bail out this crowd! This was a jam to be in!

Somebody once said that Dewey had brass guts. He was using them now. If his audacious and unprecedented procedure did not work, he would appear a colossal fool.

Well, the girls were guests of the state now. For five months the state was to board and lodge them, doctor them, fatten them up and pay them $3 a day. I suppose Dewey is the only man in all history who has maintained a string of a hundred prostitutes, and thereby accomplished a useful purpose.

ACE IN THE HOLE

Dewey knew what he was doing. As usual, when he started raising, he had an ace in the hole. He knew something few of the others in his office knew. Already he had a squeal.

For fourteen weeks that winter Dave Miller, the booker, had been in the hospital; and during that period his business had been run by his wife, Ruth. The Dewey office knew all about that. Miller had been out of the hospital just a day or so, and on Saturday morning he and his wife, with their three children, had been driving to make a call at the doctor's office, when Dewey's detectives had driven alongside and grabbed them all.

Sitting in the police station, Dave thought over his plight, his weak heart pounding and battering away with fear. He knew he was sunk. He knew he was buried.

And if he was buried, so was Ruth. They could get twenty years apiece. And then what about the kids?

"Let me see the prosecutor," said Dave to the cops. "I want to talk to Dewey."

So Dave sat down in Dewey's office that Saturday evening, a little scrawny man with a glass eye, a pattering heart, and large ears that stood straight out from the sides of his head. He talked to Jacob J. Rosenblum, and then to Dewey.

"Mr. Dewey, we got three kids," said Dave. "They got nobody to take care of them except my wife. Turn her loose, Mr. Dewey, and I'll open up. Let her go home and take care of the kids, and I'll take my rap and tell everything. They're just little kids, and they don't know anything about this business at all."

So Dewey said yes, and Dave Miller sat there with his heart pounding and jumping, and his ears standing straight out from the sides of his head, and his good eye shedding water, and he told his story. Then he collapsed and went back to the hospital.

VIII. DAVE MILLER'S STORY

A FAMILY SPAT

For five years while Dave Miller was a constable in Pittsburgh, he did very well in a business way. He and Ruth were a young couple, having babies, and salting away a little money. Being a constable didn't pay very much, but Dave had a regular income from shaking down speakeasies and cat houses.

According to Dave he got personally mixed up with prostitution, which was to be his ultimate downfall, because his wife didn't understand him. In the midst of a quarrel one day she walked out on him, and his spirited response was to go out and bring home a prostitute. The girl was there when Mrs. Miller came home the next day; and, after a somewhat strenuous scene, both women stayed on in the house, the girl earning her keep in a professional way. That's the way Dave tells it, but I think his perspective is a bit cockeyed. Even before that, probably, the Miller household was not very straightlaced. There is testimony that Ruth herself did the work on the girl's day out.

Before long the Millers were arrested for keeping a disorderly house. Some of the neighbors thought it wrong for such things to be going on in a home with small children. Dave lost his job as an officer of the law.

After wandering here and there for a while, the Millers came to New York in 1929 and set up housekeeping with their three children. Dave started out peddling dresses from house to house, and there is no better way of learning the ins and outs of the city. Soon he was especially selling dresses in houses of prostitution, for harlots were the best customers he found. Clothes were a part of their stock in trade. The girls were vain, they had money to spend, and very little sense about how they spent it. Dave always let on his goods were cut-rate, and even if they were not stolen, he hinted they were hot; because then the girls thought they were getting real bargains. The girls would buy more than they could afford, even ermine wraps and other such nonsense. Then Dave would fix it up with their bookers that they had steady work for a while, so they could pay him off.

He got along all right. Peddling dresses in brothels is really a very profitable business, having no overhead. Sam Samuels got his start that way and now he owns one of the finest apartment houses on the Grand Concourse, with city officials and judges for tenants. Sam's prosperity gave him overconfidence, however, and in 1935 he complained to the police that there was a racket in prostitution. The police, inquiring, found out Sam was running a couple of joints himself, and sent him to prison. Nobody should ever blow the whistle for the cops unless he has dropped his own burglar's tools.

BUILDING A BUSINESS

Soon Dave struck up partnership with a fellow named Harry Chicago, and they decided they would open up a joint. They supplied the credit and the backing, but they had their wives do the actual running of the place. Such arrangements of wrong-doing by remote control, so to speak, are very common in the underworld. In this case Dave and Harry Chicago were especially safe. Their joint could not possibly be pinned on them, for it is the law that a wife can't testify against her husband. But after a couple of months the cops closed it up.

Chicago and Dave had made a lot of contacts in the business by now, girls, madams, bondsmen, lawyers, and they decided to go into partnership as bookers. They started out with a string of girls and about ten houses, and soon were doing pretty well. Then they split the book and went their own ways, and Dave went on alone to develop his business as a booker.

Ruth stayed home now most of the time and took care of the children, but now and then she worked for a week or so, for pin money. If you want to make Dave Miller mad, just suggest that he ever made his wife work as a prostitute, or even asked her to. It was entirely her own idea, Dave insists, and she didn't have to do it either. He was a good provider.

Dave Miller! Didn't you have any moral scruples about all this?

"Any more what?" asks Dave.

INDUSTRIAL TREND

The ancient industry of prostitution had fallen to a low state in New York City during the twenty years after the World War. There were various reasons. For one thing the demand had fallen off. There had been a great increase in what had been called amateur competition. Also, thanks to the propaganda of Havelock Ellis and other sex psychologists and moralists, there had been a decrease in marital dissatisfaction.

Another reason for the plight of the industry was that Tammany Hall had learned, by long experience, that prostitution was a bad thing to touch. Back in the Nineteenth Century prostitution was wide open and paid regular dividends in political protection. In those days the Haymarket and other dance halls of the Tenderloin ran without restriction, and even the waitresses were wenches; gentlemen could sit drinking wine in private boxes or booths, where, in the inner recesses, ladies of the establishment would entertain them in manners we shall forbear to mention. There were joints of all kinds. Over in Twenty-third Street the Seven Sisters had their row of houses, where gentlemen must come in evening dress, and the accomplishments of the inmates included the playing of the harp. The Lexow investigation of the 90's, exposing what had been going on, to the fascinated horror of the populace, brought retribution to the city's rulers. A few years later, William Travers Jerome founded his career as a public prosecutor on the brass check, token of harlotry. The politicians, for the most part, learned it was safer to rely on less obvious forms of graft. For the population of New York, cosmopolitan as it is, broadminded as it is, and little inclined to mind other people's business, has one characteristic. The public is disposed to be tolerant, even sentimental, toward the poor prostitute; but it burns up whenever it hears about any man taking a girl's earnings away from her.

During the administrations of Mayor Hylan and Mayor Walker, Tammany ran a "clean" city. There were, it was pointed out, no women soliciting in the streets and no joints running wide open. And this was convincing to the average citizen. Your average citizen is very naive and uncomplicated. When he thinks about sin, the one thing that immediately pops into his head is going to bed with somebody he is not married to. Since the city had thorough outward order and decency, the voter decided that things were pretty clean. So the politicians were able to get away with murder in other directions.

A "CLEAN" CITY

A "clean" city turned out to be profitable for the exploiters of sex. There is always more money to be made out of the titillation and exacerbation of the sex impulse than out of its consummation. The male in heat is a generous, flamboyant show-off; but gratify his wants and he becomes a sleepy pinchpenny fellow. The cleaner New York became, the more clothes came off the girls in the Vanities, the night clubs, the burlesque houses, and the more "art" magazines there were on the newsstands. Clip joints flourished, where men on the hunt were enveigled by taxicab drivers with vague promises, where hostesses plied them with drinks, and where finally a delegation of gorillas presented a bill which seemed as big as Finland's war debt, and was as promptly paid. Taxi dance halls flourished, and there too men hunted in vain. This was the golden day of the gold digger, the teaser, the torrid virgin.

"Hello, sucker!" cried Texas Guinan. "Give the little girl a hand."

But the little girls gave nothing.

There were hustlers in the streets, of course. But they were wary.[1] They did not dare solicit openly, but cultivated a friendly, demure eye. To find them a man had to be an

---

[1] In 1939 there were still hustlers in the streets, but they were still more wary. It was their custom to pick up only those men who came along in motor cars and whistled at them; for they knew that vice cops and stool pigeons were not provided with cars and could not thus entrap them. This developed into a great nuisance for lone women on the streets at night; it became common for them to be followed along the street by whistling men in a motor car.

ogler, a nervy fellow. He had to risk having his face slapped
in public, or being denounced as a masher. And even if he
did make a girl on the street, he had no assurance that she
would deliver. She might be just a shill who would take him
to a bar where she could collect a commission on the drinks,
and then, having got him plastered, roll him for the rest of
his dough.

THE JOINTS

Then, as it has been mentioned, there was Polly Adler,
catering to the twelve cylinder trade; and as the years went
on she had a competitor in Peggy Wild. Peggy Wild is an
Italian girl of sultry, mongoloid features, whose real name
is Margaret Venti. She was once married to a traveling man,
and had a lot of time on her hands. She was renting a room
in her apartment to a show-girl who had a number of gentlemen friends, and frequently there were occasions when the
young men needed more girls to make up a party. Peggy got
started arranging such things; one thing led to another; and
the first thing she knew she was one of the town's leading call
house madams. For years Peggy ran a joint at Saratoga
during the racing season, and that made her many valuable contacts among sportsmen, politicians, and underworld
people.

At first when Peggy ran a house the price was high, but
gradually she settled down to the standard $2 joint. Anybody
who thinks that is a come-down, says Peggy, just doesn't
know anything about the business. Just as the big automobile business is in Fords and Chevrolets, so the real profits
in prostitution are in low-priced mass production. When a
John comes to a $25 joint, says Peggy, he feels as if he is
buying the place. He expects it to be luxuriously furnished,

and he wants to sit down, be entertained, talk, and have a party. He probably wants to get plastered, which will make a joint conspicuous to the neighbors. All that is unprofitable. But when you are running at $2 you can keep the overhead down, and run the customers through rapidly and discreetly. The John realizes that everything is strictly business, and he didn't come there to talk.

When a madam is running a joint at $20 and making a go of it, according to Peggy, you can be sure her chief course of revenue is not prostitution, but is probably blackmail. A high-priced joint attracts the high-class trade, and occasionally brings in an eminent citizen of high respectability and reputation. In return for a lively evening, especially in these days of fast camera lenses, such an eminent citizen may feel impelled to make contributions over a long period. But that sort of thing is outside the scope of any really honest madam.

Of course, for a price any madam is glad to close her joint for the night and entertain one party. There was one memorable night of that sort at Peggy's, when Vincent Coll, then a high lieutenant of the Schultz mob, gave her a $500 bill and bought the house for the evening. He was entertaining Al Capone and other big shots from Chicago, as Peggy remembers it, and wanted to show them a good time without making them conspicuous.

The $2 joints which sprang up all over New York, in the days when the city was clean, were small hideaways, usually in second or third rate apartment houses. Respectable neighbors, minding their own business, generally suspected nothing queer; though the building superintendent usually had to be sugared to keep him from noticing too much. These places were thoroughly unlike the wide-open houses of other

cities, such as the Four Deuces in Chicago where Al Capone
got his start; there the girls sat on crowded benches, around
a large room, and customers took their pick. Here in the
New York joints there were usually only two girls, three at
the most, often only one.

The chief asset of the madam was her list of customers,
men whom she recognized when she looked through a peep-
hole. She would accumulate her list through the years,
and when she moved, or opened up a new joint, she would
send out cards with the address, perhaps bearing some cryptic initials such as M.O., for "men only," and a sales slogan
which would be intelligible to the recipient. Such as:

GET YOUR RADIO FIXED

FOREIGN WAYS

The customers were a varied lot. There were married men
with frigid or invalid wives, who would not expend the time,
the money, or the risk for extra-mural love affairs. There
were impatient young men whose sweethearts were technical
virgins, and staid bachelors who tried to order their lives like
clockwork. There were men who could not afford wives and
sweethearts, and men who had no homes, and men so de-
formed in body and spirit that they could not find their
mates. There were men in whom welled up unaccountable de-
sires, which could not be confided even to a lover, but demanded to be satisfied among strangers, in dark and secret
places. There were many who to most of us would seem to be
just plain scum, but in whom doubtless the psychiatrists
could find traces of humanity. All these poured nightly into
the joints of New York, and then like shadows departed.
Much has been written and many tears shed, over the frail
girls who since Genesis have fluttered through their brief

days of gaudy degradation, to pass on into limbo, no one knows where. Less has been said of the male miseries and hungers which pour like a torrent through these sink holes, these furtive joints, modern bits of Sodom.

In the one-girl houses the men took what they got. In the two-girl houses they had a choice between a blonde and a brunette. But the madams sought to vary the fare. Not only did they change the girls each week, but they sought versatile entertainers. To get steady work, a prostitute had to be at least a "two-way" girl, and the more ways she had the better. Jennie the Factory used to complain about it—comfortable, fat old hausfrau Jennie, as she sat crocheting in a lull of business, chewing the rag with an old customer. Jennie didn't know what the younger generation was coming to; the old-fashioned fornication didn't satisfy it any more. Jennie blamed it on the war, and all the fancy ideas that had been brought home from France. Jennie the Factory shook her head and sighed. Ach! it wasn't like it was in the old days, when she herself was hustling. Jennie of course was subject to an illusion. Her clientele had changed. Young men did not sow their wild oats at Jennie's any more. They did that in Ford cars and tourist cabins. And more and more her customers were the misfits, the dregs of the city. Well, as in any business, the customers were always right. The girls minded at first; but as Helen Kelly told Judge McCook, they got used to it after a while. Normal or abnormal, what an adaptable creature the human animal is!

In a hostile environment, operating furtively in a vast metropolitan labyrinth of seven million people, the prostitution industry adapted itself in special ways. There were plenty of girls, there was a continual flow of them from the small towns of the East and Middle West, usually experienced before they came, eager to go to work. Almost invariably they had pimps, who put them in touch with the proper people. But even so the business of shuffling the girls up each week, and getting them on time to their hidden places of work, required special attention. Thus sprang up the specialty of the booker, agent between the girls and the madams; and if the bookie had a number of good houses, it was a very profitable business indeed.

FALL MONEY

Before the bookie would do business with a madam, he had to satisfy himself of her responsibility, be sure she would not gyp the girls and thereby start trouble. And she had to establish her credit by getting an O.K. from a bondsman, who would promise to bail out her girls if they were arrested. Usually the bondsman would require the madam to deposit with him security for $500, $1,000 or whatever the cash bail would amount to if there were an arrest. All this was necessary, so that the girls might be bailed out as soon as arrested, and not be tempted to open up and talk. For if they opened up, the booker was faced with a long term in prison.

If there were enough cash for the bail bond, that was sufficient practically to guarantee that the girls would be turned loose.

The business of springing the arrested girls and madams was in the hands of a group of prostitution lawyers and bondsmen who made their headquarters in a row of cubbyhole offices on West Tenth Street, across from Jefferson Market Court and the Women's House of Detention. It was very simple. They gave $25 or $50 to the arresting cop to omit essential parts of his testimony and $25 to the prosecutor, John C. Weston, to keep him from squawking. And the girls walked out. It was as easy and cheap [2] as that, though the lawyer and bondsman generally contrived to keep most of the cash bond for themselves, making it costly for those who put up the money.

There were always enough penniless and friendless women to go to jail and make a good record for the cops and prosecutor, and often enough they were sent away on perjured testimony. The arresting officers in these cases were plainclothes men attached to the various inspection districts, commonly known as the vice squad. Their work, entrapping women in sexual commerce, was of a sort repugnant to any red-blooded Irishman; and, by a sort of natural selection, the vice squad specialists came to include as bestial a lot as could be found in a large and generally decent army of men. They kept the city "clean" so far as outward order and decency went, and in the process many lined their own pockets.

All this was exposed in great detail by Judge Seabury in the first of his investigations, in the autumn of 1930. There was some housecleaning around Women's Court, some vice cops were sent to prison, the framing of women and the use of perjured testimony were supposed to have been stopped, but apparently the fixing of cases went right on, under somewhat more difficult circumstances. The confession of Prosecutor Weston was found to be insufficient evidence even to disbar the lawyers who had customarily paid bribes, and such leaders of the ring as Abe Karp continued to practice in the courts.

Business went on as usual. Indeed, it was better than usual

[2] Bribes paid to public officials usually are small. Once an officer accepts money, he has placed himself in the power of the crooks, and he becomes a cheap and unconsidered part of the underworld organization.

for a while. The Seabury inquiry had been confined to corruption in the courts, and had not brought to light at all the widespread operations of the bookers. But the vice squad was incapacitated. Cops quit making prostitution arrests for a while, because there was such a stink surrounding the whole matter. The madams and the bookers did business unmolested.

Such was the situation when Dave Miller came to New York, and broke into the prostitution business.

DAVE FINDS PROSPERITY

By the dreadful depression summer of 1933, Dave Miller was one of the most prosperous citizens in New York. He had a string of very good-looking girls, and was booking them into an average of about twenty houses, scattered through Manhattan and Brooklyn. His ten per cent on the girls' earnings ranged from $300 to $400 a week, and the overhead of the business was not high. Also there were the presents he got from pimps who wanted him to put their girls into good jobs. He lived with his family in a fine house at 17 West Seventy-first Street, and did a lot of his business over the telephone from there. Most of his work was done on Saturday and Sunday, when he would go around to the various houses and collect his commissions.

One day in July, 1933, a fellow named Crazy Moe came to see Dave, bringing with him another man whom he called Charlie. This Crazy Moe had formerly run a joint up in Eighty-sixth Street and Dave had sent him girls.

But now it seemed he was getting into a tougher racket. He said that a combination was being formed and if Dave would put him and Charlie on his payroll he would see that Dave was not bothered. Dave was indignant. He didn't want to have anything to do with gangsters. Not even Crazy Moe.

Dave called in the housemaid and told her to take a good look at his two visitors in case she was ever needed for a witness. You would have thought that Dave was in the most respectable business in the world the way he went about it.

"What the hell did you get me into?" said the fellow named Charlie to Crazy Moe. He got very mad and walked out of the place. Then Dave told Crazy Moe to get out too.

One night a month later, Dave and his wife decided to go to the movies. There was a good gangster picture at the Rivoli. They parked their car in Fifty-fourth Street, by the Alba Hotel, between Seventh Avenue and Broadway, and started to walk toward the theatre.

Suddenly four men came up behind them in the darkness. One of them grabbed Dave by the shoulder, spun him around, and pinned him against the wall of the house they were passing. Another gave Ruth a little shove, and she walked on down the street a few steps, out of earshot. She knew enough not to ask questions, or make a commotion, or stick her nose too much into her husband's affairs.

Dave was dumbfounded for a minute, and just stood there not saying anything. He thought at first it was a stickup. Something poked him, and glancing down, he saw a glitter. The point of a long knife was held against his stomach.

"Say, what's this all about?" said Dave finally.

"Here's what it's about," said one of the men. "You got twenty-four hours to get out of town. You got to pick up and get out of town by midnight tomorrow night."

With that one of the men gave Dave a smack in the face, and with a renewed warning to get out of town, they walked off down the street and left him there.

Dave started to go on with his wife, but then turned and walked rapidly after the men.

"Hey," he called. "Wait a minute. What is all this about?"

"You know what the boss said," one of the four told the others. "We can't tell him nothing."

"Listen," said Dave, overtaking them. "What is all this about? Who can I see to straighten this out? Who are you guys and who can I see?"

"Well, who do you know?" asked the fellow that did most of the talking.

"I don't know anybody," said Dave. "But who are you, and I will have somebody see you."

They started naming a lot of names, haphazard, big shots that Dave didn't know; and they weren't getting anywhere.

"Do you know Moey?" Dave said finally, playing a hunch.

"What Moey?" said one of the fellows.

"The only name I know him by is Moey," said Dave. "All I know him by is Crazy Moe."

"I know Moey," said the fellow. "He is all right. You tell Moey to get in touch with me."

"Who will I ask him to get in touch with?" asked Dave.

"Just tell him to get in touch with Whitey," said Whitey.

And then the four fellows went away. They were Joey Levine, who Dave later knew was partners with Little Abie Wahrman, and Whitey and a fellow known as Jersey Ralph, and an Italian fellow that Dave never did know the name of.

Dave Miller went back to his wife, and they didn't think any more about going to the movies. He drove her home in his car, and then went back downtown looking for Crazy Moe.

He found Moe on the sidewalk near Broadway and Fifty-first Street, where he usually hung out. This little neighborhood of Broadway and Seventh Avenue, just above Times Square, might almost be called the capital of the underworld, of the half world, and of all the catch-as-catch-can industries of sport and entertainment. Stand on the corner, and sooner or later there will pass by everyone who amounts to anything in the fight and wrestling games, the kingdom of jazz and swing and tap dancing, the industries of gambling, narcotics, liquor, and of the strong-arm and the snatch. Around those streets there's always a lot of angles to be straightened out. This Crazy Moe hung out there, and knew a lot of people.

"Are these fellows the combination you were talking about?" asked Dave.

"No," said Moe. "That isn't the combination, but I think I know who they are."

Crazy Moe gave kind of a grunt, and then started down the street. They turned into Stewart's Cafeteria at Fiftieth Street and Broadway, and Crazy Moe went around speaking to this fellow and that. He talked for a while to a pimply faced fellow, and then came back to Dave, and they got in Dave's car, and Moe said to drive over to Brooklyn. So they drove downtown, and across the Manhattan Bridge, and way out on Myrtle Avenue to a little flyblown speakeasy, and there in a booth across from the bar was Whitey, with the Italian fellow that Dave didn't know the name of.

"Say, you got a lot of nerve," said Whitey to Dave. "You got just so long to get out of town."

"Lissen," said Crazy Moe. "This guy Dave Miller come in here with me, and I expect to take him out the same way I brought him in."

So then they began to talk business.

"I come over to find out what this is all about and try to straighten it out," said Dave.

"Well," said Whitey. "If you give us ten grand, we'll do the same to the fellow that we was supposed to do to you."

"What fellow?" asked Dave.

"You heard me," said Whitey. "You give us ten grand, we'll do the same to the fellow that we was supposed to do to you."

"Nobody carries ten grand in his pocket," said Dave. "Besides, I ain't got $10,000."

"Well," said Whitey, "that's our offer and that's the way it stands." And he wouldn't talk any more.

Dave and Crazy Moe drove back to Manhattan. Crazy Moe told Dave he would have to pay, for this was a tough crowd and meant business. Moe said he would see Dave the next day, and meantime he would see what he could do. Dave went home to bed, but did not sleep much.

Next day Dave had a telephone call from Whitey, putting on the heat, and Dave told him to be there at his meeting with Crazy Moe. So when Dave arrived at a speakeasy to meet Moey, there were the four fellows he had met on the street the night before. Dave and Moe tried to bargain with them, but they still held out for $10,000.

"You give us ten grand, and we'll make you the biggest man in New York," said Jersey Ralph.

"I'm satisfied the way I am," Dave said. "I like it this way. I don't want to be the biggest man in New York."

So they talked back and forth, and Dave tried to talk them down, but he could not make any headway.

"Well," said Jersey Ralph finally, "you still got till 12 o'clock tonight to get out of New York."

THE COPS

Dave Miller got in a cab and rode home. He was feeling pretty sore. Here he had worked for four years and built up a nice business, and now this gang of loafers wanted to take it away from him. Damned if he would stand for it! Damned if he would run! When he got home, he called up Abe Karp, his lawyer.

"Abe, make me out a will to sign, leaving everything to my wife. I got gangsters putting the arm on me," said Dave; and he told Karp how things were.

Karp came up to Dave's house with the will. Dave signed it. And then Karp took a surprising step.

This Karp was a wise apple. He had been dealing with cops, those with the vice squad at least, for a long time. There was no more accomplished operator in Women's Court and in spite of all the charges and evidence he had just brazened his way unscathed through the Seabury inquiry. He was very bold. Karp called up the West Sixty-eighth Street station and asked them to send over a couple of detectives. Within a few minutes Dave's doorbell rang, and there when he opened it, like a pair of human mountains stood two cops. Dave knew right away they were cops. When you are in his business, you can smell a cop a mile away.

"Mr. Miller?" said the cops, introducing themselves. "Mr. Karp said you had been threatened with grave bodily harm. We are here to protect you from bodily harm."

Dave told some sort of vague story about being threatened. He took the cops down to Stewart's Cafeteria and out to some places in Coney Island as if he was hunting for the gangsters. What he would have done if he had found any of them I don't know. It is hard to imagine Dave really going to bat on a complaint to the police.

The next two days were hell. In the side streets, if Dave were without the cops, lurked gangsters ready to pounce upon him. But here in his front parlor were two officers of the law. Good Lord! What if a cop should pick up a phone call and get an earful! If the cops caught on to him, Dave knew they could hand him five to ten, maybe twenty years.

When Dave went out in the street, the cops went along, and it was just as if he had leprosy. Nobody Dave knew would talk to him. He couldn't do any business. Those cops were poison.

The second day Dave's telephone rang.

"We know you've got coppers with you, but we are going to get you, coppers or no coppers," said a man on the wire and then hung up the phone.

Dave didn't know what to do. He was scared of the gangsters but quite as much afraid of the cops. He stood it for another day and then gave the cops the air. He told them he didn't need protection any more. That was all right with the cops. They had felt kind of foolish, for Dave wouldn't tell them anything much about himself.

PROTECTION

Rid of the cops, Dave felt easier. He moved about the city furtively, staying away from his usual haunts as much as possible. Next day he got a telephone call from a fellow named Six Bits.

"Say, Dave," said Six Bits, "I got a new package, and it's a honey. We're over on Broadway. Come on over and give a look."

Now this Six Bits was a pimp who usually had pretty

snappy girls, so Dave said he would be right over to give a look at the package.

He went down in the elevator and out to his car, and he had just opened the door to get in, when Bang! it sounded as if a gun had gone off right close to his ears, which indeed was the case.

Dave dropped to the floor of his car. Two or three more bullets came spanging through the glass above him. Dave found himself thinking, vaguely, that it was a very good thing he had shatter-proof glass in his car. He lay quivering on the floor for a while, and then took a peek out. A car had been passing him, he knew, and now he saw it down the street, turning into Central Park West. He made a break and dashed back into the house.

Hardly anybody else was in the street at the time, and nobody did anything about this shooting. New York people don't like to meddle into matters that do not concern them.

Dave got in touch with Crazy Moe as soon as he could, and told him to renew negotiations with Joey Levine. This was a situation, Dave said, that had got to be straightened out.

It was several days before Moe could get an appointment, and Dave stayed in the house nearly all the time. Every time he started to go out, his wife, Ruth, went into hysterics. Finally Moey called him downtown, and Dave went to a restaurant at Sixth Street and Avenue C, on the lower east side. When he arrived, Moe was already there, with the four fellows who had put the arm on Dave.

"Well, what are you going to do about this?" said Joe Levine, tough-like, when Dave came in.

"What can I do?" asked Dave. "What do you want me to do?"

"Well, we decided to take $5,000 off you," said Joe, "and then you will pay us $200 a week protection money."

"Two hundred!" said Dave. "And what kind of protection do I get for that? Will you protect me from stick-ups? Will you protect me from the police if I get a grab?"

"No, we can't do that," said Joe. It was just as Dave thought, a shakedown, pure and simple.

"Why was I shot at?" asked Dave.

"That is the orders we got," said Joe.

"Who gave the orders? Who do you fellows represent?"

"Oh, we can't tell you that."

It went on that way for some time, and finally Dave saw he wasn't getting anywhere. He was in hot water, he was licked, and the only thing for him to do was take a powder.

"Let's have a drink," said Dave.

So Dave bought them all a drink, went home, put his furniture in storage, and took his family to California.

Thus protection came to the prostitution bookers of New York.

With the other bookers things went better. Cockeyed Louis, old, feeble, and nearly blind, paid $200 a week, and so did Nick Montana. Pete Balitzer, whose business was smaller, paid $100; but Jimmy Fredericks, who was running a small book with Danny Brooks, didn't have to pay, because there was a combination now and Jimmy was in the combination. Charlie Spinach paid. He had his hangout in the café at 121 Mulberry Street, which was also the office of Little Davie. But after a while Charlie Spinach disappeared, and we do not know what became of him.

LITTLE DAVIE GIVES THE O.K.

It may be true that life begins at forty, but it is pretty tough to be a specialist in a line of business and have everything washed out from under you at that age, so that you have to start anew. At least, so Dave Miller felt.

He stayed in the West for three months, then came back East and bought a gasoline filling station at Mineola, Long Island. That did not do so well, so he sold it at a loss and bought another at Glen Cove. That also was a bust. Dave did not know much about servicing automobiles, and there was not much money in it anyway. A year later Dave got sick, and his wife could not run the place, so he sold out again. By March, 1935, he was down to his last few hundred dollars, and had to find a job. He decided he had to get back into booking.

Dave had been in the city now and then and had run into some prostitution people, so he knew how things were. One day he had seen Bennie Spiller, and Bennie told him there was a combination now and everybody had to pay $10 a week, because that was before Bennie was taken into the combination himself.

Now Dave went to Bennie and told him he had to get back in the business, and whom should he see to get the O.K. Jimmy Fredericks, said Bennie, and he could find him at Joey Silvers's cigar store. So Dave got Joey to arrange a meeting with Jimmy and they met in Joey's store at Fifty-first Street and Seventh Avenue.

Jimmy was glad to see Dave, because things were not going so well. If you want to run a business, you have to have fellows in it who know how. Charlie Spinach's book had dwindled away to almost nothing, and now that he had disappeared, Spike couldn't make it pay. Danny Brooks wasn't able to make much money out of Jimmy's old book. Jimmy told Dave to meet him there the next day, because meanwhile he had to take it up with somebody else.

The next day Dave met Jimmy and was introduced to Little Davie Betillo, who was Jimmy's boss. This Little Davie was a slim, boyish-looking fellow, with curly hair; and to look at him at first you'd think he was just a little harmless punk, even maybe you might think he was a softie. But that would be a very wrong idea. Little Davie had been out in Chicago for five years, and it was not until just before Lucky took over that Davie came back to New York. It was said that Davie had been one of Al Capone's most highly regarded assassins out there, and that gave him a big build-up when he came back home. Just how big he was with Capone I don't know, but it was the reputation he had and traded on. Nobody questioned it. Little Davie was not a fellow anybody questioned.

"I'm broke and want to get back into booking and I understand you have to pay," Dave Miller told Little Davie. Davie went off with Fredericks and talked a little while, and then told Miller, "O.K., we're going to give you Spike's places."

"I am broke," said Dave Miller, "and how much will I have to pay? I can't pay anything now."

"You won't have to pay nothing for the first two weeks," said Little Davie. "After that you will have to pay $50 a week. Now I will have to O.K. you with downtown."

So then Little Davie went into a telephone booth and called a number, and Dave heard him ask for Little Abie and then after a wait he got someone on the wire.

"This is Davie talking," he said. "I just O.K.'d Dave

Miller. You know, that fellow you shot at. See that he is not barred. He is going to work for us."

THE NEW BOOK

Dave Miller got his orders and instructions from Jimmy Fredericks. Spike would show Dave his places. There were only about a half dozen, but Dave would soon be able to build the business up to more than that.

"All the houses that you get, you have got to call up and turn in, and then we bond them," said Jimmy.

"What do you mean, how do you mean you bond them?" asked Dave.

"Each girl pays $10 a week," said Jimmy. "Then if there is a pinch we pay half the bail and the madam pays half."

Jimmy told Dave to call up Little Bingie at the Walcott Hotel if there was a pinch at any of the joints, and then Tommy Bull would get the bail money up, for he was the treasurer for the combination.

Spike was getting out of the business. He had been Charlie Spinach's telephone boy, and then Charlie had disappeared, leaving Spike with his chain of houses, which had dwindled to a mere five or six, and not such good houses at that. Spike carried on for a while, but he could not get more than about $50 a week out of the chain; and when Jimmy Fredericks insisted on his paying $50 a week to the combination, Spike said he would throw up the book and get out. When Spike showed Dave Miller around the joints, the layout didn't look like much. Dave saw he was going to have to drum up a lot of business, and get a lot of snappier girls, if he was going to make a living. But he knew he could do it, if they would let him alone. He was a capable booker.

A couple of days later Jimmy Fredericks called Dave

down to a hangout where he was having lunch, introduced
Dave to his own assistant, Danny Brooks, and told Danny to
turn their sixteen joints over to Dave also. That seemed like
a break. He could start making money right away. But a
few days later he was called down to Joey Silvers's cigar
store to meet Jimmy and Danny and Little Davie. Davie
told him there was a new arrangement.

"You are to draw $50 a week and expenses, and Danny is
to draw $50 a week," said Davie. "And whatever money is
left over you are to give to Danny and Danny is to put it in
a slip of paper and give it to Jimmy, and he will give it to
Tommy Bull."

Dave's heart sank. So this was it. They were going to load
him up with work, and make him work on salary. He couldn't
keep his family on $50 a week. But he made no protest.
Little Davie was not a fellow anybody argued with.

"I thought I was gonna work alone," he said to Jimmy
after Davie had gone. "What's the idea?"

"Well, we weren't making any money on our book," said
Jimmy, "and that is why we are turning over these places,
and letting Danny work with you."

So he was supposed to make money for them, that was it.
Deep down in his heart, Dave cursed them all. Well, he knew
more about the business than any of them. He would make
a living.

Danny wasn't much help. He was a little Italian, whose
real name was Caputo, and he'd been in a lot of things at
one time or another, and unsuccessful at most of them. He
had been a gunman, pimp, night club operator, and also in
show business. He had owned the Thrills and Frills of 1926,
but went broke with that on the road, and then had a piece
of Texas Guinan's Padlocks. By 1933 he was down to the

point of being a one-bottle bootlegger, and then he had taken to hanging around with Jimmy Fredericks. Jimmy had been booking houses at the time, but couldn't drive a car, so Danny had driven him around. Then when Jimmy had started in the bonding racket, he had let Danny and Billy Peluso run his book and they split the money three ways. None of them had got much out of it; but when Jimmy said he was going to give the book to Dave Miller, Danny squawked, because he had just bought a new car. So he was allowed $50 a week for installments on the car, gasoline, and his own expenses.

For a few weeks Danny was around with Dave, but then he quit doing anything but come around to Dave's on Sunday to collect the money. The vice cops had got on to Danny, and Jimmy told him to lie low for a while. He stayed over in Brooklyn and made a horse book, and picked up numbers. That summer Danny ran into hard luck. He sent his girl up to work in a joint in Westchester, and then happened to go up there one night when it was raided. Danny was pinched and the girls talked. Dave paid Danny's wife $10 a week while he was in jail, and then for ten weeks he gave Danny $50 a week to pay his lawyer's fee. But Danny was convicted and got seven and one-half to twenty years in Dannemora for the crime which is called "compulsory prostitution."

The crime of "compulsory prostitution" figures a good deal in this story, and it is well that we understand what it means. There is nothing whatever "compulsory" about it. In the penal law, that word appears in the title over the definition of the crime, probably a vestigial remnant of some day long past when the Legislature was excited about the horrors of white slavery. The crime is a felony, and anyone who places a woman in a house of prostitution, or maintains a woman in a house of prostitution, or accepts any part of the earnings of a prostitute without a legal consideration, is guilty of compulsory prostitution, even though the girl is willing and eager to work in a joint and share her earnings. Pimps and madams are all guilty of compulsory prostitution, but are seldom prosecuted for it. Usually when they are sent away, it is on some misdemeanor charge, for a short term.

After he was rid of Danny Brooks, Dave soon found he was able to make a good living. He turned in his money every week, but he always held some out. He generally saw to it that the combination didn't get more than $75 a week out of him, which was more than they had been getting out of the book before.

He was able to do this because he gradually got together a classier line of girls, who were able to make more than the ones Danny and Spike had had. Also there were madams that didn't want to bond with the combination, and Dave held their houses out and didn't report them.

THE WAY IT WORKED

With all his contacts in the business, Dave soon had the lowdown on the whole situation. The bonding had started at just about the time when Dave was chased out of town, and now the bonding and the booking were two separate departments of the same business. The bookers were under control of the mob, and they were supposed to turn in lists of all their joints, so that the bond collectors could go around every week and get $10 for each girl.

As Jimmy Fredericks had explained, the $10 was a kind of insurance, or contribution for "fall money." When there was an arrest, the girls were bailed out right away, the madam putting up half the money and the combination putting up the other half. The combination also saw to it that the girls did not go to jail. As soon as a girl was bailed out, she would go to the bonding office, at 117 West Tenth Street, where Abe Karp's law office had been. Abe had been disbarred by this time, but he was still there, as chief advisor. The girl would have a lawyer and the bondsman would be Jesse Jacobs, but Abe would do the brain work. He would listen to the girl's story and decide whether she would be a good witness for herself. If the cops had broken into the place, or otherwise bungled the job, the case would be a sure turnout, and Abe would let it go right to trial. Sometimes he would coach the girl on a plausible story to tell. Sometimes he would just see that the cops were fixed. A case was never allowed to go to trial unless Abe knew it was going to be dismissed. If he could not beat the case, the girl was told to forget her bail and go on the lam. (When the Dewey office checked up, it found that not one of the girls working under the combination had ever been sent to jail, though a couple had been put on probation.)

This might seem to be a reasonably good proposition for the madams, especially since they put the $10 a week on the girls' board bills and made them pay it. But even so most of them did not want to bond. They knew it was a racket, a shakedown. And besides, there is no more rugged individualist than the average madam. She doesn't want anybody else messing into her business, and especially she does not want gangsters.

A REBELLIOUS MADAM

The bonding idea was not new. A number of bondsmen had been doing it during 1932. Dave Miller had a customer who had paid $15 a week to a bondsman on her one-girl house for a whole year before she got onto it. Then she figured she had spent more than $700 for nothing, for she had never had a pinch. This madam, Joan Garry, had learned her business from the ground up, and she knew a customer when she saw one. She always had a peep-hole, or an arrangement so she could look down into the street and see who was ringing the bell before she let him in, and thus was able to avoid trouble. So finally she gave the bondsman the air, and started saving up her own bail money.

Then in August, 1933, Jimmy Fredericks came and told her she would have to bond with him, pay $5 for herself and $10 apiece for the two girls she had at the time. He even tried to make her put down a cash deposit of $500 for her share of the bail. She refused. Charlie Spinach told her he could not book girls to her house if she did not bond, but she refused with vigor, for this Joan Garry was a hell-roaring termagant if anyone started telling her what to do or stepping on her toes. She said she would get her own girls. Little Abie and a couple of thugs came to see her, and when she refused to pay the bond money, they took the joint apart, ripped and smashed her furniture to smithereens. Joan's dander was up now. She would be damned before she would bond. Then Charlie Spinach booked Gashouse Lil in her place, and Lil introduced Ralph Liguori to Joan. Ralph came around after Lil had left, was admitted by Joan, and stuck up the joint; he hunted through the coffee cans and everything else and took out every cent there was in the place. Jimmy Fredericks told Joan she would have less trouble if she bonded, but she cussed him out, and he cracked her head open with a blackjack so she had to have ten stitches taken in it. There was further argument later, in which Jimmy blacked her eye, but she finally capitulated when he drew a revolver and threatened to shoot her dog. She paid the $15 a week, but never did pay the big cash deposit.

Even after she started bonding Joan had some trouble, and then she found the combination was of some use. Through 1934 she found it necessary to move every two or three weeks, because as soon as she was settled in a place there would be men coming to the door whom she recognized as cops or stick-up men. At last she found out that an un-ethical competitor, a madam known as Nigger Ruth, was putting the finger on her, and sicking the cops on her. So she went to Jimmy Fredericks and complained, and Jimmy put the arm on Nigger Ruth and made her stop.

Even so Joan thought the bonding was not worth while, and especially she hated to have collectors coming up to her house. In 1935 when Dave was booking for her, he had to collect the bond money himself a couple of times because the collector, a fellow named Yoke, could not get in Joan's house. She hated the collector's guts.

Joan was right, obviously, about the bonding. It was a gyp. A legitimate bond fee is 3 per cent, or $30 for $1,000 bail when security is furnished; and any madam who knows her business can get a case taken care of for a few hundred dollars. No one group had a monopoly on the arts of bribery and perjury. But once the city chamberlain had returned the bail money to the combination, after girls were turned out, the madams never got back the half that they had put up. Sometimes the combination just kept the money, and sometimes it rendered a phoney statement to the madam showing where her money had gone, charging $175 for the services of the lawyer who got $25 a case, and otherwise exaggerating its expenses.

There were enough grabs so that the bail money put up and lost by the madams was enough to pay all the overhead of the combination, for salaries were small. The money paid in by the bookers and the $10 a week paid by the girls were just so much velvet for the boys downtown.

THEORY AND PRACTICE

As Dave learned the system it became apparent that, theoretically, it was a perfect racket. Through the bookers, the combination controlled the supply of girls and kept a check on the houses, which would not be permitted to operate unless the weekly bond money was paid. And expenses could be met by chiseling from the madams, so that everything else was pure profit.

That was the theory, but it did not work out so well. Just as the benefits of mass production and centralized management sometimes fail to materialize when a lot of corporations are merged into some colossus of industry, so the bonding racket failed to produce as well as expected. For one thing the police, now under Mayor LaGuardia, were active and were knocking off joints so fast that their numbers did not greatly increase. For another thing, everybody in the whole racket was chiseling everything he could. They were stealing Little Davie blind.

Little Davie, to tell the truth, didn't know his business; and he wasn't able to tend to it properly. Operating by remote control, he was just like some banker in Wall Street trying to run a factory in Kansas or a studio in Hollywood. He knew about as much about prostitution as Richard Whitney knew about applejack and peatmoss.

The only language Little Davie knew was force. Every now and then he would call a meeting of the bookers and would sail into them. Little Davie would have big Jerry Bruno there and somber mysterious Vito, with all his gold teeth, to back him up. And Davie would tell the bookers they were all louses, and he was going to kick Jack Eller's big fat belly off him, and if any louse held out a lousy joint it was going to be a $200 fine, or it was going to be a $500 fine, and they were all louses.

Then Jesse Jacobs would make a speech and tell the bookers they should report all their joints, and tell them to sit down now and write down all their joints on a piece of paper and not leave any out.

Then Jesse would sidle around to Al Weiner, who would be writing up his list of joints, and whisper to him.

"Leave out that joint of mine, Al," Jesse would whisper. So Al would leave out Jesse's joint and whatever other joints he did not want to put in.

So that was the way it went. It did not do Little Davie any good to call them louses, because he did not know anything about the prostitution business.

BIG IDEAS, SMALL MONEY

Under Little Davie's executive direction, the racket never averaged more than $2,000 a week profit for the combination, or $100,000 a year, which was very small money for such a lot of big racket men as there were in this prostitution combination. Every time a little money accumulated in the treasury, they would whack it up into a lot of small percentages, cut the melon among themselves, and so the combination was always broke and sometimes had a hard time scraping up the money for bail bonds. This was a new racket. It was expected to produce big money, but had not done so yet.

A big-shot racket man has to have a lot of money, and he has to be free and easy with it. The bigger he is the more leeches and parasites and hangers-on he has, and the bigger he is the bigger the standing army of gunmen he has to maintain, to keep some other big-shot from taking his rackets away from him. Lots of times people wonder what becomes of all the vast sums of money that pour into the rackets, what the big-shots do with it all. But the big-shots have to have a lot of money, because they do not own the business but are the front men for combinations; and they have to whack up with the combinations, and whack up with their lieutenants, or they would not be big-shots any more. That is why the big-shots had a lot of weight and worry on their shoulders in 1934 and 1935 for bootlegging was washed up and Mayor LaGuardia had dumped all the slot machines in the bay and the cops were knocking off all kinds of joints, but there were still lots of fellows that had to make a living and couldn't be dumped out in the street the way Waxey Gordon tried to do, and they would have a hard time getting on home relief or WPA. And that is why these fellows were fooling around with a little thing like this prostitution business, which was a hot stove.

Dave Miller knew what he was talking about when he told Jersey Ralph he did not want to be the biggest man in New York, for it is a very expensive thing to be the biggest man in New York.

Dave had been doing very well when he had his own little business, before he got chased, and now that he was back he was getting along all right too.

He had to, because his family expenses were running high,

with doctors' bills and everything. For some reason or other, one of Dave's little daughters was a very nervous child. She had St. Vitus's dance. Dave had the doctor in and told him the best was none too good, and just for that one little girl, with serums and things, the expenses were running $40 a week.

That $40 a week seems like a high figure, even for a good doctor, but Dave swears to it. It is good to think that the money was going to an ethical professional man, devoted to the relief of human suffering, rather than to a lot of grasping, cruel racketeers.

THE BREAK

Dave was not thinking much or talking much about whys and wherefores that Saturday evening, while the big raid was on, as he sat there in Dewey's office making a statement to Jacob J. Rosenblum of the Dewey staff. Facts were the thing. What did you do then? What did you say and what did he say?

Dave was sitting there, spilling out his facts, and his weak heart was jumping and turning cartwheels, and his handkerchief was damp from wiping his good eye, and he had been promised that when he went to prison he would be put in a special place, under special guard, so he could not be murdered.[3]

"Who is the head of the racket?" asked Rosenblum.

"I heard once when I wanted to come back and I wanted to get started and they mentioned Charlie Lucky," said Dave. "I have never seen him."

---

[3] The prisons of New York today are dotted with colonies of Dewey witnesses, who have been given special protection against murder in prison. That is the first thing they ask for, before they agree to talk.

"Who told you Charlie Lucky was one of the bosses?"

"One time I asked Danny Brooks who was the big guy and he said: 'Don't say anything. Charlie Lucky gives him the O.K.' "

Later on, after Dave had thought it over, he was able to remember another conversation about Charlie Lucky.

"After Nick Montana and Cockeyed Louis were arrested, I got a call from Danny Brooks one night and he said, 'Pick me up we have got to go over to Mulberry Street,' " he said.

"So we went over there to that café and I saw Jimmy Fredericks and Bennie Spiller was standing there talking. I talked to Jimmy and I said, 'What is this about?' He says, 'A meeting, we are going to take the houses away from Al Weiner.' I says, 'I don't want them,' and he says, 'Why?'

"I says, 'Why his father is in trouble. This fellow has been fooling around with the police so much, what is going to stop him from going and hollering copper?'

"Jimmy didn't say anything to that, and then he and Bennie left, and Danny and I went out and got dinner. When we got back we sat there in the car, and Little Davie was talking with Jimmy, and then he came over to us.

"He came over to me and he says, 'We were going to take Al's places away,' he says, 'but forget about it. You were right and forget about it.'

"So then Davie went away and Jimmy came over to the car and we chewed the rag a while. I asked him, 'Who is going to take care of me in case of trouble?' I says, 'You know Nick got locked up and Cockeyed Louis got sent away.'

"Jimmy says, 'Aw, what are you worrying about? You cockeyed son-of-a-bitch you are always worrying.'

"I said, 'Well, you know I ain't got no money. I would

like to know what this is all about. Who is going to take care of me?'

"And Jimmy says, 'We will.'

" 'Who are "we"?' I says. 'Who is the "we"?'

"He says, 'Davie and Abie and ———'

"And I says, 'And who? And who?'

"And he says, 'And Charlie Lucky.' "

Such was Dave Miller's story. So far as Lucky was concerned, it was only hearsay up to this point. But from the first witness to break after the big raid, Dewey had heard that Charlie Lucky was in the background.

When, later, Miller told his story on the witness stand, he related his story of the talk with Jimmy; but when he came to the mention of Charlie Lucky's name, as he sat there facing the gangster himself, Dave couldn't bring himself to say it. He testified that Jimmy told him those behind the racket were "Dave and Abie and Charlie," and that he did not ask or know what "Charlie's" last name was. But such is the fortune of trying a case with human witnesses.

IX. THELMA

PRAIRIE GIRL

Somewhere in Thelma Jordan's past there is a baby. We know almost nothing about it, or how it came into being, for that is one subject she almost never mentions. But I believe it was the reason she quit going to college, the reason she left home and joined a carnival. And doubtless it was the reason that Thelma, during her years of prosperity, always made it a practice to send home $25 a week.

Her parents had no need of the money for themselves. Her father was a public official in the small prairie city where she was born and brought up. It was one of those towns with a water tower, two or three office buildings, and a lot of church steeples jutting up out of the flat plain, and a country club at the edge of town with a nine-hole golf course, very flat. A dull sort of place, to be sure; but in the years when Thelma was an underworld girl in New York, home always seemed to be the perfect distant haven of dignity and security. Twice she went home to visit, and she was welcome; one time her big brother squeezed her so hard as she got off the train that he broke two of her ribs, and then she could not work for weeks. I don't know what story she invented about herself for those occasions. She never stayed long. For one thing, it involved a lot of pretense and hypocrisy. And Thelma always hated hypocrites.

Thelma is a little, dark, cuddly girl, with large soft eyes of the liquid, melting sort. It was the eyes, rather than any intellectual power, that got her by during two years in college; for even the professors in a small fresh water college, with a heavy enrollment of theological students, are susceptible to the helplessness of little cuddly girls. She was a nice girl, too, but unhappy. If she had been in the country club set at home, or in the sorority set at college, it might have made all the difference in the world; she would have married well, have become one of the sprightliest young matrons in town, and doubtless have made her husband happy. But Thelma did not rate that high socially, nor yet could she be as free and easy as the factory girls and kitchen maids. She had a position to maintain, even if her father was only the street cleaning commissioner in what was hardly more than a one-horse town.

FLIGHT

And so she was an unhappy girl, a girl of moods, despondency and bursts of irrational high spirits. It is not surprising that she got into a jam, as girls have been getting in trouble since the dawn of time. And then, to save her family from disgrace, she went away in the summer of 1931 and joined a carnival.

There often is reason to regret that this story is not a novel. If it were, we should have no doubts about Thelma and there would be no mystery about her. We should know all about her emotional tensions, and what she thought and felt, and how the hair curled down behind the young man's ears, and why she fell for him. We should be omniscient. But that unfortunately is not the case. We know only a few things about her, and have to guess, just as we observe some and surmise much about practically all the people we know intimately and meet every day.

I should like to write fiction about Thelma. Then she would become a personification of flight, swept along and downward by strange currents over which she had no control, struggling only to keep her inner personality intact, grasping at straws and chips which she clutched as secret symbols, known only to herself, representing dignity, power and self-respect, and always secretly gratifying a grudge against men. Maybe it would make sense. Maybe it does make sense. That is the way I like to think of the real Thelma, and I may be right.

The carnival she joined was one of those half-starved shows which moves from week to week, with a portable ferris wheel, a tattooed lady, some hootch dancers, a daredevil motorcycle rider who also takes high dives into a tank, and a small army of camp followers and gyp artists with phoney gambling devices. They were rough and ready, good-hearted people of a sort Thelma had never known before, and not a bit respectable. She liked them.

Thelma did pretty well. She started selling sandwiches and soda pop at a lunch counter, but she was a good-looking girl to find in a carnival and soon was moved up to a job in a target booth on the midway. She would roll her eyes at the yokels, sell them three baseball throws for a nickel, and give the winners kewpie dolls and cheap candy in fancy boxes. Men bought baseballs for an excuse to talk to Thelma, and business was good.

Everywhere Thelma went there was sex hunger in men's eyes, and the questing impulse of pursuit. That had once been thrilling but there was bitterness in Thelma now, and calculation. She would kid a man along, and he would spend his quarters and throw baseballs until his arm was sore, while she would exclaim in approval of his better throws.

He would try to date her up, and she would string him along. It was strictly business.

A PARTNER

One day one of Thelma's bedazzled young men, after he had left her booth, let out a yelp that he had been robbed. His pocket had been picked. Two or three days later the same thing happened again, and this time Thelma knew what it was all about. She had her eyes open and her suspicions were confirmed. The pickpocket was that slick young man from New York whom she had seen around the carnival, always apparently prosperous, but with no visible means of making money. She had been curious about him, but when she had asked about him no one had given her a direct answer. They had just shrugged their shoulders. Now she buttonholed him and gave him a piece of her mind.

"Say," said Thelma. "You better lay off my customers."

Perhaps the light-fingered gentleman had a good sales talk, and maybe Thelma was a bit sweet on him and easily influenced. I prefer to think that she was the smart one, for it is my impression that she had a hard winter ahead, and only a few months in which to make a grubstake before she lost her girlish figure. Whatever happened was unethical, reprehensible, even criminal, for the conversation ended with Thelma becoming the pickpocket's partner.

Before long Thelma became a most expert decoy. She was the *femme fatale* of that carnival. There was an anesthetic quality about her eyes. Let a yokel but look into them deeply enough and he was hypnotized. When he came to, his wallet was gone. But he knew very well that Thelma had not taken it, for she had never put her hands near him.

The carnival moved down through Nebraska, Kansas,

Oklahoma, and Texas. Thelma made $30 a week out of her regular job, but in a good week her sideline often paid several times that much. By November, when the carnival closed down for the winter and turned her loose in Texas, she had accumulated a good bankroll and had learned many things which they do not teach in college. She never did any actual pocket-picking herself, for that would have been risky; and so when her past came up to bother her in later years, she was able to deny with conviction that she had ever been a pickpocket. She gave up the whole thing after that November. This was not because of any especial pity for the men who pursued her, for she thought they were fair game, but rather because it made her uncomfortable to be tied up in something dishonest. Besides, she knew her partner was cheating her all along, but could not prove it or do anything about it at all. So she parted with him, and went to New Orleans for the winter.

ENTER THE PIMP

Thelma's next year is obscure. Her family sent her some money that winter, and I assume it was in that spring of 1932 that the baby was born. Then she adventured eastward, making her living I don't know how. We find her at the end of the year in a hotel room at Washington, getting married to a big, fine-looking fellow from Texas, who went by the name of Bill Cook. She was tired of adventuring and being on her own, and the prospective security of marriage to a fine young man made her unbelievably happy. Later Thelma said the marriage was a phoney, with a fake preacher and a fake license. Whether it was or not makes little difference. It was the means by which a pimp fastened himself on Thelma.

There is an old, well-established system that men follow to get girls into prostitution.[1] First the pimp finds a young attractive girl, not too smart, who is on her own and unhappy, who usually has just been through an unfortunate marriage or love experience. He is nice to her, takes her around, spends money on her, becomes her lover. Then she meets friends of his, glamorous girls with fine clothes, and money to spend. It is a great adventure, running around with fast people. It is a shock to learn that their money comes from prostitution, but the pimp preaches tolerance, broad-mindedness. When the soil has been thus prepared, a financial crisis arises. Often the girl's lover disappears for several days, during which she is frantic with worry. Then he reappears, looking worn and dirty, with the news that he has been in jail and must go back to prison for a long time unless he can raise the money quickly to fix the case. That is the girl's cue for self-sacrifice. She is the one who can raise the money and there is only one way to do it. She volunteers. The man's cue at this point is to protest, to bewail the situation, to insist that he is going to prison. But, if he has worked it properly she insists upon saving him. The one basic rule of all this is that the man must never urge the girl to become a prostitute; she must do it of her own free will, or at least think that this is so. For, while a man may strongarm a girl or otherwise force her into a bawd's life, this does not establish the proper emotional relationship; the girl may resent it and later skip out on the pimp, leaving him without a meal ticket, right back where he started. But once a girl is started in prostitution, the chances are she will continue to do that kind of work, as long as she can get it. For it has a corrosive impact on a

[1] This explanation comes from Cokey Flo.

girl's personality, and she reacts violently, for the human
ego is a resilient thing. The girl develops a reckless bravado.
She takes refuge in drink, narcotics, or other expensive
habits, and by them is in turn imprisoned. Sometimes a girl
tries to break away, but usually she goes back. Prostitution
makes a girl much more money than working in a cafeteria
or bargain basement, and is a lot easier on the feet.

OPPORTUNITY

In Thelma Jordan's case the financial emergency was that
Bill Cook had a wonderful business opportunity in far-off
Texas, and no money to get them there. Once in Texas, they
would be fixed. There would be money, and security, and a
home of their own, and babies. But now there was no money.

Thelma fell for it, and took the leap. She made contacts
through Bill's friends, and started going on calls to hotels
in Washington. Soon she accumulated a bankroll and they
were off to Texas.

But in Texas Bill's job failed to materialize. Instead he
got her work in a joint at Houston, and came around to collect her money twice a week. Thelma's hopes for a home life
faded. She was in a worse jam than ever.

Thelma never got out of the house except when Bill was
with her; and even if she did give him the slip she knew she
would be a lone helpless girl in a strange country. She resolved upon an indirect resistance. She did not complain
about the life, but she did complain about Houston. She
knew she was good enough for a bigger town than this,
where she could make more money, Thelma told him. Bill
ought to take her back to Washington, or even to New York.
This time it was Bill who fell for a line, and so it was they

arrived in New York in the autumn of 1933, and Thelma began to work the hotels.

She soon found there was a lot she did not know about the business, but she learned rapidly. She still wanted to get rid of Bill Cook, and was just waiting for an opportunity to shake him, but the impulse to run away and get out of the business had grown weaker and weaker. It was about this time that Thelma started drinking brandy steadily. Any experienced bartender will tell you that is bad. A man can do very well on a steady diet of Scotch, or even gin, but when he starts pouring down a steady stream of brandies something is going wrong. Brandies taken one after the other make maggots in the brain, or something. Or maybe it's maggots in the brain that demand brandy. Bartenders and people told Thelma she should try Scotch for a change, that too much brandy was bad. But by that time she did not care much. From eye-opener to nightcap it was brandy for Thelma.

DECADENCE

One thing Thelma did not like about New York. In Texas a two-way girl had been a curiosity, and there had been no great demand for her services, but here in the metropolis a girl was expected to be versatile in the most degrading ways. Thelma just couldn't bring herself to it, though it appeared her squeamishness was likely to stand in the way of a successful career. Then she started observing things and using her brains, and discovered that in the craze for versatility, certain specialties had been almost overlooked. Soon, in addition to the normal run of business, she had developed herself a lucrative special clientele.

Thelma first got the idea one night when she had a call

to a drugstore on Broadway, which seemed a queer place
for a call. When she got there, the proprietor was waiting
for her in the back room behind the prescription counter.
He had there a disreputable old worn-out pair of shoes, and
all he wanted her to do was to put on the shoes and walk
up and down in front of him a few times. When she did so
it seemed to please him very much, and he gave her $10
for the job. What easy money! Thelma thought. How long
had this been going on?

Thelma now found that her education came in handy.
She could read better, had a more inquiring mind than most
other girls in the business. There were, she discovered, certain esoteric books, sold under the counter in some shops,
hoarded in libraries by strange old men, which told all manner of strange things about the sexual vagaries of mankind.
She couldn't get far with Krafft-Ebing, because every time
he got really interesting he wandered off into Latin and her
Latin had never been good. But the others were easy reading.

There were lots of peculiar men in the City of New York.
Soon Thelma developed a code of conduct all her own for
dealing with them. She would have nothing to do with men
who wanted women to degrade themselves, who wanted to
humiliate a girl, or be cruel to her. But if a man wanted
himself humiliated, or wanted to make a complete fool of
himself, that was nothing for her to worry about. She could
help him out, and probably add a few frills he had not
thought of. All this was a help to Thelma's ego. She was a
cut above the other girls.

Her work had one thing in common with journalism: she
met so many interesting people. She also had many queer
jobs. One man took her to Florida with him in the season of

1935, and all she had to do was to stand by, a nude, attentive spectator, an acolyte you might say, while he performed strange sexual rites involving the slaughter of a pigeon. She had a very nice time at Miami Beach.

FUNERAL PARLOR

But the strangest of all was a man she met but once. He was a prominent New York City mortician and Thelma was sent to see him, I believe, by Peggy Wild. She went with the understanding that she had never been there before, and would never go again; that he insisted upon.

She was received by a solemn butler, in black garb, who took her evening wrap and left her to wait in a small reception room, a stuffy little place where Thelma sat uneasily in a carved mahogany chair. As she waited she heard distant organ music, playing a funereal air. It made Thelma think of a time she had gone to a cremation over in Queens, for a little girl she knew. She felt rather out of place, in her pert little yellow evening dress.

At last the butler came again, and motioned for her to follow. She went behind him along a gloomy passage. Then he opened a door, stood aside for her to enter, and closed the door behind her.

Thelma found herself in a large, high chamber, the walls of which were hung from ceiling to floor with unbroken folds of black velvet. The organ music, though muffled, was stronger now. The only light came from two large candelabra at the far end of the room. And there, between the candles, in their ghastly light, was a coffin. It was an ornate coffin, and the lid was turned back, revealing a lining of tufted white satin.

Hesitantly, nervously, Thelma stepped forward, led to-

ward the coffin by some unseen compulsion. Now she stopped
suddenly, for in it lay a corpse. Thelma had never seen a
dead man before, and it was ghastly. The face had the blue
pallor of death, the waxy consistency, and its lips were
rouged as though to make it look more natural to the be-
loved ones of its family. Thelma drew still closer, moved
on by some horrid fascination.

Now suddenly she felt her feet gripped to the floor, herself
frozen in a rigid tension of terror. The corpse was moving!

Its eyes opened. Its lips fell apart from grinning, uneven
teeth. Its head turned. And now, slowly, stiffly, it sat up in
the coffin, and turned upon her its glaring, staring eyes.

Thelma, standing there frozen, heard a scream. It was a
long, piercing, agonized scream, a vocal convulsion of fright.
Then all at once she knew, she realized, it was she herself
who was screaming. That realization brought release. Her
knees quaked and trembled, and on her shaking legs she
turned madly and staggered toward the door, which was
opened by an unseen hand and led her into the outer corridor.

There stood the black-garbed butler, calm, cool, funereal,
holding her evening wrap for her shoulders.

"That will be all tonight, Miss," he said, and handed her
a plain white envelope.

Down the block, under a street light, Thelma opened it.
It contained a $100 bill.

LONELY HEARTS

It was Thelma Jordan, I think, who said that a girl keeps
a pimp because, when she wakes up with a hangover on a
cold, dark, gray morning, she likes to be able to look at some
one lower than herself. But Thelma had a sharp tongue, and

the remark had all the usual pitfalls of the epigram. The facts go deeper than that.

The universality of the pimp is one of those apparently inexplicable laws of nature. Practically every prostitute has one, whom she supports or whom she helps other girls to support. One fellow, who has had a certain amount of personal experience along that line, tells me that the only reason he can see for this is that the girls are dumb and haven't any sense.

Doubtless the phenomenon goes deep into the recesses of the human heart. There is no one in the world, I suppose, who leads a more lonely life than a prostitute. The men she meets are mere passing phantoms; her girl friends are insubstantial moths, here today and gone tomorrow. She is cut off from her family, from all the normal contacts of life. But her pimp is hers. He is interested in her, for a mercenary reason, perhaps, but still interested.

There are certain practical reasons for having a pimp. If a girl is pinched and taken to the police station, the pimp is the only one she can really count on to make a holler and see that she is bailed out. Then too, the girl is usually young and inexperienced when she arrives in New York, and her man makes contacts for her, sees that she gets a break. But the emotional reason is the more compelling. A girl has her man. He may be nothing to brag about, but he is hers.

Thelma Jordan had been in New York several months, and she still had her pimp, Bill Cook, who merely loafed, took her money, and fooled around with other girls when she was working. Thelma did not like him any more, she even hated him. They quarreled, for he took it as a personal affront every time she sent home her $25 a week. She thought about shaking him, but could not quite bring herself to it. He was the only person of her own in all New York, and he had got to be a habit, like brandy. It would have been easier to ditch him, if he had been a husband.

In the spring of 1934, Thelma started booking with Pete Harris now and then. Working the hotels was a very speculative business, but you could be sure of good money if you worked in a joint. One of the first places where Thelma worked was May Spiller's joint in West Fifty-fourth Street. Spiller wasn't really her name, but she used that because she was running the place for Bennie Spiller, who really owned it. All Thelma knew about Bennie was that he was a shylock who hung out and did his business at a saloon in Fifty-fourth Street, and he came to the house every day to take the money out, so it would not be there in case of a holdup. Bennie would hang around a while when he came over, kidding with the girls, and he quickly took a liking to Thelma.

LOVE WALKS IN

This Bennie Spiller was a slim fellow with a long nose and receding forehead, but was no inconsiderable person. He was hardly more than thirty years old, but already had made a lot of money. He had started out in Philadelphia, very young, in prostitution and bootlegging; and, not being a racket man, he had been smart enough to hold onto his dough. When Philadelphia got a bit hot for him, about 1930, he cashed in and moved to New York. Though he did not advertise it, he already had a bankroll of about $75,000, and soon he had his fingers in a lot of things. His brother Willie ran a horse book which Bennie backed, and Bennie devoted his main attention to the shylocking business, lending money to sporting and underworld people. If he lent $5, he would collect $6 the next week, which amounted to 1000 per cent interest, and if he lent $50 he would collect $6 a week for ten weeks, which was several hundred per cent. It was a profitable business. Then he also had May Spiller's on the side, and his shylocking gave him chances to get in on a lot of deals.

Before Thelma had finished her first week at May's, Bennie dated her up and took her out to a night club, after her night's work was done. They had a good time, Thelma was very gay, and as the night went on, Bennie got more and more fond of her. Finally they went riding home in a taxi. Thelma snuggled over against Bennie's shoulder, and he put his arm around her.

Suddenly Thelma pushed him away.

"Say, quit that!" she said. "Listen, Mr. Bennie Spiller, you needn't think that just because I work in a joint, I have got round heels to fall for every fellow that comes along. I understood that this was a social occasion!"

For that was something Thelma was very strict about. Business, she always insisted, must be a positively impersonal matter, and in society she did not expect to behave as if she were working. She remembered she had often heard it said, you mustn't mix up business and friendship, when somebody wanted to borrow some money or something. Thelma sometimes thought she would go batty if she didn't keep herself a little private life. Except when she was having one of her rattle-brained, reckless spells, Thelma was a prim girl. She was even, as girls from the prairies are likely to be, a little bit prudish.

Bennie was dumbfounded. He said good night and went

home in a daze. What a girl that Thelma was! Bennie
thought back through the years, and he could not remember
when he had ever known a girl as refined as Thelma. He
could not remember when he had been so hot and bothered.
Criminee! This must be love!

THE BUM'S RUSH

Bennie and Thelma saw a lot of each other after that.
They went to night clubs after she was done, or to a midnight movie. Thelma told him about her home town, and
college, and the carnival and Bennie told her about Philadelphia and the shylock business.

Thelma even told him about her troubles with Bill Cook,
for Bill had been raising the devil lately, out of jealousy
over Bennie's attentions to Thelma. She told Bennie she did
not know what she was going to do about him, and wished
she could ditch him.

One night Bill did not come home. The next day Thelma
did not see him. The day after that she told Bennie that
Bill was missing.

"I guess maybe he is in Texas by this time," said Bennie.
And then he told her. It had made him mad to think of
Thelma having to support that fellow Bill, especially when
she wanted to get rid of him, so he had got a couple of fellows to talk to Bill.

These friends of Bennie's were very nice fellows and had
not done anything to Bill, but they had told him to take a
powder and had gone to the train with him to see that he
got on it.

When Thelma realized that at last she was rid of Bill,
she was overjoyed. She told Bennie she did not know how
to thank him. It was very nice, she told Bennie, that she

had someone like him who was fond of her and would look out for her.

Don't mention it, Bennie said, it was nothing. Being as he was in the shylock business, he always had to have fellows around who would persuade people that they should not be deadbeats. These fellows were very strong, but they were very nice too, and they had been glad to do a good turn for Thelma.

Bennie told Thelma that any time she wanted to work, she could work at May Spiller's. He would be glad to have her, because she helped build up the business. That was nice, because May's was a good house, and most of the customers paid extra. It was a three-girl place, and took in on the average $1,500 a week, and a girl could often clear $200 in a week there for herself. Thelma did not want to wear out her welcome, but she did work at May's one week out of nearly every month that year. It was nice, too, that she could keep her money for herself, and still have a boy friend like Bennie Spiller.

Thelma and Bennie were seeing each other almost every night now, but did not live together. Bennie had his home downtown, in Twelfth Street, and Thelma lived in Ninety-sixth Street, with Red Head Mary Morris, whose boy friend was Ralph Liguori's partner, and that was how Thelma came to know Nancy Presser so well.

Bennie and Thelma were very happy when they were together, for they were that way about each other, and sometimes they would remind each other about their courtship, and how it was six long weeks before Bennie could make Thelma.

Bennie thought he was very lucky to have a girl friend

like that. Not a man he knew had a girl friend as refined as Thelma.

TROUBLE FOR BENNIE

When Jimmy Lane threatened to kidnap Bennie Spiller, in the spring of 1935, and clip him for ten grand, it started a complex and fantastic chain of events. Bennie and Jimmy had many a good laugh over it together later on.

The upshot of it was that Thelma's boy friend, Bennie, was lifted to an eminence he had never expected, and became a member of the prostitution combination itself.

It all started with the $25 a week protection which was being paid by Marty Greenfield, a brothel keeper, to a mob of strong-arm men led by one Cockeyed Johnny. This same Cockeyed Johnny mob was also on Spiller's payroll for $25 a week.

Business was very bad in the underworld in those days. New rackets were developing, but they had not yet replaced the Prohibition bonanza, and the unemployment problem was acute. Gunmen, salaried assassins who in the past had always been good for $75 or $100 a week, were in some cases working for as little as $25. Others were off the payrolls entirely, foraging for themselves, operating independently in small mobs under the loose patronage of their former bosses. The business of protecting joints was bread and butter to these groups.

One of these mobs, rivals with Cockeyed Johnny, was led by Bob Davis, who has since committed suicide in jail, and Jimmy Lane, now serving a long prison term for a jewel robbery in Madison Avenue. Lane and Davis started to take Marty Greenfield's joint away from Cockeyed Johnny, and Johnny raised a squawk. He protested bitterly.

"All right," said Jimmy finally. "You take Marty Green-field back. He ain't worth a damn anyhow. But I'm going to take Bennie Spiller. I'm going to snatch him, and I can take him for $10,000."

As news spread along Fifty-fourth Street that Jimmy Lane was going to snatch Bennie Spiller, there was hell to pay. Cockeyed Johnny knew he wasn't big enough to handle this, so he ran to Little Davie Betillo. Bennie Spiller him-self got Nick Montana to take him down to Little Davie Betillo because at a time like this protection is really wanted.

And when Marty Greenfield heard about it, he was scared too, for he was in the middle. If Bennie should be kidnapped in a quarrel over Marty, somebody then might snatch Marty to get even for Bennie. Marty grabbed a telephone and called Philadelphia. He came from there and people in Philly liked him, because he had always been good for some dough when the boys got in trouble. So he called up a racket boss over there—named Murphy, I believe—and told him what was happening.

Now this was after the murder of the Philadelphia racket boss Bill Duffy, and the top men in Philadelphia were Bug Siegel and Meyer Lansky, the Bug and Meyer mob of the big Combination. So Murphy called up Bug Siegel at the Waldorf-Astoria, and Bug Siegel got hold of Charlie Lucky, and Lucky passed the word on to Little Davie not to let Jimmy Lane put the snatch on Bennie Spiller so that Marty Greenfield would not get in trouble. That is the story that was told along Fifty-fourth Street after the crisis was over.

BENNIE GETS A BREAK

But in the meantime Little Davie was already in action, talking to Bennie Spiller himself. Little Davie needed money.

Everybody in the underworld needed money in those days.

"So they want to take you for ten grand," said Little Davie. "Bennie, you got $10,000?"

"Well," said Bennie, more frank than usual because he was on the spot, "I could get it up."

"I'll tell you," said Davie. "You bring me that $10,000. I will take care of them guys. I will kick the bellies off them louses. And we will put the money to work in the combination."

So Little Davie sent for Jimmy Lane to come downtown, and it is said that Jimmy sent back word that he hadn't got time, for Jimmy was tough. They told him Davie was very sore at him, but still Jimmy said he hadn't no time to go down. Having thus stated his position, he decided to take a jump downtown and see what Little Davie had to say. For nobody fooled around with Davie very long.

He found Davie in that café at 121 Mulberry Street, and a lot of mugs were hanging around outside there, so Davie said to come in the back room where they could talk. When Jimmy told his friends about that later, it was a build-up for him. He was tough, especially good with his fists. He could have slapped Davie all over the place with bare knuckles. But Davie did not use bare knuckles, and very few guys would have cared to go in that back room with him alone. Jimmy's friends took his version of that conversation with a grain of salt, but when they heard that he had gone in the back room alone with Little Davie, they figured that Jimmy Lane was no man to fool around with. A guy with that much guts would go far, and they thought it was too bad when he got caught robbing that jewelry store in Madison Avenue.

"Look," said Davie when they got in the back room. "I got a lot of mouths to feed here. Now do me a favor and lay off this Bennie Spiller. He is my man. There is many a favor you will want done."

Jimmy knew that Davie never had had Bennie up to now, but now he had him and he was going to clip him. So Jimmy said O.K. and they parted the best of friends.

HAPPY DAYS

Bennie's difficulties had turned into a windfall of good luck, or so it seemed to him. The percentage they gave him in the combination was a small one, to be sure. But it elevated his importance. He was in the big time now. He teamed up with Jimmy Fredericks in his shylocking, and the business did well, because they had the right kind of backing and when Jimmy or Bennie told anybody to pay up, why, he paid up.

Bennie thought Little Davie was the nuts after that. He had a case of hero worship. Davie had a smooth tongue when he wanted to use it, and Bennie was being clipped for his dough without his knowing it. It took an artist to do that. Bennie did not know until long later, when Tommy Bull tipped him off after they were in jail, that his part in the combination had been marked down for liquidation, both financial and personal, by means of a bullet. But the O.K. on that had never come down from higher up.

Bennie did not fit in with that crowd. He might be a slick article, a numbers man, a bookmaker, a shylock, a pimp or even a male madam, but he would never really be a racket man. The others felt that, and they took out their feeling in what seemed to Bennie a lot of carping criticism, hauling him on the carpet, mainly about his intimacy with that prostitute, Thelma.

"Bennie, are you pimping for that girl?" they would ask.

"Naw, I just like her," Bennie would say, but that did not satisfy them. So at one of their regular Tuesday evening meetings in November they told Bennie to go get Thelma and let them talk to her. Bennie went uptown to Thelma's apartment and got her, for she was not working that week, and took her downtown to Celano's Restaurant, in Kenmare Street, around the corner from Mulberry. There sitting at a table in a back corner were Little Davie, Little Abie and Tommy Bull. Bennie introduced her. She knew Jimmy Fredericks, but it was the first time she had met these bosses.

"Thelma," said Little Davie, "have you been giving money to Bennie?"

"No," said Thelma, "I don't give him any money."

"You know, you can't give any money to Bennie," said Davie. "Bennie can't take money from you and stay in the combination."

"I know you been making a lot of money here lately," said Tommy Bull. "If you ain't giving it to him, what are you doing with it?"

So Thelma told them she was spending her money on clothes and brandy, and sending the rest of it to her folks at home.

"Well," said Little Davie, "if we ever hear of Bennie taking any money from you, he will get kicked out of the combination. And if you are going to go with Bennie, work as little as possible."

Because they did not want to associate with a pimp.

X. THE GIRLS

NANCY SAYS NO

If only because she was the best-looking girl in the lot, Nancy Presser would have stood out from the crowd. But Nancy also had that vague, indefinable amalgam of qualities which, for want of a more specific term, is called personality. After the first mad night and day of the great raid, Nancy was quiet, subdued. She stayed by herself. She had a lot on her mind and she was worried. There was an intensity about Nancy's silence.

There are women who, sitting silent in a corner, can exude more magnetism, attract more attention than another female who is trying to be the life of the party. Nancy was that kind.

Luck had it that, on the night of the big raid, the questioning of the inmates of Polack Frances's house was turned over to Harry Cole, the good-looking yachtsman on Dewey's staff. Now, as I have indicated, Harry Cole is the sort of fellow almost any girl likes to talk to; he is, moreover, a lawyer with the utmost skill at putting people at their ease; and he has had unusual success in persuading criminals, both men and women, to open up and tell all. Later, as a jury lawyer, he was to win an astonishing percentage of convictions. It's the human warmth about him, largely, I suppose. At any rate, you would have thought that if any man could get the truth out of Nancy Presser, it would be Harry Cole.

164

Several times in the fortnight after Nancy's arrest, Cole questioned her. After her medical report came through, showing she was badly infected with both gonorrhea and syphilis, she could hardly maintain any longer that she was a good girl; but she refused to give any information whatever. Cole would talk to her, get nowhere, then send her back to the House of Detention for a few days more. It was boring, but still Nancy kept her mouth shut.

Here was Nancy, the girl who would do any damned thing you'd ask her, who had lived for eight years at the beck and call of any and all men; she was talking to a good-looking man and all she would say was no. Here was Harry Cole, using all his powers of persuasion on a dizzy blonde, and he could not get to first base.

It was, doubtless, a novel situation for both of them.

MEDICAL OPTIMISM

For the first week after the big raid, everybody in the Dewey office dropped what he had been doing and worked on the prostitution case. There was so much to be done. There were girls and madams coming back and forth from the House of Detention every day. There were defendants negotiating to take pleas. There were numberless other witnesses being hunted, picked up, and questioned.

There were so many girls around the place all the time that Dewey had to take additional quarters on the floor below for waiting rooms. That space was needed, if only to provide separate toilet facilities for the witnesses, away from those of the secretaries and stenographers. Such insulation was not available for Dewey and his men. They had to share the facilities down the hall with all the pimps and other underworld men who came pouring through their office.

This was not a minor matter. When the medical reports on the girls came in, it appeared that more than two-thirds of them were suffering from venereal disease, and more than half of those had both syphilis and gonorrhea. With some of them the diseases were not in communicable form (though that is a matter of medical opinion) but many of them were practically falling apart. These girls had been charged $5 every week they worked for medical examination by doctors who specialized in that line of business; many of them had health certificates. About all that can be said for the doctors is that they appear to have been confirmed optimists.

One of Dewey's men always wore gloves when questioning the girls. I expect he had never got over the shock of the pictures he was shown in some college hygiene course. Another of Dewey's assistants carried, long afterward, a faded and washed-out looking fountain pen. He had a girl sign a statement with his pen one day, then later could not find the pen. His secretary had sneaked it away, taken it home and boiled it. He got it back the next day.

After the first rush was over, things settled down to a more normal basis. A few men were assigned to prepare the prostitution case for trial, and the rest went back to their other investigations. Harry Cole resumed his work on the restaurant racket case. Sol Gelb was put in charge of the case for trial. The main brunt of associating with these women and questioning them was to fall on Frank Hogan.

Hogan was engaged to be married at the time, but for five months his fiancée saw very little of him. Night and day, at his office and at the House of Detention, he was trying to keep a hundred women happy.

THE PEOPLE'S DIGNITY

The first legal, technical job which fell on Hogan was to get the evidence for specific counts in the indictment. You can't just accuse a man of being a racketeer. As a matter of fact, there is no such crime as racketeering. You have to accuse him of a specific act, or acts.

The first count in the indictment eventually was to read as follows:

"THE GRAND JURY OF THE COUNTY OF NEW YORK, drawn for the EXTRAORDINARY SPECIAL AND TRIAL TERM OF THE SUPREME COURT OF THE STATE OF NEW YORK, by this indictment, accuse THE SAID DEFENDANTS OF THE CRIME OF PLACING A FEMALE IN A HOUSE OF PROSTITUTION WITH INTENT THAT SHE SHALL LIVE A LIFE OF PROSTITUTION, committed as follows:

"The said defendants, in the County of New York, on or about the 22nd day of April, 1935, feloniously did place a certain female, to wit, one Betty Anderson, in a house of prostitution, to wit, in premises located at 1 West Sixty-eighth Street, Borough of Manhattan, City, County, and State of New York, with intent that she, the said Betty Anderson, should there live a life of prostitution; against the form of the statute in such case made and provided, and against the peace of the People of the State of New York and their dignity."

The time, the place, and the girl were the same in the second count of the indictment, which accused the defendants of "the crime of receiving money for and on account of placing a female in a house of prostitution for the purpose of causing her to cohabit with male persons to whom she was not married," the sum of money being "not less than One Dollar."

The third count again dealt with the same time, place, and girl, and accused the defendants of "the crime of knowingly accepting, receiving, levying, and appropriating money without consideration from the proceeds and earnings of a woman engaged in prostitution."

Thus, in the same act, the crime had been committed in three different ways.

The indictment which eventually went to trial had ninety counts in it, setting forth specific instances of such exploitation of twenty-five different women.

The prosecution was to undertake to show that each of these acts was carried out as part of a conspiracy in which each of the defendants was a member. For it is the law that any conspirator is equally guilty with all others, of every act which is committed as a part of the conspiracy.

This indictment was to be the first one of the sort ever tried in the New York state courts. A racket is not a single crime; it is a complex, a series, of small crimes all rolled into one. Dewey saw this, and knew that to present a full picture of a racket to a jury, a change in court procedure would be necessary. He had a bill prepared and presented to the Legislature which permitted a number of crimes of similar nature to be joined in one indictment, so that the charges could be tried simultaneously. There was nothing new about this. It had been federal court procedure for a long time. But prosecution of that sort had been unknown in the New York state courts.

This bill later became the widely discussed Dewey Law. It was what made possible the spectacular Dewey racket trials. The prosecution case was appealed to the highest courts on the ground that this was unconstitutional, but the appeal was unsuccessful.

Governor Lehman sponsored the joinder of trial bill for Dewey. It lay dormant on the legislative calendar for a long time. Seemingly nothing was being done about it. Dewey was getting worried. He could not understand it.

Then, suddenly and unexpectedly, the bill was called up one day and put through the Senate without opposition, without a dissenting vote.

It happened that on that day certain Senators were absent, off on some junket or other. Maybe that was just a coincidence. At any rate, I don't doubt that every member of the Legislature was recorded as voting for the Dewey Law. That is customary with unopposed legislation.

THE SCHOOL

Faced with the task of transforming a motley crowd of girls and madams into a series of counts in an indictment, Hogan went about it in a canny way. He did not figure it out in terms of crowd psychology, but rather sought a method by which a vast number of cases could be winnowed and sifted down to a few, air-tight and copper-riveted. But he might have taken his method right out of the book.

Three madams had confessed on the first night, and by now these had been augmented by a couple more. The idea of giving testimony in exchange for immunity, while firmly cemented in the law's practice and traditions, was something new for these girls; and it took time to penetrate. The madams caught on more quickly. Indeed, they realized that this prosecution was down their alley. The gangsters were their natural enemies; and now, in a totally unexpected way, they were being given the help of the law in throwing off the parasites who had preyed on them.

Roughly, there were thirty-five madams and sixty-five girls among the material witnesses. The questioners started by getting all the madams in one room at the House of Detention. Among them were the madams who had decided to help, Betty Winters, Molly Leonard, Jennie the Factory.

Then into the room, one by one, were brought those girls who had agreed to be helpful. In the presence of all the others, and encouraged by Hogan, the girls would converse with the tame madams. They would refresh each other's recollections, and thereby isolate from a confusion of memories some specific date and place in which the crime of compulsory prostitution had been committed.

Anyone who has ever been to an old-fashioned testimonial meeting will know that when people start confessing their sins in public the impulse of other people is to do the same. Something of this sort began happening to the madams.

Then the girls who had confessed began putting the heat on the madams. One by one they walked around among the crowd, identified one madam after another, talked to them.

"You remember me, don't you?" a girl would say. "I worked for you last April at —— West Eighty-sixth Street. Rita was the other girl that week."

Before long the madams were confessing, one after another; and each one who did so was eager for company.

Now the tables were turned. The girls were brought into the room, and the tame madams were brought in one by one to go through a reversal of the process. Fingered by the madams, the girls too began to talk. Day by day they went to the meeting room. They called it "the school."

Soon there was plenty of the basic prostitution testimony.

It was an open and shut case against the bookers. But the bookers knew it, were confessing, offering themselves to testify. The important thing now was to develop the case as it related to the conspiracy, to the gangsters.

The racketeers' molls were slow in talking, and even when they did talk they were not immediately frank. They knew more than the others, but they had more reason to remain silent.

The other girls pointed them out. Mildred Harris, Pete's wife, was certainly important; the investigators already knew that. So was Frisco Jean Erwin, Pete Harris's sweetheart; she knew more than she was telling. That Thelma Jordan was the girl friend of Bennie Spiller, who hung out with Little Davie. The madams had missed Cokey Flo Brown, Jimmy Fredericks's sweetheart; she had been arrested a couple of weeks before and had jumped her bail.

And that blonde, said the girls, that blonde Nancy Presser, she was a gangster's girl certainly. She and that boy friend of hers, that Little Ralph Liguori, certain knew a bellyfull.

Some of the madams made things tough for Nancy. Up in the cell block they spoke bitterly to her. They called her names. They said she worked in joints to get the lay of them, and to put the finger on so that Liguori could go and stick them up.

FEAR

Hogan sought out these girls and talked to them especially. He wanted to persuade them to tell the truth. But even after they admitted being prostitutes, they would not be entirely frank. After he got by the first brazen resistance, he saw something else in their eyes. It was a cold, stark fear.

As Thelma Jordan was to say later, when a defense lawyer upbraided her for not telling the truth at first and demanded why she had not done so:

"I was afraid to talk, because I knew what happens to
people that talk and who tell things about the members of
the combination, about racket people. I know times girls
have had their feet burned and their stomach burned with
cigar butts because they talked, and their tongues cut, and
things like that, and I was afraid of it, and that is why I
didn't talk."

"Why are you talking now?" her cross examiner was to
ask.

"Because I have confidence in the people that are behind
me."

"Who are the people that are behind you?"

"It must be Mr. Dewey and his District Attorneys that
are on my side."

For cross examiners often put their feet in it.

The fear was real, and it was general. As Al Weiner was
to say, when asked what he had been promised in exchange
for his testimony—Al Weiner, the young booker who had
taken over the family business when his father went to
prison:

"Well, Mr. Dewey said he would recommend some leni-
ency, and that he would also recommend some sort of a jail
where I would not be murdered."

For that was what all these fellows demanded, before they
would plead guilty and testify for the People.

The fear was real, and there was good reason for it.
Things had happened to underworld people who squealed.
For instance, consider the case of the man who had been
arrested during January, three weeks before the Dewey

raid, while mailing a package of narcotics at the post office. Under questioning by federal prosecutors, he confessed and agreed to testify for the government. But it seems that news of his confession leaked out. He then was bailed out promptly and was taken to Mulberry Street, and what happened then we do not know. But a few hours later he was taken to a hospital, badly beaten, and shortly thereafter he died. When Tommy Bull was arrested in the big Dewey raid, a slip of paper was found in his pocket, with cryptic pencil notations on it. What they mean, why they were written, we do not know. First there was the date of the arrest of the narcotic man who had been beaten to death. Following this were written the date of his release, the date he was taken to the hospital, the date of his death, and the date of his burial. Small wonder that women feared to talk.

When Thelma Jordan said that she had confidence in the people who were behind her, she was stating the basic principle of successful criminal prosecution. With all the idealistic intentions in the world, no prosecutor will get very far unless he can persuade people to trust him, rely on his protection, virtually put themselves at his mercy. A successful prosecutor must deal with criminals, with underworld people; and they must be sure that they will not be double-crossed. Victims of criminals must be willing to trust him, be sure they will not be betrayed.

Dewey's basic and most important job was to convince criminals and the victims of criminals that he was a tough guy and a square shooter. And that went for everybody on his staff.

For this purpose, among the hundred women in the House of Detention, no man could have been better than Frank Hogan. There is in every Irishman, I suppose, a touch of the wild Corrigans, the showy Walkers, and the mystic Synges; but you would not know it with Hogan. He is a quiet, mild fellow, and he turns on no neon lights when he goes to work. You can be sitting in a room full of people, who all seem to be talking up and making impressions for themselves; and Hogan will be sitting quietly in the corner, listening. And you would never suspect that a murderer had once confessed to him, after going free for three years, and that Hogan had then comforted the murderer's bride. You can find out some of these things if you talk to men who work with Hogan, and a little bit more if you pump him. Then if you talk more, he is likely to come out with something, in calm, matter-of-fact fashion, that will make the hair on your neck stand up. For there is in him somewhere also a melodramatic touch of Dion Boucicault. Take the matter of Margaret—

MARGARET

The women were of all types. There were harsh-voiced madams from eastern Europe, with black mustaches. There were blowsy madams and stringy madams, and a thin-lipped spinster from New Hampshire, still under thirty and good-looking, who ran a joint. There was a gentle-mannered, gray-haired woman, who was worried lest news of her predicament come to her son, in military school. Among the girls were blinding blondes, and dark, gloomy girls with soulful eyes. They seemed to come from almost anywhere but New York. Some were rovers. They might work New York this month, Cincinnati next month, and Philadelphia the month after that, traveling around with their pimps. They came from Kansas and Iowa, South Carolina and Michigan, Hungary and Italy, California and Connecticut.

And many came from the mine towns of Pennsylvania. Nearly all had felt the pinch and bite of poverty, the blight of underfed slatternly homes. Economically they had bettered themselves, or so it seemed on payday. They were accustomed now to making more money in a week than their fathers, brothers, and old boy friends could make in a month.

Only a few of the girls came from New York, and one of them was Margaret. She was a small, dark Latin girl, with quiet manners and earnest eyes. With most of the prostitutes, it was apparent that they had come to the logical end of their dizzy ways. However innocent they may have been at one time, there was clearly no white slavery about this business. They were in it because they wanted to be. But Margaret seemed somehow cut from a different piece of goods.

She was among the first girls who admitted they were prostitutes, said they wanted to testify and put their past behind them, start out anew. She was very helpful in the early stages of the work. Clearly she was telling the truth about everything.

Margaret went through grammar school in New York, studied six months in business college, then worked two years in an office. When she was seventeen she quit her job, for she was going to get married. She had a beautiful wedding dress, with white flounces of lace, and a great veil. She had put away linens, and looked at furniture. The flowers were ordered, the cake was baked. Then, the day before the wedding, her fiancé died.

After Margaret's weeks of weeping, life all seemed changed. She was out of work, and could not find a job. At home she seemed superfluous. She was a girl of eighteen, with no apparent prospect of getting married. That was serious, for those of Margaret's race marry young, and an unwed girl of twenty is an old maid.

A fearful despondency came over Margaret. She loved her parents and they loved her, but there was a constraint between them. She left home and went to live with a girl friend, still hunting desperately for a job she could not find. Hope seemed gone. One night in a cheap restaurant, after a meager, lonely meal, she broke down, put her head on the table and cried.

"What's the matter, dearie, can I help?"

A girl was sitting beside her, was speaking to her. Margaret found herself pouring out her troubles, and the girl was sympathetic. She knew a place where Margaret could make some money, she said, and Margaret went with her.

Whether she had an inkling where she was going I do not know. Perhaps she did know, and still did not, for despair paralyzes the human spirit. That night she went to work in a joint.

News traveled fast among the customers, and in her first week Margaret took in $400. She attracted so much business that she was kept over for a second week. The third week she went to the hospital.

Physically she was patched up in a few weeks. Spiritually something much more serious had happened. Margaret felt she could never face her family again, she could never face anyone respectable. I don't profess to understand her reaction, but it was something old and trite both in fiction and in fact. She was out on her own, hopeless, friendless, emotionally crushed. She went back in the business. A few months later she was picked up in the Dewey raid.

Now that Margaret had given her testimony, told her

own personal story, poured forth her troubles, been transmuted into three counts in an indictment, she changed day by day. There was a glint of hope in her eye. All the girls were talking now about "going straight," making plans for the future. Margaret seemed especially serious.

So many fragments of human life and human problems poured in upon Hogan and burdened him down, matters far distant from the dry pedantries of the law. From a distance one might regard this feminine round-up with emotions of horror, with the feeling that it was a gaudy, bawdy affair filled with salt and gusto, with feelings of pity and sentimentality. But close-up, of course, it was just plain human, a collection of frail, helpless personalities; and it got under your skin.

But the thing that got under Hogan's skin the most was not the girls at all; it was the letters that came in. Within a day or so after the raid, the mail began coming, from all parts of the country. Fathers and mothers of lost girls, reading in the newspapers about the Dewey raid, had found in it a ray of hope. Perhaps the lost daughter could be found, in a New York brothel!

Day after day the letters came, each containing a picture. Hogan looked at the pictures, sent them back. He recognized none of them. He was finding no lost girls. Then one day a letter came with a New York postmark. Hogan sighed as he looked at it—another family tragedy. He unfolded the picture, glanced at it. It was Margaret.

Margaret broke down in tears when she saw the letter, wept hysterically and bitterly.

"Oh! Mr. Hogan! You won't tell them! You won't tell my mother I am here!"

"No, Margaret, certainly not."

So Hogan wrote a polite little note to Margaret's mother, returning the picture, and saying he could not recognize it.

But he could not get it out of his mind, and neither could Margaret. She loved her mother, but could not bring herself to face her. Surely her mother had some inkling of what had happened; but to know it for a fact and certainty, that would be too cruel. Hogan and Margaret discussed the situation and a few days later they decided to do something.

Accompanied by a policewoman, a middle-aged motherly person, Margaret went uptown and rented a hotel room. Then she sent her mother a telegram, saying she just happened to be in town, and please come to see her. So the mother came, and Margaret gave her tea and talked to her and heard all the news about the family. Margaret was employed, she told her mother, as companion to a woman who lived in California, and they were traveling. And Margaret's employer was there with them all the time, and told Margaret's mother she was so sorry that they must hurry away, but they just had to catch a train that afternoon.

So Margaret's mother went home happy, and Margaret was happier than she had been for a long time, when she went back that night to her cell in the House of Detention.

Where Margaret is now I do not know, or what eventually became of her. So many of the girls had such good intentions, and so few of them made the grade. But after the big trial was over, a couple of weeks after Margaret had been released, she turned up at the Dewey office to call on her old friends.

Proudly and happily, she displayed a marriage certificate, and proudly she introduced her new husband. He seemed a decent, solid fellow, though somewhat embarrassed as he stood there twiddling his hat in his hands.

I hope that he was as decent and solid as he seemed, that he did not put Margaret back to work. I hope they lived happily ever after.

SAWDUST TRAIL

There is no more obvious or venerable fact of psychiatry or religion than that confession is good for the human spirit.

Day by day now more girls were confessing, and receiving legal absolution in the Grand Jury room. It was as though a cool, fresh breeze had started to blow through the House of Detention. These girls had touched the depths. They were the dregs of society. Yes, they had just about everything possible wrong with them. But they were still girls, and girls who were now hitting the sawdust trail.

They became not unlike a lot of girls in a college dormitory waiting for graduation. They were going to start life anew. Two of them were very good at knitting. They taught other girls to knit. Pretty soon they all were knitting. These two thought when they got out they would start a shop for knitted goods and teach women how to knit. Jennie the Factory spent her time crocheting. She taught some of the girls to do that too. Some of the girls thought they would open tea rooms. Others, as in any graduating class, thought they would just like to have nice positions. Doubtless they dreamed about marrying the boss.

The girls began to look and feel healthier. They were practically on the wagon now, and all were off narcotics. Some of them were getting plump and healthy-looking, although some were getting too fat. They were having a holiday from sin.

With most abrupt impact, all these girls had come in contact with two dozen young men—as high-grade young

men as could have been found in New York City. It was a
new, doubtless a shocking, experience. For the first time in
years they had met young men who were interested in them,
not as meal tickets, not for abrupt carnal pastime. That had
its effect.

It does not do to think of these girls as strange, outland-
ish, abnormal creatures. They had little brains. Certainly
they were ill-prepared to meet life. They were dizzy blondes
and over-ambitious brunettes who did not know what to do
in the world or how to do it. They had been through experiences which to cloistered folk might seem the ultimate in
self-degradation. Yet the human animal is a strange, varied,
adaptable creature. In Japan, prostitution is an almost respectable means by which a girl may pay off her father's
mortgage and collect herself a dowry. In phallic temples of
India it may be the function of a priestess to be a prostitute. All that is Oriental. But even among the white folk of
the older European countries, a girl of the bagnio is accepted, tolerated as a commonplace, perhaps even as a useful member of society. Maybe these girls did not feel as
much besmirched, some of them at least, as some sheltered
folk may feel just in reading about them.

All the women, old and young, had such simple, human
foibles. Old Jennie the Factory, friendly from the first, had
her apartment uptown on the west side in which were four
Pekinese dogs, and I do not know how many canaries. To
keep Jennie happy, it was necessary for a detective to drop
up to her apartment every few days to see that Jennie's
maid was taking proper care of the family.

One day Bobby Connolly came down to the Woolworth
Building to be questioned. She just could not seem to make
sense or keep her mind on anything. It developed that Bobby

had a run in her last pair of stockings. A policeman had to go out and buy her a new pair before the examination could get under way.

The girls thought a lot about clothes. There was a primitive communism among them and when any girl was going out for some special event, she borrowed from everybody and was welcome to do so.

Later on, when the big trial started, a newspaper writer pulled a gag that you could tell the girls were not ladies because none of them wore gloves. After that a team of horses could not have dragged any girl to the witness stand unless she had her hands modestly covered.

THE LITTLE RED BOOK

Nancy Presser was scared. She could not understand all these things that were happening to her. People were telling her every day, even the girls were telling her, that she ought to open up and tell the truth, tell everything. She did not want to tell everything. She was scared, for one thing, of Ralph Liguori.

One day when Nancy was down at Dewey's office, her boy friend Liguori called there to see her, for the witnesses were permitted to have some visitors. Ralph said he could not understand how his girl Nancy could have got in a mess like this. Nancy told the prosecutors Ralph did not know anything about this prostitution business.

So he was not detained, and he went uptown with Nancy escorted by a detective and matron, when she went to their hotel room to get some clothes. Nancy got herself only four or five dresses and a few other odds and ends, for life was simple in the House of Detention. She left behind (as later listed by the hotel) two coats, five slips, five blouses, six chemises, two jackets, two skirts, four nightgowns, eleven sweaters, twenty-six dresses, fifteen hats, and four pairs of shoes.

As she rummaged through her things, Nancy chatted with Ralph and got him over next to her. Then, when the cop was not looking, she slipped a little red memorandum book into Ralph's hand. It was Nancy's business book, filled with names, addresses, and telephone numbers of her friends and customers. That was one bit of evidence Mr. Dewey would not get!

While other girls grew healthier and happier, Nancy grew pale and wan. When other girls were being questioned in mass, Nancy sat off by herself, refusing to participate. Often at night she poured out her troubles to Jennie the Factory, and old Jennie would tell her she ought to talk. And Jennie would tell Hogan.

"Ach, Nancella," Jennie would say in a wheedling and endearing tone. "Be a good girl. Tell the gentleman, please. You know me, I'm like a mother to you."

But Nancy would not. She would still hold back and Jennie would become impatient.

"Nancy, you dirty whore," Jennie would shout, "you god-dam so-and-so."

Then Hogan would talk to Nancy, tell her she ought to quit stalling and tell the truth. He knew that she knew plenty. Other girls had told him so.

"But, Mr. Hogan, you don't understand." Nancy would say. "You're legit and you don't need to be afraid. You don't know how it is with we girls."

And Hogan would try to reassure her, tell her she would be given protection, tell her she did not need to be afraid of men who were in jail.

"But, Mr. Hogan," said Nancy, "these people are not all

in jail. They got friends outside, friends bigger than them. You think you're keeping things very secret here, but there is girls upstairs flying kites out every day through their boy friends. Those people know what is going on in here. I've seen them right outside here on the L platform, shaking their fists at the windows up here."

So Hogan told Nancy, as the Dewey men told all the girls, about how Dewey prosecuted Waxey Gordon, with more than a hundred witnesses, and none of them was touched.

"Now, Mr. Hogan, I know something about that. When Waxey was arrested and sent to jail, he was through already. But this case is different. These people are big people, and they are not through. Do you realize what you are asking me to do? You are asking me to sign my own death warrant."

He could not persuade her. Day after day girls were being taken before the grand jury, there to win immunity by testifying. Clearly Nancy would have liked to go too, and tell about the routine details of employment, as other girls were doing. But nobody was being taken to the grand jury unless the investigators were convinced she was telling the whole truth. And Nancy so obviously was not being frank.

Finally Hogan suggested that she go down and talk to Dewey. Perhaps he could persuade her that she would be protected. She agreed.

Nervous, upset, and scared, Nancy was taken down to the Woolworth Building. She had to wait to see Dewey. But as she came into a waiting room she saw a familiar face. It was like meeting a friend in the wilderness. It was that nice Mr. Cole! Nancy went straight to him, talked to him for fifteen minutes, until Dewey was ready to see her. Then Cole and Hogan went in with her to see Dewey.

When Dewey undertakes to persuade anyone, he can be very convincing. He turned on all the lights for Nancy. He talked to her for a long time, assuring her that she would be safe. Cole and Hogan talked to her. Finally Nancy said maybe she would talk. But she did not want to do it while she was staying at that House of Detention. It was decided that she would be taken out to live, under police guard, in a hotel, and that Harry Cole would be in charge of questioning her.

After Nancy had been in the hotel a few days, she was lonely for congenial company. She would like to have Thelma Jordan with her, for they had got to be good friends in the House of Detention. So Nancy and Thelma, who was the sweetheart of the defendant Bennie Spiller, were put in an apartment together.

Nancy and Thelma grew very close to each other during the next few months. They went through troublous times together.

Thelma was with Nancy one day in Dewey's office, after Ralph Liguori had been picked up and held as a material witness, and Ralph was with them a few minutes.

"Nancy, are you talking?" asked Ralph in a whisper, so their guard would not hear.

"No, I'm not talking," said Nancy.

"Nancy," said Ralph, "you better not talk, about me or any of them fellows. Did you read in the papers about that Nancy Titterton that was murdered in the bathtub?"

Cold chills ran through Nancy and Thelma. The mere mention of Nancy Titterton and her fiendish death was enough to send cold chills through any woman in New York that spring. Thousands of them got new locks for their doors.

"Remember that girl was murdered," said Ralph. "That's what happens to people that talk.

"Nancy," said Ralph Liguori, "if you talk, I'll see that your picture, and all about you, gets in your home town paper."

XI. MILDRED

A WOMAN SPAT UPON

The time that Charlie Lucky spat in the face of Mildred Harris is an occasion, we may be sure, that he has since regretted. For it was Mildred who gave Lucky the works.

Mildred Harris is as good a name for her as any, and it will avoid a lot of confusion. Not counting one-night hotel stops, Mildred had used no less than ten surnames in as many years, and to at least four of them she was legally entitled. Her last husband was the prostitution booker whose professional name was Pete Harris.

Mildred had so many names because she had so many men, and because her men used so many names. She went from one man to another. Once she was the mistress of a prominent well-known business man, a sporting man about town, and when the Dewey men picked her up she was sharing her apartment with one of the city's most prominent homosexuals, Phil Ryan, a night club entertainer and master of ceremonies. Mildred had been around.

Out of all the men in Mildred's life, it is said that the only one she ever cared for deeply was Murray Marks; and that was where Lucky came in. It wasn't only that he spat in her face.

This Marks was one of the opium-smoking crowd that Mildred hung out with at the Century Hotel. He had been a Waxey Gordon lieutenant, but in the spring of 1933 bootlegging was on its last legs and so was Waxey's mob. Men had to shift for themselves, and Marks started out aggressively to become a big man in the opium business. That was dangerous, because drugs were regarded by the Italian mob as one of its exclusive preserves.

Mildred and Marks were that way about each other and during this period she was sitting in a speakeasy one night, sipping a brandy and waiting for him to join her. She felt someone near her and, looking up, she found herself staring into that drooping right eye of Charlie Lucky.

Lucky spoke to her, and just what he said I do not know. He knew her, and he knew she was going with Murray Marks. He spoke in sharp, bitter, cutting words. And he spat in her face. Then he turned and walked out of the saloon, followed by two dark men who had been standing at a discreet distance.

A few days later, on June 29, 1933, Murray Marks got off a bus at White Plains Avenue and Pelham Parkway, in the Bronx, and started to walk along the street among a crowd of women shoppers. A motor car which had been following the bus drove up behind him. There was a burst of pistol shots, and Marks fell to the pavement with five bullets in him. He was dead before he could even reach for the .38 revolver which he carried in a holster under his armpit.

There were few enough clues for the police. Marks had a pistol permit from a judge in Troy, and he carried a courtesy card from the Patrolmen's Benefit Association of Westchester County. Tracing a key in his pocket, detectives found his apartment hideaway in the neighborhood and in it was a pound of opium. One clue led to a house in the East 60's of Manhattan, elaborately outfitted for opium smoking, occupied by a brother of Chink Sherman. The killing was just another unsolved racket execution.

But Mildred had no doubts. After that she always hated Charlie Lucky. At his trial she told the jurors that she hated him. She did not tell them why.

GIRL OVERBOARD

Mildred was a Catholic, though not a good one. It is a strange thing: through all the years she was batting around, Mildred had a little holy water cruet which she carried with her, a tiny flat one-ounce bottle set in a metal frame, which was embossed with an image of the Blessed Virgin. After Lucky's trial, when Mildred went back out into the world, swearing she would go straight if it killed her, she gave the cruet to Frank Hogan of Dewey's office. She said it was a keepsake from a bad Catholic to a good one.

Sometimes Mildred went to confession, tried to straighten herself out. But that never lasted. She would go haywire again, and when Mildred went haywire she did it in a big way. She had had careful religious and moral instruction when she was young, but when she went overboard, she did so thoroughly, beyond her depth. There was nothing in the catechism to tell a girl how to behave after she became the mistress of a prostitution man.

Mildred came from a small town in the South, and she had that way with her which southern girls have. Before she had fooled around so much, and put on too much fat, she was a tantalizing minx. She was not little, but was a good-looking brunette on the well-built style. And she was a lady. That is, she had the manners of a grande dame. A man could take her anywhere and not be ashamed. That always helps.

When she was seventeen years old Mildred came North

and went into training as a nurse, but within a few months she met a young business man and married him. He was a Jewish fellow and they were married in the Temple Emanu-el on Fifth Avenue, then went to Pittsburgh to live. After three years Mildred got a divorce, sent her baby daughter to live with her parents, and went on to New York. That was in 1925.

A gay ex-wife, twenty years old, Mildred was soon in the thick of the city's party life, and in almost no time she was being kept by a prosperous cloak and suit man. After a year or so she married him, and it seemed as if she were doing pretty well by herself. But I guess he expected her to settle down, give up her old friends, live the dignified existence of a wife. So she ditched her husband and went to live in a fine apartment of her own, provided by her prominent sporting merchant. That lasted less than a year, however, and late in 1930 she took up with a fellow she thought was a Broadway gambler. Later she found out he was a prostitution man. That was Pete Harris.

There are people in the prostitution business who lead ascetic lives. Dave Miller, for instance, was a well domesticated family man. Then there are madams like Stone-faced Peggy, the thin-lipped spinster from New Hampshire, young, good-looking, but cold as ice. But Pete Harris was not that way. He was a girl fancier. He went at his business like a gentleman farmer, trying to make his hobby pay for itself. Just what his sex appeal was is difficult for other men to imagine; maybe it was just business magnetism. He had the best-looking string of harlots in New York, and though he always had three or four who were his special pets, he chippied around with a lot of them. Mildred used to bawl him out for it, told him he was like a tippling bartender, and the business would ruin him in the end.

After living with Pete a few months and getting a new slant on life, Mildred went in for prostitution herself. She knew she was not cut out to be a harlot, so she became a madam.

For a week she worked for Pearl Woods, one of the town's more prominent madams, as a prostitute. She did not like the work, but she thought it best to begin at the bottom, and at the end of the week she felt she knew the routine of the business pretty thoroughly, for Mildred was no dumbbell. Then she opened up a house herself.

After a while Mildred and Pete got themselves a penthouse apartment in Fifty-fifth Street, just west of Sixth Avenue, and Mildred ran her joint in an apartment on the floor below. Pete was able to give her some good tips on the business, but she always kept her business affairs separate from family life and got her girls from other bookers. She had an experienced maid to do the actual running of the joint, and her own part of the job was to bring in business. Mildred knew a lot of bartenders and men who ran speakeasies and clubs, and they always had men asking for a good address. Soon she had developed a long list of good customers. Once she was offered $1,500 just for her list.

In the spring of 1932 Mildred started to smoke opium. She had gone pretty thoroughly off the deep end by now, and also she had a lot of time on her hands. She knew a man and woman who lived in the Century Hotel and kept equipment for opium smoking, and a lot of minor racket people would go there to kick the gong, as smoking was called.

Mildred took to going there about once a week, just for

fun, and then more and more often. Other people paid the freight, for she was popular, and so it was very easy. These opium evenings were sexual orgies. Men and women would lie on the floor to smoke the pipe. Sometimes they would take off all their clothes. Then the party would get all mixed up.

Pete Harris began criticizing Mildred. He did not approve of opium smoking. It offended his moral sensibilities, it was expensive when it got to be a habit, and there was always danger of the law. But the main trouble was that Mildred seemed to have lost all her inhibitions. The thing came to an issue one night when Mildred, in front of a room full of people, took what might be called an unpremeditated roll on the davenport with one of her gentlemen friends.

"Mildred," said the humiliated Pete when the guests had gone, "you ain't got no ethics."

And he packed up his clothes and moved out of the penthouse.

NEW PLAYMATES

During the next eight months or so, Mildred went in for the Italian mob in a big way. Gus Franco, a former drug peddler who was now in the numbers racket, moved into the penthouse with her and they were sweethearts for nearly a year. Every Sunday Gus would take her down to have a big spaghetti dinner with his family, who ran a restaurant in East Eleventh Street, and Mildred got very fond of Gus's mother. It was to her she turned after her arrest in the Dewey raid, to have a lawyer sent to her.

Mildred soon gave up the penthouse, and she and Gus lived around in various hotels in the Broadway sector. In each hotel they lived under a different name, as though they were fugitives, but last names did not mean anything to their own crowd, who all used phoney names anyway. They smoked opium in one place or another every night. Mildred was thoroughly addicted to it now.

It was during this period that Mildred got acquainted with Little Davie Betillo and Tommy Bull. As she remembered it, Gus took her down to meet them and buy some opium, for they were big fellows in the drug racket. Mildred cultivated their friendship, often went on smoking parties with them. Opium had become a big item in her budget. Now she could buy it wholesale.

In the later days of her terror, Mildred thought often of those opium nights with Davie and Tom. Tom was an old-time thug, with heavy jowls and paunchy belly, who had a police record thirty years long, covering everything from homicide to seduction. He had been in prison six times. He was now supposed to be a big wholesaler in the drug business, big enough at least so that he could and did sometimes refuse to let import consignments of narcotics come ashore, because he wanted to maintain the market price. Little Davie handled the gun and muscle end of the business, so he was Tommy's boss. He said his boss was Charlie Lucky.

Tommy Bull was sinister enough, but the terrifying one was Little Davie. He was much younger than Tom, a slender young man with high cheekbones, curly hair, and slim hands. He had eyes that could be soft as an antelope's, eyes that could spit venom. Mildred could remember him lying there, sucking on the opium pipe and talking to Tommy Bull about the days when he had been a torpedo for Capone in Chicago, about guys that had been knocked off, guys that ought to be knocked off. Men who have spent their whole lives in contact with convicts and ex-convicts tell me they have very seldom met a really vicious man. Even in the underworld it is a rare person who takes pleasure in the contemplation of homicide. Little Davie was one of those.

In the spring of 1933 Mildred tried to pull herself together. She left Gus, took a cure for the opium habit, and went back to live with Pete. Relatively speaking, she had become respectable again; but it did not last long. Soon she was slipping away in the afternoon to take just a few puffs of opium, just a pleasure smoke; and before long she had the habit again. That was when she was playing around with Murray Marks. After his death she turned over a new leaf and started taking morphine. That was still the drug habit, an even more severe habit than opium, but at least it was more discreet. She would slip into her bathroom three times a day and take a shot in the arm. That wasn't the same as sprawling around the floor with a lot of people.

Mildred continued living with Pete, opening up a house every now and then when she needed extra money; and in 1934, after her husband had obtained a divorce, she and Pete went to the Municipal Building and got married.

The matter of a prostitution booker and a madam getting married struck a lot of people funny. There was a lot of talk about it, too, for there are cats and gossips even in the underworld. In their circles, Pete was a good catch, and other women were jealous. People said Mildred did not care about Pete, she had just married him for a meal ticket. They said Mildred had been putting the arm on Pete for money, even threatening to expose him.

But Pete and Mildred said all that was nonsense, they had got married because they loved each other.

Pete always denied it when people said he had married Mildred in self-defense, because somebody told him that, under the law, a wife cannot testify against her husband.

HOW TO INFLUENCE PEOPLE

Pete Harris was not a very big booker, but he dealt with the quality trade and made a pretty good living. So he always had parasites leeching on his back. He always had to buy tickets for benefits and testimonial dinners. There were vice cops he had to sugar. And, hanging around the telephone office which he maintained in West Sixty-ninth Street, were always three or four broken-down pimps, who used it as a place to sleep. But that was charity. It always seemed to Pete there was nothing more pitiful than a pimp who had lost all his girls.

The real blood-sucking, however, began in August, 1933, when Pete met Little Abie Wahrman, partner of Joe Levine, the fellow who had chased Dave Miller.[1]

Abie was a small fellow with blond, curly hair, nineteen years old at this time. He looked like any kid you might see around a corner drugstore, but he had been a mobster for five years, and had a reputation as a strong-arm man. He was helping support his parents in Brooklyn, he had installed his wife in a nice apartment in the Beekman Place neighborhood, and he himself had the opium-smoking habit. So he needed a lot of money, and Pete was one of those who were to provide it.

Pete first encountered trouble one afternoon on West Fifty-fourth Street, in the same block where Dave Miller had his encounter. Joe Levine and Abie wanted him to pay

---

[1] Joe Levine dropped out of the picture after the original strong-arming of the bookers, and Little Abie took over leadership of that mob.

$250 a week, but Pete told them they were crazy, he did not make half that much. After some dickering at a meeting over in Brooklyn, Pete agreed to meet them again in his own neighborhood, in Seventy-first Street, Manhattan, near Broadway.

A pair of Pete's tough friends had gone with him to Brooklyn, but for this appointment they did not show up, and Pete had to go alone. When he arrived, there were so many gorillas there it seemed to him the whole block was surrounded. Pete bargained with them until they came down to $100 a week, but when he refused to pay that, they raised the price again to $200.

"We shot Dave Miller out of town," said Little Abie. "We got all his joints."

"Well, I can't pay it."

"Then you will have to get out of town."

"All right," said Pete with a shrug. "I will go home and pack my clothes and leave town. I will leave town, because I don't make that much money."

So Pete turned and started to get in his car, which was by the curb. As he opened the door, somebody pushed him from behind and tossed him over into the back seat, and then there was a fellow on top of him shoving a gun in his stomach.

"Sit quiet," he said.

Then four or five piled into the car, and they drove him up to his apartment at 290 Riverside Drive. They all went up in the elevator with him, and when they got in the apartment they all pulled out guns.

Pete went into his bedroom and started throwing clothes into a traveling bag. His brother Eddie and Mildred's brother Art came rushing in, asking what was wrong; and when they saw the pistols they threw up their hands.

The visitors started pushing Eddie around. They told him to get ready, they were going to take him out of town too. This Eddie had done a slight bit for manslaughter himself, but he was no match for this crowd.

"Hey, what do you want from my kid brother?" cried Pete. "He's got nothing to do with me. He is just here visiting me."

"Hurry up, we're going to ride you out of town," said Little Abie.

"Oh, no, you are not going to take me in no car out of town," said Pete.

He was scared now, both for himself and Eddie. He was afraid they might take him out and dump him by the side of the road somewhere, just for an example. So Pete started to talk business with them again, and finally agreed to pay $100 a week. He said he would start paying the next week.

"Oh, no," said Abie, "you got to start paying now, starting today."

Pete looked in his money box, found $100 there, and handed it over. With that, the whole atmosphere in the room changed. Everybody put away his pistol and smiled.

All Pete's visitors, one by one, came up to him and shook hands.

"We will be your friends," said Abie. "We will take care of you and protect you."

"Nobody will bother you, nobody will shake you down," they told Pete. "You come down to 108 Norfolk Street,[2]

2 There is, there must be, a genius loci, or a contagion, which hangs over certain places in a great city. We find Little Davie hanging out at 121 Mulberry Street, just a stone's throw from Mulberry Bend, which was the gang hangout of an earlier generation. And it is coincidence, of course, but also we find Abie operating from 108 Norfolk Street. Only a few paces

and make your weekly payments there. There is a candy store there, a cigar store. We will be down there."

So they departed, and as soon as they were out the door Pete just plumped down in a chair and sat there for a long time. His knees would not hold him up any more.

A BIRTHDAY GIFT

Always after that Pete paid his money every week at the Norfolk Street store, sometimes giving it to Abie, sometimes leaving it for him in an envelope. Soon after Pete started to pay, Abie told him they were forming a combination for bonding houses, and he was going into partnership with Little Davie. He took Pete over to the café at 121 Mulberry Street to see Davie, and after that it was plain that Davie was Abie's boss. One time when some other gangsters tried to shake Pete down, demanding $1,000 and threatening to kidnap him, Pete told Little Abie about it. Abie took him over to see Davie, and it was Davie who sent a man uptown with Pete to straighten things out and tell the other mob to lay off.

Pete did not know anything about Davie when he first met him, and he was concerned about seeing that the people who got money for bonding were able to deliver the goods. The bonding of girls at $10 a week was nothing new. Pete had done a little of it himself. Various groups had undertaken it, and often they had welshed when bail money was needed. But it was something new to consolidate the control of booking and bonding under one combination, and that was what Little Davie was undertaking.

from the front door of this candy store, in 1927, Legs Diamond and Little Augie Orgen were shot down. From that wounding, Legs went on to notoriety; and from that death of Little Augie, Lepke and Gurrah rose to their great underworld power.

"You know it is a serious thing, them girls going to jail," Pete told Little Davie. "A bookie can't take a chance on any girl going to jail. He faces twenty years if a girl will open up on him. I want a guarantee on no girl going to jail."

"Positively," said Little Davie.

After they had left, Pete asked Abie who Little Davie was.

"Who is going to put the money up for the bond?" asked Pete. "You know they have got to put money up. If they get six or seven pinches in a day, they will have to put up a lot of money on them bails. Some bails are $500, some are $200, some are $100."

"Don't worry about that," said Abie. "Charlie Lucky is behind him. He is behind Little Davie."

So Pete quit worrying about that, because he knew that Charlie Lucky was about as big as they come. And in the meantime this little fellow Abie was giving him plenty to worry about.

One day Abie told Pete he was going to have a birthday. It was plain he expected a present, and Pete thought it would be a good idea to give him one. So he got a handsome wrist watch, bought it wholesale through his brother, paid $55 for it, and gave it to Abie.

Abie opened up the package eagerly, and then when he saw the watch his face was suddenly contorted with rage.

"This is a cheap watch!" he cried. "A secondhand watch!"

Pete's heart sank. He should have known Abie would want a watch with diamonds.

Abie jerked his arm petulantly, threw the watch at Pete. It crashed against the wall and fell tinkling to the floor.

"Just for that I'm going to fine you," said Abie. "I am going to fine you $300. And for the next six weeks you will pay me $150 instead of $100."

Soon after Pete had finished paying this $300, Abie put the bite on him again. Abie said he had to have $750 in a hurry, to help a friend out of a jam, and he wanted to borrow it from Pete. Pete said he was broke, could not lend any money. So Abie said that was all right, he would borrow it from a shylock, and Pete could give him $60 a week for fifteen weeks to take care of it. Pete paid the $60 a week, including $150 interest, which made it $900 in all. After it was all paid off, Pete asked Abie to pay it back to him.

"Oh, that was a donation," said Abie.

"But I loaned it to you."

"It was a donation," said Abie. And that was that.

During this period Mildred and Pete were getting ready to get married, and the whole situation gave Mildred a pain in the neck. By working hard and drumming up a lot of new business, Pete had been able to scratch along and pay off the $100 a week, but all the extras were getting him down. Pete was not a fellow to live economically, he had to keep up a front. He liked to drive a Packard, and give fur coats and platinum watches to his women folk. As a result, he was up to the ears in debt to the loan sharks, the combination's own loan sharks.

Mildred told Pete he was a fool to stay in the racket. All he was doing was make money for other people, and get deeper and deeper in debt to their own shylocks. She wanted him to get out and open a saloon somewhere else, so he could lay something by for the future. But they wouldn't let Pete get out unless he paid his debts, and they kept shaking him down so he could not get out of debt.

When Pete had to run away in January, 1936, Mildred told him this was his chance. They were still good friends, though they were not living together, and she told him to use his trouble as an excuse for getting out of the racket and staying away from New York.

For one thing, Mildred hoped that if Pete got out of the racket she could win him back again. In his business there were entirely too many office wives.

A SLIP OF THE TONGUE

Mildred refused to tell anything after her arrest as a material witness on February 1. Then for the next ten days she was going through a drug cure and convalescing, and she was not much use to herself or anybody else. When she went back to the Dewey office again, she found that evidence had piled up against her husband. She and Pete's brother, Eddie, who was also held as a witness, talked it over and decided the thing to do was open up. But they never did open up thoroughly until March 5, when Pete was extradited from Philadelphia and decided to tell all and throw himself on the mercy of the court.

Sol Gelb was now in general charge of preparing the prostitution case for trial. After a long talk with the Harrises about the advisability of their telling the truth, in hope of mitigating Pete's sentence, he settled down to take long statements from the men concerned. He turned Mildred over to Charles D. Breitel, one of the junior assistants, to make a statement. In this statement came the real beginning of the downfall of Charlie Lucky.

Mildred told Breitel that she had had a talk with Little Davie, asking him to let Pete get out of the business. She said Davie had refused, unless Pete first paid up all his debts. Breitel asked her what there was to stop Pete from leaving town anyway.

"For fear of these people," said Mildred.

"Well, they wouldn't follow him out of town, would they?"

"Of course," said Mildred. "Absolutely."

"What makes you say that?" persisted Breitel.

"Well, that's the understanding I've always had. They weren't only New York people, understand."

"What makes you think they weren't confined to New York? Who were they?"

"It's a general rumor," said Mildred. "This I can't truthfully tell you but it was general information that Charlie Lucky was the head of it; that he was Little Davie's boss, but that I can't—"

"And by Charlie Lucky do you refer to the Unione Siciliana?"

"Yes," said Mildred.

Charlie Breitel is a small dark fellow with glasses, a very business-like, clipped, efficient manner, and a poker face. Here was something big and exciting, but he was casual.

"Where did you get that information from?" he asked.

"Through hearing people talk."

"What people?"

"Well, rumors, after all, go around."

"Was it Pete that told you Davie was one of Lucky's men?"

"No, Pete has always believed it too."

"Well, then, he must have told you that, if you know he believed it."

"Yes."

"What did Pete tell you about it?"

"Nothing directly," said Mildred. "You see the position I was in. I didn't realize, when he used to tell me these various things—I used to think he was just telling them to me but he was trying to impress upon my mind the seriousness—the type of people he was mixed up with—how deep he was really in it."

Mildred had clammed up. Her tongue had slipped. She had said more than she meant to say. Breitel pressed her no further. After the stenographer had left, he thought she might talk about it more freely. But she would say no more.

Sol Gelb was busy questioning Pete and his lobbygow,[3] Jo Jo Weintraub, for some days. When he finally got around to reading Mildred's statement, he saw the importance of the mention of Lucky. He questioned her about it. He wanted to know the source of her information.

Even before Little Davie and Tommy Bull were arrested, the Dewey office knew that they were Lucky's men, though it had no evidence of it. On the night of the arrest, Dave Miller said he understood Lucky was the boss of the racket. A prostitute named Patsy Day asserted repeatedly that Dewey did not have the real boss, that he was Charlie Lucky. There were other straws, all pointing in the same direction, but no evidence. Most of the assertions that Lucky was the boss traced back to the leading defendants awaiting trial, Jimmy Fredericks, Little Abie, Little Davie. Pete Harris said that Abie and Jimmy had told him Lucky

---

[3] People tell me this word should be defined. The word *lobbygow*, I believe, originally was applied to Chinese pimps. It is now commonly used to refer to a stooge or underling of someone in illegal activity. For instance, a corrupt judge may have a lobbygow who hangs around him and takes care of fixing cases. The term was commonly used by those in the prostitution business.

was top man. Pete did not know. He did not know Lucky. If anyone in the Harris family knew, it would be Mildred, because she always had run around with the Italian mob.

Hearsay. Hearsay. How much of what we all know is hearsay! Everything we read in the newspapers is hearsay. Everybody knows that President Roosevelt has a brain trust, but to almost everybody that knowledge is hearsay. To almost all the employees of General Motors it is only hearsay that the duPonts control the company. Could anyone be found who could testify, and would testify, concerning the boss of the prostitution racketeers? It was Dewey's job to go to the top.

Mildred, questioned by Sol Gelb, began telling things she had not told before. She said Davie and Tommy Bull were not the head men in the racket, that they were working for a boss. Gelb asked her who the boss was. She replied that Dewey had missed him. Gelb asked her if she knew who the boss was. She said she did not. He then confronted her with the statement she had given Breitel. She went off into evasive answers.

Gelb tried a new tack, started questioning her about her past life. She began telling more. She had said she knew Davie and Tommy only slightly. Now she told of knowing them for years, buying narcotics from them, smoking opium obtained from them. Repeatedly she said Dewey did not have the boss of the racket under arrest. She admitted she was not telling all she knew.

Mildred said she did not trust the Dewey office. She was afraid she would be double-crossed. Unlike other women who had been before the Grand Jury, she had not been given immunity; she had signed a waiver. Gelb was surprised. That was a mistake. It was the open, announced policy all through this case to give immunity from prosecution to all the women who told the truth, even to the pimps and other minor figures.

Frank Hogan was with Gelb at the time, and together they assured her she would not be prosecuted. She insisted she wanted something more than oral promises. So Gelb sat down and wrote out a promise that she would not be prosecuted. He signed it and Hogan witnessed it. Mildred said that made her feel better.[4]

"Mildred, are the rumors true that Lucky is the boss?" he asked.

"Yes," said Mildred.

But she would not talk more about him. Mildred now said she was afraid. She revealed that she had a small daughter living in the South. The Dewey office might be able to protect her, but it would not protect her child. Mildred talked more and more about herself, told details of her past, though omitting her own activities as prostitute and madam. She never did admit those until just before the trial, when Dewey insisted she must tell the whole truth. She drew a picture of her child out of her pocketbook to show, tearfully talked about the little girl. That child she said was the one sacred thing left in her life. She said she was glad to have Frank Hogan there, because he also was a Roman Catholic.

4 The defense found out about this letter, and when asked on cross examination whether she had any such written promise, Mildred lied about it, for some unexplained reason. Neither Hogan nor Gelb heard this testimony, and Dewey did not know about the letter, so the denial went uncontradicted in the record. Later the letter turned up, as an apparently important point in the application for a new trial: the charge was made that Gelb told Mildred to conceal the letter and commended her for doing so. There was no reason to conceal it, and in view of all the surrounding circumstances, the charge was absurd.

Both Hogan and Gelb tried to reassure her that she and her child would be safe.[5]

Gelb asked her again what prevented her husband from getting out of the business.

"You have no idea of how I tried to get him out of it, how I begged and pleaded for him," said Mildred. She said she never would forget the sneer of the man who refused her.

"Was it Charlie Lucky you pleaded with?" asked Gelb.

"Yes," said Mildred.

But again she refused to tell more. She told Gelb he had no conception of the power of Charlie Lucky.

Gelb and Hogan suggested that she talk to Dewey. Maybe he could satisfy her. She agreed.

Mildred was very nervous after this talk. She was jittery all the time those days. She was still weak from the narcotic cure, and was under the most strenuous of emotional pressures. Gelb gave her a couple of drinks of brandy to brace her up. He often had to do that.

The next day Gelb took Mildred to see Dewey. She told Dewey she knew Charlie Lucky and could testify about him, but she could not bring herself to do so for fear of what might happen to her. Dewey talked with her at length, told her she and her child would have all necessary protection, and she need not worry about that. Finally she agreed to talk.

MILDRED'S STORY

It was during the fall of 1932, said Mildred, that she met Little Davie and Tommy Bull and after that she saw

[5] This account is based on lengthy affidavits on the subject by Gelb and Hogan. This interview later became a subject of controversy, when Mildred gave a different version, and said she was alone with Gelb.

a lot of them. They often came up and spent the evening at her place. One night she was in the downtown Italian section with Little Davie and they went in a restaurant, and sitting there at a table was Charlie Lucky.

"I want you to meet my boss," was what Little Davie said in introducing them, she remembered. Davie and Charlie talked for fifteen minutes or so, and then they left. That, of course, was before the beginning of the prostitution conspiracy.

Mildred said she saw Lucky five or six times after that, with Davie and Tommy, and they merely exchanged greetings.

Late in 1932, said Mildred, she heard Davie and Tommy talking about prostitution.

"Tommy said to Davie that he heard there were a couple of fellows bonding houses of prostitution. They took $10 a week from each girl," said Mildred. "He thought it was a very good thing for them to get into; and Davie said he didn't want to be bothered with it, because he didn't think there was enough in it. So Tommy said it could be worked up into a very good thing; they could take over practically all the houses in New York. And Davie said to him that he would talk to him about it later."

Long after this, said Mildred, in the fall of 1933, after Pete had his trouble and started paying protection money, she went downtown to see Little Davie. She went on:

"I said to him, 'What is this I hear about this bonding of houses and protection of bookies? Pete is having a lot of trouble with the east side fellows, and I hear that you are interested in it, is that right?' And he said, 'Yes.' I said to him, 'They are asking Pete for a lot of money; he isn't making that kind of money; he can't pay it; I would like for you to do something about it.' So he said there was nothing he could do about it; he had to pay like the rest of the other bookies.

"I said to him, 'Who is behind this? Are you still working for Lucky?' And he said, 'Yes.' I said, 'Is Lucky behind this?' He said, 'Yes.'"

In the fall of 1934, when she and Pete were planning to get married, said Mildred, she went down and talked to Davie again:

"I told him that Pete and I were going to be married, and I wanted Pete to get out of the business. So he said, 'He can't get out; he owes too much money.' So I said, 'Well, give him a chance to pay the money.' Davie said, 'He can't get out as long as he owes money.' Well, I said, 'That is ridiculous. Every week there is something else. They constantly shake him. There is tickets; there is donations from week to week, and there is more and more money, and then he has to borrow back from your own shylocks. There is no possible way that he can ever get out. He can't pay the money, because it goes around in a circle.' So he said, 'Well, he can't get out until he pays the money.' So I said to him, 'I am going to see Lucky, I am going to make it my business to see Lucky.' He said, 'It won't do you any good, because anything I do is all right with him.'"

So Mildred could not get anywhere with Little Davie. She and Pete were married. A few weeks later, in January, 1935, she went to Miami, taking Pete's eight-year-old nephew, Eddie, who had been sick. She took a month's supply of morphine with her, and Pete sent her $40 a week to live on down there, and she lived in a cheap hotel, but she ran into a lot of fellows she knew and had a good time batting around night clubs and the Roney Plaza. Her picture got in the newspaper, identified as a former Ziegfeld Follies girl.

One day at Hialeah race track, Mildred saw Charlie Lucky from a distance, and she decided that now was her chance. She asked about where he hung out, and was told he could be found, late at night, in the Paddock Bar and Grill. A night or two later she went there. She said he was sitting at the bar, and when he saw her he left his two companions and sat with her at the bar for a few minutes.

"I started talking to him," said Mildred. "I said, 'You know I am married to Pete now; I want Pete to get out of the business.' And I said, 'I have been to Little Davie and he won't do anything for me. He says there is nothing he will do about it. I told him I was going to see you, and he said that it wouldn't do me any good.'

"I said, 'He can't get out because of the money that he owes. They constantly shake him down. There is no way of his ever getting out unless you do something for him.'

"So he said he would see Little Davie when he came back to New York. So I said, 'Well, where can I see you?' He said, 'I will see you in New York.' So I said, 'Where?' He said, 'I will see you in New York.'

"He said, 'Well, as long as he owes the money he can't get out.' He says, 'You know the racket.'"

That, said Mildred, was all she could remember of the conversation, but in May of that year, when she was back in New York, she saw Lucky one night at the Villanova Restaurant, in West Forty-sixth Street, where he hung out, so she talked to him again:

"I recalled to him the conversation I had had with him in Miami about Pete, that he was going to see Davie, see what he could do for me. So he said that he had talked to Davie, and there was nothing he could do about it, he had to pay the money. I said, 'Well, that goes back to the same argument again.' I said, 'There is no such thing as him paying the money. He can't get out, he can never catch up, he can never pay.' So he says, 'Well, he can't get out unless he pays the money.'

"So I said, I pleaded with him. I said, 'Well, you are the only one who can do anything for him. Please do something for me.' So he said there is nothing he can do or would do about it.

"So he says, 'You know the racket. Let him alone.' "

That was Mildred's story, just as she later told it on the witness stand, and substantially as she told it to Sol Gelb now in his office.

There were other things she told, of course, things which were hearsay, things which would have been irrelevant, incompetent, and prejudicial if mentioned at the trial. She told of Charlie spitting in her face, and the death of Murray Marks.

She was told before the trial, I assume, that she must not tell things like that, or tell about the opium smoking of Tommy and Little Davie. Such things might cause a mistrial, and it is the duty of a prosecutor to protect his record.

As she was to tell her story at the trial, there was a weakness in it. It seemed surprising that, if her acquaintance with Charlie was so slight, he should have recognized her so easily at Miami Beach. Dewey on his redirect examination tried to bring out more on that, but he was held down by objections, and bound by the original answer of his witness.

In private Mildred had told that the occasions she met

Lucky with Little Davie and Tommy Bull were opium-smoking parties. She had told of Lucky, back in those days before the prostitution racket started, lying at his ease with an opium pipe, declaring that he was going to be a bigger man than Al Capone.

XII. ARREST

GOOD-TIME CHARLIE

Good-time Charlie was a pimp.[1] His wife was a prostitute and she stuttered. She stuttered so badly that the Dewey people never could make much sense out of what she was saying. But that did not keep her from making a living for Good-time Charlie.

In the light of Charlie's later behavior, his wife became an important witness. The Dewey men had a good idea why Charlie acted as he did, but because his wife stuttered so much, they never could be certain. So sometimes it is advantageous to have a wife who stutters.

According to various accounts, Good-time Charlie was in on the ground floor of the prostitution bonding combination which started up in the late summer of 1933. Moving spirit in this venture (which belied the common impression that economic enterprise was dead in that blighted year) was Jimmy Fredericks, who later was to assume prominence in the industry by such methods as blackjacking a madam and threatening to kill her dog.

This Fredericks, or Frederico, had been a criminal since childhood. He always blamed his own anti-social tendencies on the brutality of a parental school where he was sent for

[1] "Good time," along with its other meanings, is a technical term used by vice cops in their testimony in Women's Court. It used to be, at least, that whenever a vice cop found a prostitute with a man he asked him what he was doing there; according to testimony, the man almost invariably replied: "I came for a good time."

211

truancy, though that may be discounted, since he had a feeble-minded brother who was sent away for assaulting a child. So far as I know, Jimmy had only one job in his life. Paroled from a burglary term in Elmira, when he was seventeen, he worked at $9 a week as a machine helper for a refrigerator company, but soon decided that was too tough. So he started sending prostitutes up into vacant rooms of the tall loft buildings in the garment center, where they would be convenient to men in the clothing factories, and took 25 per cent of their earnings. After serving another prison term, five years at Sing Sing for grand larceny, with a bit extra tacked on for an escape, Jimmy ran a string of cordial shops on Staten Island, apparently as a blind for other activities.

Fredericks was now a squat, fat, bull-necked mug in his late thirties, with oily hair and a dark, beetling brow. He hung around on the sidewalk in front of a chain drugstore at Seventy-second Street and Broadway, and people around there had him figured out for a shylock. He did shylock, with other people's money; and if he told any debtor to pay up, the debtor tore everything loose to get the money, for Jimmy was that kind of guy. He also had his little business of booking prostitutes, out of a doctor's office in Thirtieth Street; but he let his assistants run that and just took his cut on the profits.

So now Jimmy decided to go into the business of bonding prostitutes. According to various witnesses his associates included Diamond-toothed Eddie, Yock Goldstein, Tony Pisanelli, and Good-time Charlie.

JIMMY LOSES A DECISION

This venture was to be on a bigger scale than any of the sort that had been operating before. The promoters knew that, to make real progress in biting every prostitute for $10 a week, they had to have financial backing and to stand in right with the mob downtown. So, the stories go, they went to see Jerry Bruno and he thought it was a good idea.

[All through the prostitution trial, witnesses mentioned this Jerry Bruno, one of the Mulberry Street bosses, as a member of the combination. But all this came from accomplices; there was never enough corroboration to arrest him and bring him to trial. Eventually, Jerry Bruno was tried and convicted by the federal authorities as a boss in the narcotics business, and in that same drug case Ralph Liguori, Nancy Presser's boy friend, was brought down from state prison and also convicted.]

Everything seemed to be going fine, but then one day Jimmy Fredericks came to his stooges in the booking office, Danny Brooks, Billy Peluso, and Little Bingie, with a sad announcement. He said he had "lost a decision downtown" and had to get out of the bonding business.

Now, more than two years later, as the Dewey men pursued the prostitution case, they wanted to know what happened at that meeting downtown, when Jimmy Fredericks lost the decision. So they sent out cops to look for men that might have been there, and they brought in Good-time Charlie.

Yes, said Good-time Charlie, he had been in that combination with Jimmy, and one day they had all been called downtown to a meeting. They did not know what it was all about, but they went to a restaurant in Mulberry Street and were put to wait in a back room.

Then, accompanied by Little Davie Betillo, into the room came a dark, intense-looking man with short legs and a squinting right eye. It was Charlie Lucky, said Good-time Charlie.

"It was funny," said Good-time Charlie. "We were sitting down there, but when Charlie Lucky came in, all the Italians stood up.

"He talked to Little Davie awhile, and then he turned to us.

" 'You guys are through,' he said; 'I am giving the business to Little Davie.'

"Then he turned around and walked out again. We were sitting down, but all the Italians were standing up."

So Jimmy Fredericks and his crowd were out of the bonding racket, for Little Davie was the boss now, not Jerry Bruno. According to Good-time Charlie, Little Davie hated the guts of Jimmy Fredericks and said he would keep Jimmy from making a living if he went broke doing it.

But after Little Davie had been running it awhile, the guy who was managing the bonding was not getting anywhere; so he hired back Jimmy Fredericks to do the work. After that Jimmy was busy. He had collectors, Yoke, Teddie, and Chappie, who went to all the houses every week to collect; and then he turned the money over to Tommy Bull. He had Little Bingie on the telephone, and when a joint was pinched Jimmy would get word of it through Bingie. Then he would have to hunt up Tommy Bull and get the money to bail the girls out.

They would not trust Jimmy to keep a supply of bail money on hand, and that was a pain in the neck. Because when girls were pinched, Jimmy would have to hunt all over the place for Tommy; and lots of times he could not find him, because Tommy would be somewhere sleeping off an opium jag.

MORE WITNESSES

The investigation of a criminal case is much like prying the lid off a paint can. Once you get it started, it comes fast.

Mildred Harris had inadvertently mentioned Charlie Lucky and the Unione Siciliana; Good-time Charlie had talked, and though Good-time Charlie was not the easiest man in the world to believe, everything now was pointing at Lucky.

Danny Brooks, who was brought down from Dannemora, Little Bingie, Billy Peluso, Dave Miller, and Pete Harris all said that they had been told, by bigger men who had been arrested in the racket, that the boss was Charlie Lucky. They had all wanted to know about that and had asked questions, because they wanted to know whom they could rely on for backing if they were grabbed by the cops.

Now Thelma Jordan was talking too, to Harry Cole. She too had been told that Lucky was the boss. Jimmy Fredericks had told her. And Bennie Spiller, after he was taken into the combination, often had mentioned Lucky. He had talked about the regular Tuesday night meetings of the combination, told of meeting Lucky there. She and Bennie had driven Fredericks to the Waldorf one night, when he said he had to meet Lucky.

Dewey, stalking the big shots, had undertaken to smash a minor racket by the way; and the trail had led to the biggest shot of them all.

HUMILIATION

Charlie Lucky had not been seen in New York since he had slipped away in November, after the murder of Dutch

Schultz. He had been in Miami since, had registered with the police there in December. He had stayed there with a friend who ran a gambling house. Undercover inquiries brought forth that Lucky was now taking the waters at Hot Springs, Arkansas, a favorite winter resort of the bigger criminals.

A trusted detective of the New York force was at Hot Springs for a holiday. Word went out from Dewey to grab Lucky. The racketeer was found sitting with friends on Bath House Row, was arrested, and was promptly turned out in $5,000 bail.

When he heard of that, Dewey nearly burned up the long distance telephone wires. He sent word to the Arkansas authorities that Lucky was "Public Enemy No. 1, the most powerful and dangerous racketeer in the country." Thereupon the judge hastily called Lucky back and held him in $200,000 bail.

In New York witnesses were quickly taken before the grand jury, an indictment was voted, and extradition papers were started west by airplane. Bad weather forced the plane down, delayed the papers two days.

Big money and the friendliness of Hot Springs to its paying guests were at work for Lucky. He had a half dozen of the town's most prominent lawyers working for him, including members of the Legislature and city officials.

Attorney General Carl E. Bailey of Arkansas entered the lists in behalf of Dewey. Lest something untoward occur, he sent twenty state troopers at dawn to take Lucky away from the Hot Springs jail and spirit him away across the mountains to Little Rock. Bailey did not deny reports that he had been offered $50,000 to lay off, but announced that "Arkansas cannot be made an asylum for criminals" and

the state's honor was "not for sale for blood money." The
whole thing gave Bailey a buildup which was probably de-
cisive when, later that year, he was elected by a narrow margin as Governor.

For ten days the extradition fight went on. It was delayed
by court orders and stays of execution, proceedings in both
state and federal courts. Then Dewey noticed a law point.
They were bound by a court stay not to take Lucky away
for two days, but legally that did not mean forty-eight
hours. At a minute past midnight, ten hours before Court
met to consider the matter further, they were free to remove
Lucky. At a nearby junction there would be a train at midnight. Hold the train!

With the approval of another court, Charlie Lucky was
taken from his cell at midnight.

"I am being kidnapped!" he shrieked, as he was rushed to
the waiting train for New York.

Back home, Lucky maintained a pose of injured innocence.

"I may not be the most moral and upright man who lives,"
he said, "but I have never stooped so low as to become involved in prostitution. I have never been mixed up in anything so messy."

That was to be the rallying note in future months for his
friends in the underworld, his friends in the sporting world,
his lawyers, as they spread the inevitable cry that Lucky
was being, had been, unjustly prosecuted. He was a racketeer, a crook, all right, said his supporters, but in this case
they had him wrong. Many people along Broadway still
say that.

Lucky's arrest was indeed a shocking, humiliating thing.
Gangster though he was, his position in the underworld car-

ried the dignity that went with power. He was a big man in big things. But here he was arrested, accused of being mixed up in a little, dirty, cheap-jack racket. For though the prostitution racket might some day have become big and strong and successful, it never really did. But a conviction for failure would be just as serious as a conviction for success; prison would be just as confining, just as cold.

Back in New York, Justice McCook held Lucky in the unusually large bail of $350,000.

"I am in a fog!" cried the master of the underworld, and covered his face with his hands.

XIII. TALES OF THE
WALDORF

NANCY TALKS

"Yes," said Nancy Presser. "I know those fellows you arrested. I met Tommy Bull and Jerry Bruno and Jimmy Fredericks with Ralph Liguori. I know Davie and Little Abie.

"And I know Charlie Lucky too."

Nancy was talking now, and it was as though the gates of a dam had broken loose. It was not just about the Luciano mob. That was only incidental in her life. This was a racket girl talking about the underworld.

As Nancy began telling her story, Harry Cole sent out and had Liguori, her boy friend, grabbed as a material witness. Perhaps he would even be a defendant. Though he was small fry, he seemed to have an in with the big mob; and if he could be persuaded to talk, if his resistance could be broken down, he would be much more important than any mere prostitution man.

A girl from a $2 house said she knew Charlie Lucky? Was that credible? Yes, it was, if you knew the rest of the story—that she had been a high grade call girl, and a friend of the Waxey Gordon crowd.

There are two facets to an investigating prosecutor's job. First he has to go out and get the testimony. Then he has to examine that testimony, check it, decide whether he believes it. A prosecutor cannot bring forward a witness he does not believe. That would be not only unethical and dishonest, it would be downright stupid. Nothing blows up in the prosecutor's face more certainly and embarrassingly than a lying witness, for the art of cross examination is a highly developed one and, in a big underworld case especially, the defense is likely to know more about the witnesses than the prosecution can.

Nancy was convincing. What she told came forth, not full blown and complete, but as isolated facts combed bit by bit from the crowded tangle which is anybody's memory. And as the bits came forth they fitted into a consistent pattern. Where there were known facts to check with, Nancy's stories agreed with them. She told about Gashouse Lil; and when Lil was picked up, they got her insurance policy and the check Nancy had forged for Ralph. Her stories about dope running fitted police suspicions, though they were not to be confirmed until Ralph was convicted in the Jerry Bruno case long later. Nancy told a fantastic tale about going to Great Meadow Prison with Waxey Gordon's theatrical troupe, and inquiry revealed that such a trip actually had occurred. Nancy knew the ins and outs of the Gordon mob. She could describe the apartment of Joe the Boss to the satisfaction of a detective who had been to Joe's funeral. She described Ciro Terranova's pink stucco villa. She drove around the Mulberry Street neighborhood with detectives and pointed out a lot of mob hangouts they knew, and some they did not know. This baby evidently knew her stuff.

Nancy said she had known Charlie Lucky ever since her girl friend, Betty Cook, had been going with him. Later he had been bodyguard to Joe the Boss, she said, and after Joe's murder had become the real boss of the rackets throughout the country, succeeding the imprisoned Al Capone as head of the Unione Siciliana.[1] Nancy said she had first heard of Little Davie as a bloodthirsty killer, when she was running around with some of the Capone crowd in Chicago. She said she would never dare to go on the stand against them, for fear of being murdered.

It was in 1934 that she got to know Charlie Lucky really well, said Nancy, and that came about through a fellow named Charlie. She had his last name right on the tip of her tongue, but just could not remember it. It was a long Jewish name. He had lived in the Hotel Alamac, on the fourteenth floor, and she had his name and room number in that little memorandum book she had given to Ralph Liguori. She said she had Charlie Lucky's name and address in that book too.

Nancy had met this fellow named Charlie through Willie Weber, one of Waxey's mob, at the Palace Hotel, and Willie had lent them the key to his room so they could go up there. After that she was often called to this Charlie's room at the Alamac, and she often saw him at Kean's Tavern, a gin mill at Forty-ninth Street and Eighth Avenue, across from Madison Square Garden, where a number of gangsters hung out. Charlie told her he owned a piece of Kean's.

Thus Nancy led up to the story which, bereft of all its irrelevant and incompetent, but clarifying, details, she was eventually to tell on the witness stand.

NANCY'S STORY [2]

One afternoon at the end of 1933 or early in 1934 (said Nancy Presser) she was in Kean's Tavern with the fellow

[1] Joe the Boss was supposed to be head of the Unione Siciliana, but Al Capone may have been Joe's boss.
[2] As developed on cross examination, as well as direct.

by name of Charlie; and there, sitting at a table drinking, were Charlie Lucky, Abie Wahrman, Little Davie, Jimmy Fredericks, Jerry Bruno, and Tommy Bull. They invited Nancy and her friend Charlie to sit down and have a drink. She sat there talking with them for about an hour, about nothing of any consequence.

It was the first time in years that she had talked to Charlie Lucky, but she was a girl who had known him when. Naturally she played up to him, now that he was a big shot. She slipped him a bit of paper with her phone number on it. He smiled at her and winked.

Ten days or two weeks later, Nancy ran into the same crowd in Kean's again, and again sat down to drink with them.

"Davie said to Lucky," recalled Nancy, "that a lot of the houses don't want to bond, a lot of the independent houses. 'We will have to go and get the independent houses and get them to bond.' He said that he was having trouble with a woman by the name of Dago Jean, because she would not bond.

"So Lucky turned around and told him to go ahead and wreck the joint." [3]

Nancy did not remember any more of that conversation. That much had stuck in her head because she remembered Ralph saying something about Dago Jean a day or so before that.

It was some months later (Nancy's tale continued) that she saw Lucky again. It was October, probably, and he called her up late at night and asked her to come to his place

[3] Dago Jean was brought in the Dewey office and admitted having trouble with the combination, including the wrecking of her joint.

at the Barbizon Plaza. It was a high floor, she could not remember which.

They had a few drinks and talked and kidded around. (Nancy was not permitted to tell any conversations except those relating to prostitution.)

"I told him that I needed money, that I was going to go to work in a house; and he told me not to go to work in a house," Nancy remembered. "I asked him why, and he said if ever I needed money he would let me have it.

"Then I asked him how was the bonding coming along, and he says, 'It is coming along fine.' "

Nancy sat there talking with him an hour or so, and they had no sexual relations, and he gave her $50 when she went home, and it was nothing unusual for a man to give her money without going to bed with her.

Two or three times more Nancy was called up to see Lucky at the Barbizon Plaza late at night, but on none of these occasions did they go to bed. Lucky couldn't, he had something wrong with him; or anyway, Nancy refused. (Lucky's probation report set forth that he had a chronic condition which "lighted up" now and then.[4])

The last time Nancy went to the Barbizon Plaza, she and Lucky had a few drinks of champagne, six or seven, about two bottles; and Lucky got so drowsy that he just keeled

4 Among the first things a prostitute learns are certain primitive principles of diagnosis. It was in connection with this hygienic point in Nancy's story that I was so struck by the tale about Lucky's hospitality to the Purple Gang of Detroit. Assuming Nancy's testimony to be true, was he again displaying chivalry toward his usual feminine playmates by staying away from them in his time of distress and turning his attentions to a call-girl?

This is pertinent; for, considering Lucky's station in life and Nancy's, her story was naturally subject to ridicule at his trial and among his friends along Broadway. He could have had fancier girls than Nancy; but, if he was sick, that would hardly be a friendly act to them. There are so many things we don't know, can only guess.

over and went to sleep. Nancy went home and left him there, and did not see him again for about six months.

The following summer, in 1935, Lucky called her up again; and he was now living at the Waldorf-Astoria, on the thirty-ninth floor, as Nancy recalled it. Late at night, seven or eight times, she visited him there; and he was no longer incapacitated.

One night Lucky was talking on the telephone, and Nancy heard him saying only yes, and no, and O.K. But then he turned away from the phone and seemed very angry, and said he had been talking to Little Davie and he couldn't depend on Davie and would be better off if he went on the thing himself.

Another time they got to talking about prices in houses and "he said that the two-dollar houses were going to be raised to three dollars, and the four-dollar and five-dollar houses were going to be raised to higher prices, and that he was going to go and put the madams on salary and take the joints away from them; he said Little Davie was going to take care of it for him."

And that was Nancy's story, so far as it related to Charlie Lucky in reference to the prostitution case.

BELLHOPS AND MAIDS

There was more than this, of course, to Nancy's stories of her visits to the hotels. Sometimes, she said, men would come up to see Lucky while she was there; and then she was told to go in the bathroom and keep the water running, so she would not hear. She remembered once hearing, though, some discussion about the split on the $400,000 armored truck hold-up in Brooklyn. And there was a certain prominent citizen who came up sometimes to see Lucky, and who got off the elevator some floors below, maybe at the apartment of Bug Siegel, and then walked upstairs to see Lucky, with much puffing, panting, and redness of the face.

The elevator operators in the Waldorf Tower were able to identify the picture of this prominent citizen as a man they had carried as a passenger, but they did not know what floor he had gone to; and nobody but Nancy could ever put him in Lucky's apartment.

After Nancy had told her story about being at the Barbizon Plaza and the Waldorf-Astoria, an obvious idea occurred to Dewey. Maybe employees of the two hotels had seen other defendants in Lucky's company.

Investigators were rushed uptown, to find all those hotel workers who had had contact with the Luciano apartments, waiters, bellboys, elevator operators, chambermaids, assistant managers.

They were brought down for Charlie Grimes to question. Before each of them he dropped a bundle of twenty photographs with no names on them, to see whether they could make identifications.

"Who? Me?" exclaimed a bellhop. "I should identify fellows in Lucky's room!"

None of them was eager. None of them wanted to do it. But Charlie Grimes is a big dark fellow, who can make his face look like two or three thunderclouds.

Within a few days Grimes reported that a half dozen witnesses had picked photographs out of the batch, as those of men they had seen in Luciano's apartment. And the identified pictures included nearly all of the prostitution case defendants. This was a gold strike. It was tremendous. Reputable persons were identifying the racketeers with Lucky.

They were the only respectable witnesses that had been turned up in the whole Luciano case!

One night Grimes and Cole were questioning Fred Seidel, for years the operator of an elevator in the Waldorf Tower, and they had a detective bring Nancy Presser and another girl into the room.

"I do not know the girl with the darker hair, but I have seen the blonde," said Seidel. "I have seen her several times in the hotel but I don't recollect the occasion."

"Don't you remember me when I had the white fur around my neck?" asked Nancy.

"I remember her now, but I can't tell you what the date was," said the elevator operator.

Grimes and Cole left the girls alone with Seidel a while.

"If you are trying to protect me, forget it," Nancy told him. "Others have recognized me. You may as well tell the truth."

But the elevator operator could not make his identification any more positive; it was one of those disappointments, those close approaches to evidence, which happen all the time in an investigation. It was too bad, for corroboration of Nancy was desperately wanted. Her story was circumstantial, it was convincing to those who heard it; but the least bit of independent evidence to support it would add immensely to its value.

There was a former employee of Kean's Tavern, brother of a Waxey Gordon mobster, who admitted seeing Nancy there with members of Waxey's mob. Admitted it off the record, that is. He declared that if ever called as a witness, he would swear exactly the opposite. That was too bad, too, for except Nancy's testimony there was nothing in the case even to show that Lucky's crowd ever frequented Kean's.

It was not until the Luciano trial was nearly half over, when Dewey was preparing to introduce in evidence some papers found on the defendants when they were arrested, that Dewey picked out a card no one had ever before noticed. It was just a plain printed card, found in Little Davie's pocket, a business card of Kean's Tavern.

XIV. TENSION BEFORE
TRIAL

"HE WENT AND PUNCHED ME"

Nancy Presser had a frightful pain in her side. She was
in bad shape altogether, with everything coming on top of
that narcotic cure in December, which had shaken her nerves
apart.

First there had been the discovery, after her arrest, that
she was in a violent stage of syphilis. She was surprised at
that, because she had had her blood tested lots of times. Of
course, said Nancy, it was nothing to be ashamed of. Anybody could get that. You didn't have to go to bed to get
that.

Now it was the pain in her side. It really wasn't anything,
said Nancy. But it kept getting worse. The doctor looked
and shook his head. These occupational ailments! An operation was indicated.

An operation three weeks before trial? God forbid! Get
consultation. Get a specialist, the best that can be had. Yes,
said the specialist, diathermic treatments would bring her
along all right. She must have them. Nancy had been many
a man's darling for the moment, but now she was a precious
package for the People of the State of New York.

Nancy was going to help restore the public peace of the
People of the State of New York, AND THEIR DIGNITY.

"My side still hurts, but it is getting better," said Nancy.

"The reason for it is that it is right where that Ralph
Liguori went and punched me."

RALPH IN THE POT

A month from the time Charlie Lucky was brought back
from Hot Springs, the prostitution case was to go to trial.
That was a short time for preparation, but it had to be
rushed. Already the witnesses had been incarcerated for
months. Late night and early morning, seven days a week,
all the men in the Dewey office worked under pressure to
complete their case.

Ralph Liguori was under indictment now, along with the
rest. Nancy remembered his telling her that he was one of
those who shot Dave Miller out of town. Joan Garry recognized him as the man who had stuck up her joint as discipline from the combination. There were other bits of testimony which tied him up as an odd job man, a stick-up man
for the combination.

SNEAK THIEF

Now was found another witness who talked about Lucky.
Not a prostitute, not a madam, not a woman, but a sneak
thief who was lodged in Tombs Prison.

Joe Bendix, through a career of twenty-two years, had
been one of the most industrious hotel thieves in the business. From the time when, at the age of eighteen, he stole
a bicycle from a Western Union boy and went to jail for
it, Joe had been to prison so many times that he had lost
count.

This time he was in a real tough jam. He had looted the
apartment of the manager of one of New York's most fashionable hotels, and as an habitual criminal he was eligible

for life imprisonment. Joe was doing everything he could to ease up his rap.

He had sought to ingratiate himself with the District Attorney's office by giving information about the $1,500,000 Bank of Manhattan bond robbery. Now he had sent a note to Dewey's office, hoping to acquire still another friend at court, only to discover that this had done him no good with the regular District Attorney's office. They did not like Dewey over there.

Joe Bendix was a talented thief and his great misfortune was that his picture had been memorized by house detectives everywhere. He did not get wise to that until late in life.

In his early years as a thief it had been his practice to wander around the hotel corridors, trying the doors as he went until he found one that was open. Later he began to use keys. He would walk through the hotel hallways until he found a door open with the chambermaid's key in it. He would steal the key and then would be able to enter any room where he had spotted a prosperous occupant. He specialized in taking jewelry, though he was not above taking sables and silver fox. The key method was more effective, but more risky, than the earlier sneaking. Opening a locked door made his crime burglary, which was a felony.

Joe was a talented fellow. As a youngster he studied art at night school and during later years in prison he whiled away the months by improving his talent. He became so good that later he sometimes got jobs painting murals on speakeasy walls.

One time Joe had a good, honest, respectable position. He was art editor of the *New York Central Railroad Magazine*, and was paid $20 a week. So he decided to settle down and get married.

Three weeks after the wedding he was sent out to Cleveland to make some photographs for the magazine and got caught looting a room in the Statler Hotel. He went to prison and his wife got an annulment. After that Joe didn't try much being respectable. He had other wives and women, mostly vaudeville and night club dancers. During the late 1920's, Joe ran a photograph studio in Brooklyn. He was on parole and had to have a front. But he hung out a good deal around Broadway, familiar with many of the mob men there.

It was during this time, according to Joe, he met Charlie Lucky. He was introduced to Lucky, he said, one night at the Club Richman when Lucky was there with a man known to Joe only as Captain Dutton. After that, Joe said, he often did business with Lucky, meeting him on the sidewalk in front of the drugstore near Forty-ninth and Seventh Avenue.

Lucky, according to Joe, at that period was a very active fence. Besides being a narcotic runner, a bootlegger and all around mobster, Lucky was a fellow who would never turn down a chance to make a quick profit. Joe said that when he had a nice piece of jewelry Lucky was always ready to take it off his hands quick for a fraction of its value. According to Joe, Lucky had an interest in three drugstores around town which he used not only to push dope, but to get rid of stolen perfume and cigarettes.

In 1930 Bendix got caught stealing again and went back to prison, while Lucky went on to attain his mastery of the mobs.

When Joe Bendix got out of prison the next time he had reason to worry about his future. Another felony conviction and Joe could say good-by to the world for most of his remaining life. Joe said he wanted to get out of the thieving business. So he talked the matter over with his friend Charlie the Barber.

Joe said he figured that if he got a tie-up with a good safe mob like Lucky's, he would not need to worry about further arrests. So he asked Charlie the Barber to put him in touch with Lucky, thinking that maybe he could get a job, a steady job, as a collector from houses of prostitution.

Joe said he talked to Jimmy Fredericks and then talked twice to Lucky in the Villanova Restaurant in West Forty-sixth Street, where the big boss hung out.

"Lucky said that Fredericks talked to him about me," said Joe. "He understood that I wanted a job as a collector in some of these houses of prostitution and he understood that I was a little too high hat for the job and what was the idea of my looking for that as a job, that it only paid $35 or $40 a week.

"I said, 'It is better than going back to stealing. I would rather work for $40 a week than go out and face the Baumes Law which I was facing as a fourth offender.'

"He said, well, he said, 'If you are willing to work for $40 a week, it is O.K. with me. I will tell Little Davie to put you on. You can always meet me here; you can always see me here; I will see you here in a few days.'

"I went there about four or five times and tried to see him, but he was not in. I saw him about two weeks later. He was there with some people, but I walked over to him, and we walked aside. He asked me where I had been the last few weeks. I told him that I had something on. I had some money on the side, and I kind of overlooked it for the time being, but I needed money again; whether it was still all right for me to go to work.

"He said, 'I have given a list to Little Bingie at the Wolcott Hotel. If you go down there he will take care of you.'

"I said, 'O.K.'

"He said, 'Well, when you go around to collect, if you get wise to things, after a while, you can make yourself a little extra on the side, from the madams.' "

Bendix said that he tried several times to see Little Bingie at the hotel but never could find him in. He remembered especially one Sunday that he tried. Meanwhile he painted some murals at the Stadium Café, did some stealing, and went back to jail before he ever did see Little Bingie or talk to anybody else about the prostitution racket.

Joe Bendix was certainly no great shakes as a witness. But he convinced the men in Dewey's office. His character would be torn to shreds on a witness stand, not to mention his obvious motives for testifying. But there was his story— Little Bingie at the Wolcott Hotel, Jimmy Fredericks and Charlie Lucky at the Villanova Restaurant. How would he know those things if he weren't telling the truth?

Dewey was later to argue to the jury that either the Dewey office was corrupt or Bendix knew those things of his own knowledge and was testifying truthfully.

MORE WOMEN

Just before the trial the police picked up another girl, a pretty little narcotic addict from a Kansas farm, who had occasionally been the plaything of Tommy Bull. Her name was Mildred Curtis. She was in very bad shape from narcotics and it was not entirely clear that they would be able to use her as a witness.

She told about being in a restaurant one night with Tommy Bull and Lucky and heard Lucky tell Tommy to "straighten out" some madam who would not bond. A few days later, she added, Lucky asked Tommy Bull whether he had straightened out the madam and Tommy reported that she was in the hospital and Lucky told Tommy to find out from her doctor how badly off she was.

There were others who said they knew Lucky. Frisco Jean Erwin, a little blonde girl from the West Coast, who had edged Mildred Harris out of the affections of Pete Harris, said that she had smoked opium with Lucky and Little Davie.

But when Jean was asked what went on at these parties, what the gangsters said to each other and to her, she clammed up. Pressed with questions, Jean became an abject figure of terror. She was afraid to talk any more. One day she went into hysterics, had a fight with Jeanette Lewis, Jo Jo Weintraub's sweetheart, and screamed all over the office.

This Jeanette Lewis talked very freely. She was a newcomer in town but she claimed to know a lot because she was a sweetheart of Pete Harris's assistant. Jeanette told an amazing story about how she came to New York.

In the summer and early fall of 1935, she said, she had been working in Cincinnati and there became very intimate with the handicapper at the Coney Island race track, Otto Berman, known as Abadaba.

Abadaba, a clownish, bizarre fellow, was the mathematical genius who was to obtain posthumous fame as the man who fixed the parimutuel payoff figures at the track for the benefit of Dutch Schultz and his policy racket in New York. Abadaba's juggling of the parimutuel odds kept the "bad" numbers from coming up in the policy lottery and cheated thousands of players who would have made hits in an honest game.

Jeanette said that while she was running around with Abadaba, Charlie Lucky was out in Cincinnati; and several times the three went out together.

One night while sitting in a hotel room, said Jeanette, she expressed a desire to work in New York and Lucky said he could fix it up for her; so he put in a long distance call to New York and then said to the party at the other end of the wire that this was "312" speaking. Those figures, said Jeanette, were code for C. L., the third and twelfth letters of the alphabet. According to Jeanette, Lucky was calling Bennie Spiller to see that she was put to work when she came to New York.

Fantastic as this was, it seemed for a while as though the story might be corroborated. Night club employees at Covington, Kentucky, identified photographs of Abadaba and Jeanette as people they had seen there together, and they thought they had seen Lucky there with the couple too. Lucky had been in Cincinnati about that time.

Jeanette came to New York in early November, 1935, and was startled to find out that her old friend Abadaba had been rubbed out along with Dutch Schultz in that shooting affair at Newark. So she went up to the bar and grill on Fifty-fourth Street where Bennie Spiller hung out, and was put to work in May Spiller's joint.

There was something fishy about Jeanette. But she was sufficiently convincing so that she was put before the Grand Jury to tell about the times she was booked. Three of the counts in the indictment were based on Jeanette's business experiences.

As Jeanette continued to be questioned, it seemed as if

her story might be too good to be true. There was doubt about whether to use Jeanette as a witness. She might be just a publicity-seeking psychopath. When Jeanette sensed that she might not be called to the stand her story suddenly improved. She said that she had been specially commissioned by Charlie Lucky to spy on Pete Harris to find out about his holding out joints. That settled it. Jeanette was not a girl a prosecutor would want to vouch for.

Weeks later, after the trial was over, when everybody was waiting to see whether anything happened to the witnesses after they were turned loose, a sensational news story flashed into the headlines. From Washington, D. C., it was reported that a girl witness from the Lucky trial had been branded with the mark of the mob.

It was Jeanette, who had not been used as a witness. The news story blew up quickly. With a fingernail file Jeanette had scratched, not too deeply, the figures 312 on her own stomach and the initials C. L. on her legs. She had made the headlines after all.

MILDRED'S JITTERS

As the date of the trial drew nearer, pressure grew heavier and heavier. Most of the people in Dewey's office were working on the case, chasing down new angles, checking up on details, preparing for the great battle in court.

There were 125 witnesses who had to be questioned and prepared for possible use at the trial and an infinite number more were called in and questioned without result. And such witnesses as had been broken, who had agreed to testify, had to be kept in a courageous frame of mind.

Mildred Harris had the jitters. She worried about herself;

especially she worried about her daughter. Some days she said she just could not bring herself to tell the true story in court.

Mildred was being kept now in an apartment in Queens along with Peggy Wild, Jennie the Factory, Thelma Jordan, Nancy Presser.

Everything was done that could properly be done to keep the girls happy and contented. All of them were being credited with $3 a day as witness fees and half of that was advanced to them in cash for current use. From time to time, from the House of Detention and from the hotels in which the important witnesses were being kept, they were taken out to the movies, taken on shopping expeditions.

Soon after the girls had started getting their witness fees they had complained about not being allowed anything to drink. They were not prisoners, they had declared. It was their own money and why shouldn't they have a cocktail before dinner and a highball afterwards when they were outside the prison? And often they were outside the prison. Their questioning at Dewey's office kept them away from the House of Detention's meal hours. Dewey had to admit that this was good reason and after that the girls had their cocktails which they paid for with their own money.

Mildred Harris not only liked to drink, but she needed a drink sometimes. She was no longer having her morphine and she was in a bad state of nerves. Sometimes Mildred overdid it and drank a bit too much when she was out to dinner or out for the evening. There was one cop who was often her bodyguard, named Patrolman George Heidt. Sol Gelb had to bawl him out several times for letting Mildred drink too much.

THE THREAT

One afternoon, late in April, Mildred was uptown doing some shopping on the way back to the apartment in Queens, guarded by Patrolman James F. Cooney. Coming through Times Square, Cooney stopped to buy a newspaper and as he did so a sleek young man stopped and engaged Mildred in a conversation.

Cooney did not interrupt them. After all, Mildred was not a prisoner. She had a right to talk to people. The young man was Mildred's old boy friend, Gus Franco, dope peddler, policy racketeer. Mildred did not sleep a wink that night. It was a night of terror.

The next day she again said to Gelb that she could not testify. She had met Gus Franco and he had told her that if she talked her life would be worth nothing; if she talked about the gang, her child's life would be worth nothing. Franco knew about her little girl. He was a bad guy.

All that day Gelb spent reassuring Mildred, promising her protection, promising her child protection. She was in such a state that day that he could not quiet her down. That evening he took her into Dewey's office and asked him to talk to her. She was there more than three hours.

"You have no idea of the power of that Italian mob," she said. "Lucky controls the Unione Siciliana. Its killers are in every city of the world."

Gelb and Dewey made light of her fears. She challenged them; told them she would call Gus Franco up on the telephone and let them hear for themselves, listening in on the wire.

She called up Franco's house but only his mother was at home. Mrs. Franco seemed glad to hear from Mildred. She talked garrulously to her about her health.

"Mildred," said Mrs. Franco, "there is no fear of you any more, is there?"

"No," said Mildred.

Mildred stayed and stayed at the Dewey office the nights after that. She was afraid to go home. One night Gelb left the office with her and her bodyguard Patrolman Heidt. They took a taxicab and Gelb asked them to drop him off uptown on their way.

As they drove uptown Mildred said she needed a drink; she had to have a drink; she insisted on having a drink. Gelb finally told the cop to take her somewhere and get her one. The cop was insistent that Gelb should go along. He didn't want to be on the spot for going out drinking alone with a witness after midnight.

Sol Gelb is a very smart fellow but this was one time he let himself in for something. He never could remember whether it was the cop or Mildred who suggested the place. But before long they found themselves sitting at a table having a few drinks in the Fifty-Second Street night club known as Leon & Eddie's.

Gelb must have been very tired that night to have let himself in for this one. But there were a lot of angles about that situation he didn't know. For some reason he didn't know that Leon & Eddie's was one of the hot spots in town. He didn't know it was a favorite hangout for Moe Polakoff, Charlie Lucky's lawyer.

Mildred had not yet told Gelb what she later swore before Justice McCook, that their companion, Patrolman Heidt, had told her he used to be payoff man for Ownie Madden's mob.

The incident was to have repercussions.

XV. THE RUN-OUT

"THE MEN WHO RAN THE BOOKERS"

The trial of Charles Luciano and his co-defendants opened on the morning of May 11, 1936, before Justice Mc-Cook in the County Courthouse, in Foley Square, Manhattan. A blue ribbon panel of jurors, so-called because the talesmen were specially selected for experience and intelligence, had been summoned for the occasion, and talesmen filled the courtroom as they waited for the process of selecting a jury.

The trial opened with the appearance of the three bookers, Pete Harris, Al Weiner, and Davie Miller, who stood before the court and pleaded guilty—ninety times guilty, for there were that many felony counts in the indictment. Of course they were thousands of times guilty in reality, for each time a girl was booked three crimes were committed.[1]

Ten defendants were left. They had eleven lawyers to represent them.

Dewey had four assistants on hand to help him in court; and over in the Woolworth Building practically all the rest of his staff was at the job of marshaling the 120 available witnesses and working up last minute angles of the case.

Before the prospective jurors were questioned, Dewey explained something about the theory of the case. He made it

---

[1] Before the case against the other defendants went to the jury, twenty-nine counts were dismissed, for there was no need of dragging the case out too long with repetition.

clear that the girls in the case had not been forced into any house; that they were prostitutes and wanted to work at their trade.

"It is not contended by the People that each of these named defendants personally placed a woman in a house," Dewey explained. "That was left to the underlings. The actual mechanics of the business was left to the underlings.

"Beginning at the top, Charles Luciano will be proved not to have placed any women in any house, not to have directly taken any money from any women, but to have sat way up at the top in his apartment at the Waldorf as the Czar of organized crime in this city where his word, and his word alone, was sufficient to terminate all competitive enterprises of this kind.

"We will show you in the case his function not as the operator of anything, but merely as the man whose word, whose suggestion, whose statement, 'Do this,' was sufficient; and all the others in the case are charged as being his servants.

"David Betillo, known as Little Davie, was his chief lieutenant, the man who really ran the racket. He did not place any women in houses. He merely ordered the men who did.

"Thomas Pennochio, known as Tommy Bull, was the treasurer of the combination. We do not charge that he placed any women in houses. Of course, he received the proceeds of the bonding combination and of the money taken from the bookers of women each week for being allowed to engage in the business of prostitution.

"Abraham Wahrman, known as Little Abie, is in the same category.

"The defendant Bennie Spiller we do not charge with running houses of prostitution. His primary function was to invest capital in the corporate enterprise, by which all prostitution in New York was organized into one racket by strong-arm men and gunmen.

"James Frederico, known as Jimmy Fredericks, was what you might call the general manager of the enterprise. He gave personal orders. He stood out in front. We are now getting down to the men who actually did things other than mere giving of orders. He did not actually place many women in houses of prostitution. His primary function was to tell the bookers of women what to do, send the collectors around to the houses and collect their weekly toll, collect their toll from the bookers, to discipline the madams, to conduct the beatings when people did not behave and stay in line.

"Ralph Liguori had a separate and unique function. He was the hold-up man for the combination. If the madam did not book and did not bond with this combination and accept its protection, Liguori stuck up the house.

"Now, of the other defendants, Jesse Jacobs and Meyer Berkman ran the bonding and legal end of the business. They ran the machine by which these women when arrested by the police, were immediately bailed out, advised, coached how to testify. They provided the lawyer to try the case, and turned the women out. So that they aided and abetted in keeping the women available to work and in making it safe to engage in the business of organized prostitution on a colossal scale."

Dewey then went on to list the three bookers who had pleaded guilty, and the remaining booker, Jack Eller, or Ellenstein, who had chosen to stand trial.

"These four bookers of women are the men who actually ran the chains of houses of prostitution, who actually received the telephone calls from day to day from the prostitutes and told them where to go," Dewey continued.

"They actually did the business, with their assistants. None of the assistants of the bookers have been indicted.

"Now the purpose of all of this outline here is so that you will know that the principles of law upon which this case is founded are not that you get the tool, the underling who actually goes out on the street and takes a woman by the hand and puts her in a house. He is the type who usually gets caught. The principle of this case is the theory of law upon which we are getting as aiders and abettors the men who ran the bookers, and the bosses of the men who ran the bookers."

It took two days to get a jury and then Dewey outlined in some detail the facts he intended to present, rounding out the whole story of the racket through its minor participants.

He set up a chart in the courtroom listing the names of the defendants and their various co-conspirators to make the case as little confusing as possible.

Defense counsel had made cautious openings denying the charges. George Morton Levy, trial counsel for Lucky, was less cautious than the rest. He said Lucky did not know any of his co-defendants, except Little Davie, whom he had once met when Davie tried to interest him in a gambling boat off the Jersey coast.

Doubtless that was what Lucky had told him. But it was a mistake which, long after, was to cause vain regrets.

"I WAS JUST UNDRESSED"

The first girl Dewey put on the stand was an Italian girl who went by the name of Rose Cohen. She was more confident and self-possessed than most of the other girls and was a good one to start out with.

Rose related that she was brought up in Philadelphia and when she was eighteen came to New York to live with a man. Four years later they busted up and Rose went working on the streets to make a living.

After a few months she got a job one week working in Molly Leonard's place and Molly introduced her to Pete Harris who agreed to book her regularly.

Rose took in $260 that week, of which half went to Molly. Out of Rose's $130 the madam deducted $18 for board, $5 for doctor and $13 for Pete's 10 per cent commission. The rest of the money was Rose's. That was early in 1933.

Later on, Rose said, the board bill was jacked up $10 in all the houses to cover the weekly bond payment. She worked for many madams, Peggy Wild, Jennie the Factory, Little Jennie, Jean Bradley, Elsie, Cokey Flo, Nigger Ruth, and a lot of others. In July, 1935, Rose related, she was arrested by a cop, who came in and posed as a customer, at Jean Bradley's place at Central Park West.

"I hadn't done anything improper yet when he arrested me," said Rose. "I was just undressed."

She was bailed out after this arrest, Rose related. She was taken to the office of Jesse Jacobs across the street from the prison. Jimmy Fredericks told her to come back in a few days and Abe Karp would tell her what to say at her trial.

Rose was planning to say that she was a seamstress working at Twenty-sixth Street and Sixth Avenue. Karp had told her that was all wrong because that was a fur district where seamstresses didn't work. Rose said she didn't know any place to work in New York so they decided she should say she was a seamstress working in the tailor shop in Gimbel's in Philadelphia, and just over in New York for a visit.

So Rose had taken the stand and told that story and the judge had dismissed her. The combination had protected another one of its girls.

Now, one after another the girls were coming to the stand. An amazing procession of women, modestly dressed, wearing no make-up, relating coldly and objectively that they had been engaged in the business of prostitution; telling about the people they met; what their business arrangements were. Madams, some young and pretty, some old and motherly-looking, some crass and blowsy, came on the stand and told all about their business; about how the bookers and Jimmy Fredericks carried on their business.

Little Marie Dubin told about how Jimmy Fredericks one night bawled out the madam for whom she was working because she had illegal pin ball machines in the place. The bonding combination's responsibility did not cover pin balls and if the cops found them there it might be serious.

Al Wiener, a dead pan youngster, who limped on one short leg, related that he had not gone near his father, Cock-eyed Louis, when the old man was arrested as a booker, but had merely taken over the family booking business and carried it on. Joan Martin told her story and exhibited her scalp to the jury to show where Jimmy Fredericks had black-jacked her. Dave Miller told of his experiences.

It became very clear within a few days that the defendants were sunk, buried, except maybe Charlie Lucky. The prosecution had not come to him yet.

THE RUN-OUT

Now, thought Dewey, it was time to smash at the big shot. He would call Good-time Charlie to the stand to tell how a mere word from Lucky had been enough to chase out competition, win a monopoly for the combination; how the Italians had all stood up in awe of the boss.

Good-time Charlie was in the witness room outside the courtroom. The afternoon session was about to begin. Dewey was there, speaking a word or two to his witness before he put him on the stand.

"Mr. Dewey," said Charlie, "I can't tell that story."

"What!" exclaimed Dewey.

"I can't give that testimony," said Good-time Charlie. "It isn't true. I just made that story up."

"But you swore to it before the Grand Jury!"

"Yes, I swore to it, but it isn't true. I just made that story up. I didn't go down and get chased out by Charlie Lucky."

There was consternation in the Dewey camp that night. They had only four primary witnesses against the chief defendant—Good-time Charlie, Nancy Presser, Joe Bendix, and Mildred Balitzer. Mildred Curtis was still on dope, and could not be used. But Good-time Charlie had run out.

It was not a terrific surprise. Charlie was a bad character, a poor witness anyway. That sort of thing happened in prosecution of gangsters all the time. Witnesses were threatened, witnesses were scared, witnesses were bought. Sometimes, even, witnesses lied in the first place. But it was the sort of thing that was not supposed to happen in the Dewey prosecution. Everybody felt pretty low about it. Good-time Charlie's story had been promised in Dewey's opening.

"Well, cheer up," said Barent Ten Eyck, one of Dewey's chief assistants, "my new witness is better than Good-time Charlie ever was."

For, as Ten Eyck had left the court on the day when Joan Martin testified, he had heard that a prisoner in the

House of Detention wanted to see him; and on his arrival there he had been handed a note. It read:

"Mr. Ten Eyck
"DEAR SIR:

"I would like to see you on a matter of great importance in the Dewey vice case.

"I am, and was, for three years, James Frederico's sweetheart.

"I can help you a great deal. Some of the witnesses saw me today. I know they will tell you anyway. *I* might just as well tell you myself.

"Please excuse writing.

"Respectfully,

"FLO.

"P.S.—Here under name of Fay Marston, 4th fl."

James Frederico was the real name of Jimmy Fredericks, and his girl, Cokey Flo Brown, was a key figure in the vice investigation.

XVI. COKEY FLO

FLO LEARNS ABOUT MEN

Cokey Flo Brown operated in New York City for six years before she ever was pinched, and came to be known as one of the smartest madams in town.

The real reason why she tied up with Jimmy Fredericks and became his sweetheart is something one may only guess. He had the build of an ape but he was a fat slob and a greasy one; the real tough guys around Seventy-second Street and Broadway used to chase him away until after he had made his tie-up with the mob downtown. After that he was more than welcome, a tough guy himself by virtue of his connections. Maybe that had something to do with Flo's love for him.

Flo was a small, steely, brown-haired girl in her twenties, who lived always by her wits and on her nerve. Except perhaps when she was smoking opium, there never was anything languorous, amorous or voluptuous about her. She was a keen dashing little figure whether on a sporting expedition to shoplift furs on Fifty-seventh Street or driving up Broadway in her smart little car.

Flo had more brains than the average. At fourteen she had finished two years of high school in Pittsburgh with good marks. Then she felt ready to go out in the world, and she joined up with one of the oldest and most sure-fire of the boob hoisting rackets—selling hand-painted enlarged photographs to the simple miners of the Appalachian coal fields.

It was her job to get the pictures, find a prospect and string him along. Later the high pressure boys would make the killing by selling a handsome gilded frame to go with the new family portrait.

At fifteen Flo formed a partnership with an older girl called Pearl and they started a speakeasy in Cleveland. They had a brownstone house with a bar on the ground floor, and lived upstairs. Pearl had a boy friend who lived there with her. Flo tried that out too when she was fifteen but soon ditched the man. Always, so far as she was concerned, sex was very highly overrated.

Flo and Pearl steered very clear from anything like prostitution business in those days. It was too risky and there was plenty of money in liquor.

Peddling drinks became a bore and at eighteen Flo again heard the call of adventure. She gave her share of the business to Pearl, took $5,000 which she had saved up in the bank and set out for Chicago. Within two months she had three men at once keeping her in a hotel on Michigan Boulevard, all fellows with underworld tie-ups. After she got the first one the other two were so much velvet, and she was careful to pick busy men who were out of town a lot and had not much time to spare for her, so that they did not get in each other's way. That lasted nearly a year, and then Flo ran up to Duluth, Minnesota, to see what that town was like. Within a few weeks there she had attached herself to a local bootlegger.

Duluth is a pleasant place, cool in the summer, and since her friend liked to get away from his wife, she went on trips with him to Hot Springs when the winter weather got down below zero. This went on for three years until he took her on a trip to New York. The big town fascinated Flo and

challenged her. She was twenty-two now, had learned a lot
about men, and knew a lot of the angles of the underworld.
She was ready to back her wits against Broadway.

BUILDING UP A BUSINESS

Through her Duluth friend, to whom she bade good-by,
Flo met a girl who was running a brothel; and she often visited the place to see how it was done. It was a furtive business, which took keen wits and quick thinking. It appealed
to Flo and she decided to try it herself.

One day she encountered a blonde named Dolly whom she
had known in Chicago, and decided that she would begin
then and there. Flo had learned the business angles and
Dolly was an experienced girl who could handle the more
personal end of the business.

Flo rented a small apartment on the east side, in York-
ville, and she and Dolly started out prospecting in the cafés.
As soon as Dolly had taught her a few tricks about the art of
picking up men, in which Flo really was no novice, Dolly
stayed home and Flo went to the cafés alone. Flo would sit
at a table or stand by a bar and when a prosperous looking
man undertook to flirt with her she would kid with him a
while and then invite him to her apartment.

"Come on up," she would say. "I would like to introduce
you to a girl friend of mine."

When she had taken him up to see Dolly, Flo would say
she had to go out for a few minutes and would be right back.
Then she would go out hunting for more business and before
she returned to the apartment she would telephone and make
sure that Dolly's visitor had departed. It was very clever. In
that way no cop could ever get any evidence on Flo.

Flo did not take long to build up a list of customers.

After two months she quit soliciting. A good many customers came back to see Dolly and some of them brought their friends. Flo's business was now a steady going concern and she had built it up without attracting the attention of the police. Flo got other girls through her friends. Before long she had moved into a brownstone house on sedate West End Avenue. There, unlike most madams, she made her home as well as her place of business. She still had only one girl at a time, and operated on a completely independent basis at a $5 price. But the depression got to her toward the year of 1933; so she cut prices, got a booker and went on a mass production basis. The time was to come when Flo would boast that she could remember the voices, names and faces of three thousand customers.

A NEW PASTIME

Flo's gentleman friend from Duluth had sent her money at first but soon he faded out. Before long she had another sweetheart who came to live with her. He was an opium smoker and it was he who taught Flo the pleasure of kicking the gong. He told Flo it was a very pleasant thing, and one night after she had closed up the joint she tried it with him. He had the gum, the pipe and the lamp and when he gave her the first lesson he made the pills small and held her down to only four or five so that she did not get sick as new smokers usually do. He taught her carefully to puff in the fumes with short, jerky breaths. After he had broken her in with a few evenings of smoking he brought up another couple to join them. After that they had parties of two or three couples, sometimes once a week, later three or four times a week, at Flo's place after hours. Although the vice of chandu may be to the Oriental a solitary pleasure, it is usually to the white man a communal pastime.

According to Flo, all the common ideas about opium smoking are cockeyed. She had no hangovers, she had no fancy dreams, she was not transported into another world. It just made her sleepy and relaxed her nerves. Maybe it also broke down and relaxed the masculine protest which was always obvious in Flo. Maybe it lessened her natural bent to be a sharpster, made her softer, more acquiescent and pleasurable. I don't know. To hear Flo herself tell about an opium smoking party you would think it was something like a Puritan prayer meeting.

Flo always lived under tension. She could be sometimes the most charming companion and other times she was shrewish. Some of the girls who worked for her thought she was swell; others found her a termagant. Sometimes, she would be so tense that she would not let her girls step off the rugs, because of an irrational fear that the clicking of their heels might attract attention to her place.

Flo says she just smoked opium for pleasure. But maybe she was taking refuge; maybe she was seeking relaxation. Perhaps it made things easier to seek oblivion in the drug. She played around with it for two or three years as a pleasure smoker before she finally became an addict.

Then Flo began taking morphine. She would take a quarter of a cube in a hypodermic three times a day. People began to call her Cokey Flo. She always hated that name.

INSURANCE AGAINST TROUBLE

Flo first got into trouble soon after she began booking, though she was not arrested herself. Sometimes she left the place in charge of her maid, and one evening, in her absence, the joint was pinched. Flo hadn't been smart enough to save up her money and she had a tough time with her booker, Charlie Spinach, to get the girls bailed out, especially since one of the girls wanted to go on the lam. The forfeited bail came to $500 altogether and Flo had to pay Spinach off, at $50 a week.

At this time Spinach told her about the combination and brought Jimmy Fredericks to see her. They gave her a hot selling talk and Flo was glad to join up for $10 a week per girl.

She and Jimmy Fredericks took to each other right away. Flo had busted up with her sweetheart a few days before that and she fell for Fredericks on the rebound. Within a few weeks he started to live with her and during the next couple of years he stayed at her place four or five nights a week. Often she drove him around in her car, for Jimmy never did learn how to drive.

It seemed that Jimmy let on he was a very poor man in those days. He told her he was only getting $35 a week on his job. They talked it out and he said he liked the job because he was in with very good people and also it was nice to be in a legal thing like the bonding business.

During this time Jimmy maintained his own family residence in a nice apartment down in Twelfth Street. Flo never weaned him away from his old girl entirely. On Christmas, 1935, Jimmy gave his wife a mink coat. Flo gave Jimmy $100 but didn't even get a Christmas card herself. That made her angry, but soon adversity was to make her forget all jealousy.

THE LAW GETS TOUGH

Disaster came to Flo in January, 1936. The cops came to her joint, arrested the girls, arrested the maid and grabbed Flo along with her opium pipe, hypodermic, and morphine. It was a tough rap and altogether it took $2,800 for bail.

Flo only had $1,500, but Jimmy, through the bonding combination, got up the rest. Flo decided she had better get cured of the drug habit before she went to trial because the cure in jail is very tough. So she went into a sanitarium on Central Park West.

When she started reducing her morphine her first reaction was a violent stomach ache.[1] She found out she had a very bad gall bladder. She was flat on her back and her strength had gone, her nerves were jittery and there were sharp biting pains in her legs.

She could not eat. When they gave her anything to eat she could not hold it on her stomach. She had weighed 118 pounds when she entered the sanitarium—now she could feel herself wasting away.

One day, just after February 1, her doctor came in and told her there had been a big raid on most of the joints in town and that Jimmy Fredericks was in jail along with the rest of the combination. Their bail was so high that they couldn't get out. Then it seemed to Flo as though the world had ended. She was in the worst jam of her life, worst suffering of her life, and the one person in the world on whom she could depend was a prisoner.

She had never felt so alone. She didn't want to write to anyone or communicate with anyone because she didn't want

---

[1] The importance of morphine to the addict is more evident in its absence than in its presence. Flo always said she felt perfectly normal when she was charged up but when she didn't have the drug it was hell.

them to know she was taking the cure. She just lay on her back and felt as though she was dying.

Flo stuck it out for two weeks more, then she sent word for a friend to come and see her. Her friend was horror struck. Flo weighed 92 pounds now. She hadn't eaten or slept for three weeks. Her friend whispered with her, went out, and came back and slipped Flo some tablets of morphine. Flo swallowed one and felt like a new woman. She was able to eat some dinner that night. In three or four days, sneaking in a bit of morphine when the nurse was not present, she had enough strength to leave the hospital.

Once she was out, Flo felt like a hunted rabbit. Dewey's office would want her, she knew. She would not dare to appear for trial even if she did have the case fixed. She moved about furtively to keep the police from finding her. She stole some stationery from the Hotel Ambassador on Park Avenue and used it for writing letters to Jimmy at the Raymond Street jail. She wrote impassioned letters to Jimmy on a typewriter, addressing him as "Dear Cousin" and signing herself just as "Cousin" on the typewriter too.

Flo had to make a living. Her doctor got her a job at $25 a week as companion and assistant to a Mrs. Calvert, more widely known as Dorothy Russell, daughter of the actress Lillian Russell. Dorothy Russell was in troubled times, in her declining years, and an invalid. Her assets had recently been sold to pay her debts. She was trying to make a go of it by writing fiction and scenarios for the movies. Flo lived with her in a hotel room and did her typing and other chores.

Often she would sit down and dash off on the typewriter a letter to Jimmy. She wrote:

"THE AMBASSADOR
"Park Avenue
"51st to 52nd Streets
"New York

"Monday Night.

"MY DEAR COUSIN:

"Well, its the day after Easter, and everything is still the same. There is nothing new. I feel very melancholy tonight. Very blue. I'm disgusted with the whole world. There is no justice at all. I wish Uncle Dee would die of cancer, the louse! He should of died from leprosy when he was a baby.

"I think its terrible to make a person do time before they are even convicted. Its not fair. They let lousy murderers go free. But a person that never did anyone any harm in their life, has to rot in jail. Look at that Vera Stretz case. A confessed murderess! She even admitted doing it, on the witness chair, yet she is freed. But a person that hasn't even been convicted yet has to stay in jail, until some louse gets good and ready to bring them to trial! Look at all the money that was spent on Hauptman! The Governor himself intervening for a filthy foreigner of a baby-killer. The worst kind of a killer there is. Thats why I say there is no justice in this world.

"Gee, I'm so blue, and lonesome for you. I don't know what to do. Believe me, if I had about five minutes, with a few certain people, alone, I'd know just what to say and do. There would be just five rats less, to bother people.

"Well, its no use wishing. I'm going down to see Seigal Wedsday, I guess. I want to know what he intends to do. What defense has he worked out? I want him to get busy, and try to get his head to working. Not to think he is going to get money for nothing. He should never mind bull shi-ing so much, but get something done. I can't stand this suspense and inactivity much longer.

"Well, dont worry, old pal, everything will be O.K. Just have faith and courage. Thats the main thing. Maybe you'll thumb your nose at all these louses that are lieing like hell, just to save their own skin.

"Take care of yourself, and ask them if they will allow you to buy some linement, so you could rub your legs. Maybe if you massaged them with something, you'd get a little relief, so you could get some sleep. I worry about your legs an awful lot. I wish I could rub them for you.

"Regards from all, and all my love,

"your Faithful,

"Cousin."

The man that Flo was going to see was Samuel J. Siegel, Jimmy's lawyer. She wanted to help in any way she could with Jimmy's case. But her talks with Siegel seem not to have been very successful. It didn't seem as if Jimmy's sweetheart, even though she knew a great deal about the prostitution racket, could be of much help in his defense.

Flo poured out her energy in her "Dear Cousin" letters. The "Cousin" business is a habit of underworld people writing prison letters. They think it will help them get things past the censors. She wrote:

"We always were more to each other than just plain cousins. I want you to always remember this, that no matter what happens you will always mean everything to me. Everything that is good, and fine, and sweet in this world, will be embodied in your image, for me. Some of the happiest moments of my life were spent in your company, perhaps some unhappy ones too, but thoughts of them fade away when the image of your smiling face comes to my mind.

"Thats the way I always want to picture you, head up, and smiling. I know you will come through this thing with all your colors flying!"

STILL MORE TROUBLE

Once she was back on dope, Flo could eat again and during the next two months she gained back twenty pounds. She got along all right with Dorothy Russell and she later remarked that for the first time since she was fourteen "she was living a clean and decent life."

The only trouble was the cats and dogs. Her employer had several of them and Flo also had a dog. Altogether they were pretty crowded in their hotel space. But Flo went around the corner on Seventy-fifth Street and rented herself a basement room with a back yard in which her dog could play.

Calamity fell on Flo the next evening. A plainclothes policeman picked her up on the sidewalk in front of her rooming house and charged her with soliciting on the street. Flo always denied her guilt. She said the cop propositioned her and grabbed her when she told him he had the wrong girl and started to walk away. As to that, we may well surmise the probabilities. Flo was in debt. She needed money for expensive drugs and the dog's playground.

Anyway, she was convicted. It made her pretty sore that Sam Siegel didn't come up and do anything for her. He sent only one of the most junior youngsters in his law office.

Flo was back on the drug cure and it wasn't any considerate private sanitarium this time. They put her on a standard five-day reduction treatment, a little bit less dope each day. It is effective, it is quick, and it is torture.

Flo quit eating again. In the next two weeks, as she remembered it, all she could swallow was four or five spoonfuls of lousy prison cereal, and a few mouthfuls of milk. Day by day she grew weaker.

The Women's House of Detention is a modern skyscraper prison and one of the best; but even so, it is hardly a pleasant place for a narcotic addict. Flo lay day by day in a tiny cell, four cold walls and an iron door which had a slit in it near the top, about four inches wide and ten inches long. Flo was thirsty. She didn't have enough strength to call for a matron. There was running water in her cell, but she didn't have enough strength to get up and push the button.

Opiates had never given Flo visions or dreams, but now the lack of them sent ghosts galloping through her brain. All the grotesque melodrama of her life tumbled and surged about her. It seemed as if she was going nuts. Sometimes, at first, she was able to get up and go out of her cell. Some of the Dewey witnesses were on the same floor but not in the same corridor. Some of the girls saw her and slipped her a note telling her that Mr. Ten Eyck and Mr. Hogan were very nice and she ought to get busy and help herself out of a jam.

Flo grew angry, made a tart reply. She didn't want to meet any nice young men; she didn't want to be a squealer; she never would be a rat.

It seemed to Flo as she lay alone at night as if a thousand cats were clawing at her stomach, as though a thousand devils were inside her legs, forking at her muscles, tearing them apart. The drug devils had her. And day by day, the less the drug the more the devils.

Flo saw the newspapers. The trial was on now. The girls, bookers, were opening up and were telling all. Jimmy was buried. Every witness, it seemed, was a gravedigger.

A fierce struggle was going on inside of Flo. All the traditions, all the loyalties of her adult life, were those of the underworld. She still was fond of Jimmy but she was angry with him too. Here she was in jail and he had paid no attention.

"None of them had ever given me a second thought, not even Jimmy," she recalled later, thinking of that struggle in her mind and the resentment which surged up in her.

"I had found out that they had sent money in to some of the witnesses to try to keep them from talking by being nice to them. Jimmy knew I was in jail, broke and sick, but he hadn't tried to send anything in to me, had he? Davie Betillo I hated. He was a killer of the worst type—a human life meant nothing to him—with a vicious, rotten, murderously warped mind. Lucky Luciano I had always hated, even before I knew him. He had been the one to order the death of two of my best friends, men that he had made a deal with, that he would spare their lives if they left town. They kept their end of the agreement but he didn't. He was a dirty double-crosser. He had sent his killers after them when they left town and had killed them in spite of his word not to. Now they were dead, killed, murdered by his killers with bullets in their backs. Not even a chance to fight back for their lives. Tommy Bull? I hated him for a different reason— a reason connected with dope. I cannot tell this reason but what he had done to some morphine he had slipped me— what it had done to me—made me hate him the rest of my life." [2]

[2] What Tommy Bull did to Flo's morphine remains a mystery. One of the men whose death she referred to was Mildred Harris's friend, Murray

Flo sat down and wrote her note to Ten Eyck offering her testimony. It was the fifth, the most strenuous day of the cure. Later Flo forgot all about having written that letter. It was on that same day that Joan Martin went to court, shouted maledictions at Jimmy Fredericks, and showed the jury the stitches on her head where Jimmy had blackjacked her. Flo read about it in the paper and frothed with indignation at Joan. But still it was clear Jimmy was buried. Flo was on her own.

That evening Sol Gelb found waiting in a corridor a thin, pale, wasted woman in gray prison dress and flat shoes. It was Cokey Flo Brown, smartest of the madams, offering to tell her story.

TO TALK OR NOT TO TALK

"I know Charlie Lucky," said Cokey Flo.

"Yeah?" said Gelb.

One thing a prosecutor always has to watch out for is the volunteer witness, the willing witness, who may come in like a gift from God and wreck his case. A send-in witness is an old shyster trick of defense lawyers.

Gelb started to question Flo and got bad results. She was jittery, she was nervous, she still did not know whether she wanted to talk or not.

Flo turned away from Gelb and started to walk away and Ten Eyck came along and stopped her. She said she was going back to her cell. He told her he would be there very late that night if she wanted to talk to him again. Flo went up-

Marks. These quotations and other references to Flo's state of mind come from an account written by her and made a part of the supplementary record on appeal.

The chronology of events in the actual occurrences of these days was later a matter of dispute and it is clear that Flo's own memory of actual events in this high tension period was confused.

stairs and thought it over. Toward midnight she wrote another note:

"Mr. Ten Eyck
"DEAR SIR:
"Must see you. Have decided to tell you the truth. I lied to you and Mr. Gelb. Have thought and thought and now I feel stronger and better able to think and finally I decided to tell you the truth about what you wanted to know. This is the last nite you can send for me.
"(Flo)   FAY MARSTON, 8th fl."

Ten Eyck had her brought down to the psychiatrist's office which he used for interviewing witnesses. She told him she had got off to a bad start with Gelb because she was so nervous and because she was irritated by the way he cross-examined her. She was calmer now and had decided to go through with her plan to talk.

Flo said she knew all of the defendants. On a sheet of yellow legal scratch paper Ten Eyck wrote down the names, leaving four lines for what she might say about each of them:

> Charlie
> Davie
> Abie
> Tommy
> Eddie
> Jack Eller
> Jesse Jacobs
> Meyer.

But this outline did him no good at the time. Before her story was finished, he had filled that page and three others with pencil notes [3] practically all about Charlie Lucky. Flo talked about hardly anyone else. Ten Eyck talked with Flo until two o'clock in the morning. The next day he got Eunice Carter to go into court and get a postponement of Flo's sentence in the soliciting case. Naturally, it was understood that Flo was talking in order to try to get a break for herself.

FLO'S STORY

Flo was such an important witness that Dewey wanted to talk to her himself before he put her on the stand, examine her carefully to be sure she was O.K. Why she was testifying was a question. She might be out for revenge; she might plan to get on the witness stand and exonerate her sweetheart.

On the night of May 20, he had her brought down to his office, and there in the presence of five assistants and a stenographer, Dewey and Ten Eyck questioned her. This was twelve days after her arrest.

Flo said that the reason she had got in touch with Dewey's office was that she hoped by giving testimony for the people she might win consideration from the judge by whom she was sentenced. She understood that nothing was being promised to her and that nothing was wanted but the absolute truth.

In a question-and-answer statement, like testimony that would be given in court, Flo told about her early life, about her opium smoking, about the joints she had run, and about the years she had lived with Jimmy Fredericks. A thin, wispy girl, still weak and wan from her suffering, Flo sat there answering all manner of detailed questions.

---

[3] Fortunately, Ten Eyck kept these pencil notes, which were to serve as documentary evidence of how Flo told her story, when it was later contended that the testimony was dragged from her in several nights of high pressure questioning.

It was in the spring of 1934, soon after they had started living together, Cokey Flo said, that she had first met Jimmy's business associates. It was in a Chinese restaurant, somewhere on upper Broadway, in the neighborhood of 130th Street; she could not place it exactly. She went there with Jimmy late at night, driving him herself in Bennie Spiller's car. Seated at a table in the chop suey place they found Charlie Lucky, Little Davie and Tommy Bull. Jimmy introduced them to her. "Meet the girl friend," he said.

They sat there eating and talking for some time, said Flo. Most of the talk she couldn't understand, for it was in Italian. But in English there was a little talk about gambling and bonding and some inconsequential matters.

When they left the restaurant, said Flo, they all got into the car and she drove them downtown, and then they started talking about bonding. She thought it was Little Davie who brought the subject up.

"He said some of the madams are holding out, and then Charlie spoke up and said: 'Well, can't you get them together?' and Davie says: 'Yes, we will. It takes a little time.'

"Charlie Lucky said something about 'get them together' —said something like—'Will get them together' and 'I don't like them stalling in the payments and some not wanting to bond' and stuff like that—'get after them.'

"And Tommy spoke up and said, 'That's all right, we'll take care of them!' "

"Remember any mention made of bookies?" asked Ten Eyck.

"Jimmy said some of the bookies were holding out joints; that Nick Montana would collect bond and keep it and if the place was pinched, they would run to the bonding company and Nick would make himself scarce and there would be a big fight about it."

"What do you mean by bonding?"

"Well, combination."

"Did anybody say anything to that?"

"I believe it was Charlie said: 'Have a meeting and get them all down and get them on the carpet,' because later I remember Jimmy told me they had all these bookies down and bawled the devil out of them and Nick thought he would get away with it, because he had a brother—big shot in Harlem. They didn't care whether he had fifty brothers—he had to kick in just the same."

Two times, said Flo, she went down with Jimmy to a garage, somewhere on the lower east side. She did not know quite where. The first time Jimmy left her outside the place to wait for him.

"He said he would be out in a while and I stayed there a while and got tired of sitting in the car," said Flo,—"started to prowl around to get an earful or other, and heard them say to Bennie that he should cut out being so much of a pimp and try to get his mind on shylocking. They were trying to get some money out of him to put up for something or other."

Flo said she then got back into the car and after a while the men came out and she saw they were Tommy Bull, Little Davie, and Charlie Lucky.

The other time outside the garage Flo said she again did some eavesdropping. They were all inside talking at once, arguing, and she heard them talking about Nick holding out joints and things about madams not wanting to bond. She heard Jimmy also talking to them about a crash raid the cops had just made on a lot of joints that were running in the house at 124 West Seventy-second Street. Those raids had taken place around Easter in 1935.

Another time she saw Charlie Lucky, said Flo, was about four o'clock in the morning when she and Jimmy went down to a restaurant in a basement in Chinatown. She couldn't remember the address but she remembered the big figure 21 outside the entrance. (Flo's description, it was later determined, tallied with the restaurant at 21 Mott Street.) So far as Flo could remember, this was in the summer of 1935. She and Jimmy found Lucky, Little Davie, and Tommy Bull sitting there eating, and again they talked mostly in Italian. But there was some talk in English about bonding. It was a discussion, Flo recalled, about making the madams pay up and getting more places.

"They were speaking of bonding and madams being stubborn and not paying, and Charlie said to Jimmy: 'I told you just talking won't do any good—that you have got to put the screws on them a little bit.' "

"Do you remember whether that was his precise language as far as 'putting screws on them' is concerned?"

"I would not say he said 'screws' exactly, but he didn't use much proper English. So Jimmy said: 'Well, maybe it's better policy if you talk to them a little bit. Things are a little tough now. You want to go a little easy. Of course, when things let up you can go down on them hard.' Charlie Lucky said: 'All right, then.' Davie said: 'We'll make a go of this thing. Bound to go, because it's a good proposition. It's got to.' "

"Remember whether any specific madams were mentioned in this connection?"

"Yes. I remember Peggy Wild refused to pay bond. She was supposed to be closed and Jimmy said he found out from different girls she was operating at the time in the building across the hall from where she was supposed to be closed. Jimmy said he sent a collector up and she would not even let them in the door. Said: 'I'm not doing anything—get away from here.' So I think Davie Betillo said: 'Well, that's all right. I'll take care of her. She'll bond.'

"After we left the restaurant, when Jimmy and I were alone in the car, he told me that he had been annoyed quite a bit with Peggy because of her man Bill Wild running downtown about paying a bond and that he tried to get people to get to Davie and to get to Lucky, because everybody knew Davie was under Lucky."

"Who said that?"

"Jimmy—everybody knew that."

"Any mention of any other madams doing the same thing?"

"Jennie the Factory."

"Remember anybody saying she was trying to be wise?" asked Ten Eyck, refreshing Flo's recollection a bit.

"Yes. Lucky said: 'Oh, she's a wise guy.[4] We will have to take care of her.' Jimmy said: 'That's all right, we will.' "

Again, in the early winter of 1935, between Thanksgiving and Christmas, Flo said she met the same men. She went with Jimmy to meet Lucky and Davie about three o'clock in the morning, again in the basement restaurant, No. 21.

"At that time," she continued, "Charlie Lucky said he was tired of having his name mentioned so freely in connection with the bonding combination. He said: 'It's getting hot. It's not paying and it's getting tough. This Dewey investigation

---

[4] Peggy Wild and Jennie the Factory really were wise guys with connections. Both of them paid bond for a while but both of them quit doing it before the time of the Dewey raid.

is going along and it's taking in all the rackets and liable to get to this too.'

"Jimmy said: 'Oh, the Dewey thing. There won't be anything to that,' and Davie said: 'Well, you can never tell but after all, if worst comes to worst, they will probably be looking for the phoney bondsmen, there won't be anything to that.' "

Flo said that the profit at this time was only $500 or $600 a week and Charlie Lucky complained that there was not much money in the racket and that they had to get the joints together into a more profitable set-up. But Davie thought the time for that had not come yet. Lucky, said Flo, wanted to drop the matter for the time being, and then go into it in a big way and syndicate the houses the way they did in Chicago. She continued:

"So he said: 'We can take joints away from madams, put them on salary or commission and run them like a syndicate —like large A & P stores, and there would not be any bonding or booking of houses. In Chicago there were three or four combinations had those syndicate places. In New York there would only be one, of course. Just us.'

"So Davie said: 'Well, why don't you wait a little while and see how it works out? Your name won't be mentioned any more so far as that's concerned. Why don't you give us a chance, and try a couple of months? I am sure we can work it out because we got it pretty well going now. We're just on a little hard luck now with pinches and so on.' So Charlie said: 'Well, all right, I'll let it go a couple of months and then if we don't make more money out of it than we have, then if it looks as if it's going to get tough, we'll cut it out for a while.' "

As Flo understood it, the money that was taken in by the

combination was split up among ten or twelve different people in varying percentages, including the bosses of mobs in other parts of town. She said the reason why Lucky was complaining about his name being used was that madams were sending their pimps around town to talk to racket men and see if they could not persuade Lucky to let them out of bonding. That was very foolish because the other racketeering combinations had a split in the profits.

Wispy little Flo, weak and wan, had sat there for two hours answering questions, straining her memory, telling her story.

Now she was taken back to jail. The stenographer hurried off to type up her notes. The next day Flo was to read over this statement, make corrections in it in her own handwriting, sign and swear to it.

Dewey sat in the office with his assistants. He was satisfied. He was sold. Cokey Flo was an honest-to-God witness.

"All right," said Dewey, "we will put her on the stand tomorrow."

XVII. THE POINTING
FINGER

A SURPRISE WITNESS

Samuel J. Siegel, counsel to Jimmy Fredericks, was a squat, gray, stoutish man, somewhat inclined to be pompous. He was one of New York's most prominent criminal lawyers and he always made a point of not accepting whorehouse cases unless they were important.

In the late afternoon of May 21, Siegel slipped out of the courtroom briefly for a smoke on the stairway near the door.

At the moment a pretty girl named Shirley Mason was finishing her testimony, in which she told the sad tale of how she had flunked her Wassermann test and been thrown out of her job in Atlantic City and how Jack Eller had sympathetically brought her up to New York, and put her to work on West Eighty-sixth Street. Soon she had to quit work, not because she had syphilis, but because she had caught typhoid. After she got out of the hospital Shirley and Jack had gotten very fond of each other and she had lived with him until he stole her watch.

All this was interesting and very tough for Jack Eller. But it was not Jimmy Fredericks's funeral. So Mr. Siegel could afford to relax and let someone else represent his client for the moment. Suddenly the courtroom door flew open and an excited defense colleague burst out.

"Sam," he cried, "they've got Cokey Flo!"

The story has it that Mr. Siegel sat down, plop, very hard, on the courthouse stairway. The thought that Cokey Flo should have turned state's evidence, even though she was in jail, was one of those unexpected things. Flo had been in a very different frame of mind the last time he had seen her.

An instant later Mr. Siegel was up again, pushing into the courtroom, ready to meet an emergency.

TRIAL BY ORDEAL

Flo was on the stand. She said that she knew nearly all of the defendants. She was telling about her early life; the men she had known; how she acquired the narcotic habit; and how she met Jimmy Fredericks. She was on the stand only twenty minutes before the court was adjourned until the next day.

Flo had been on the verge of collapse all that day before she came to the stand to testify. There still were shooting pains in her back and legs. She had black spots before her eyes as she lay weakly on a couch, waiting for her ordeal. She had asked for a drink of brandy and Justice McCook had let her have it. That had helped.

Now that her first minutes in the courtroom had passed, Flo felt better. The police guard took her out for a ride and then to a restaurant for dinner. For the first time since her arrest she ate a meal that tasted good, and she was able to keep it on her stomach. Flo slept for about an hour that night, the best night's sleep she had had in a long time. She ate a little breakfast that morning and before she took the stand the judge let her have another little carefully-measured shot of brandy.

"When I took the stand I felt as though it wasn't me, at

all, it seemed to me that I was someone else," Flo said later. "I was in a daze, I was numb, I couldn't feel. I was so weak, my eyes were even weak. When the attorneys for the defense were cross-examining me, I looked at them and couldn't see them, there seemed to be three or four of them at a time, instead of one at a time.

"I answered mechanically, whatever was asked me. It was a good thing I had told the truth, for if I had been lying, as they were trying to say I was, they would have trapped me, caught me, hundreds of times.

"Even the defense knew how sick I was, and felt sure I wouldn't have the strength or courage to stand up, that I would break down. I can't tell you how I stood it, but I did. It was just sheer will-power that kept me up, that's all. It was the will to make good now, so that I would have a chance in life to get a break and get away from it all. When one of the defense attorneys said, 'If you didn't get immunity before the Grand Jury, as all the other witnesses did, then why are you testifying?' I answered, 'Because I'm sick of all this, this kind of living, I want to make a clean breast of everything, and turn over a new leaf, with a clear conscience.' And I meant it.

"I stood up under it all. I didn't mind anything. The defendants staring up at me, and making threatening faces at me, the attorneys trying to belittle me for my use of drugs, their hammering at me with questions, trying to trap me, my own pains, and aches, and weakness. I stood up under it all."

Flo was on the stand all day. It took only forty-five minutes to finish her testimony for Dewey. Then began the long weary process of cross-examination.

But for two hours of recess time, the defense lawyers, one after another, nagged at Flo, from eleven o'clock until nearly seven in the evening. Time was taken out also for an examination by doctors to find out whether Flo had had any narcotics. Flo was questioned in detail about her technique of smoking opium; taking morphine; about all the girls and madams she had seen in the House of Detention; about how she set up her business in New York, and her experiences in it.

It was all a very highly developed form of intellectual torture. She had to tell all about the cures she had taken, what pains she had had, where they were located; all about her arrest and conviction; how Sam Siegel's office had got Dorothy Russell to rescue Flo's dog from the back yard.

It was really an astonishing feat of endurance the way Flo, in her weakened condition, stood up under it all. One after another the lawyers matched their wits with hers. None of them, either then or in the brief hour of questioning the next morning, trapped her in any strong inconsistencies.

A GOOD GIRL

Cokey Flo's nine hours on the witness stand were over. She was the twenty-eighth woman who, in the course of two weeks, had come before the jury to tell the details of a life of harlotry. Now a new witness was awaited.

"May we suspend a moment," said Dewey, "while the defendants move around and change places in the courtroom?"

The gangsters rose uneasily, moved about. The bustle and whispering filled the chamber. Necks were craned in expectancy toward the door of the witness room. Abie Wahrman hitched nervously at his polka-dot necktie. Jimmy Fredericks, bulging a bit in his bright green suit, took the seat next to Abie. Little Davie, also in bright green, sat farther up front, near Luciano.

Now to the witness stand came a young girl. There was something vaguely different about her from all the rest, a certain pink and white freshness. Her name was Molly Brown and it was her job to clean bathrooms on the thirty-ninth and fortieth floors of the Waldorf-Astoria. She looked about the room, nervously, uneasily, as all eyes converged upon her.

Molly commuted every day from New Jersey and she scrubbed up ten or eleven bathrooms every morning. You would not think that was a very exciting life, even at the Waldorf. But in this last year, drama had come into the life of Molly.

It was that Mr. Charles Ross in apartment 39-C. All the girls were interested in him, especially Molly. Just to look at him you could tell that he was different from most of the other guests at the Waldorf, and the strangest people came to see him.

Molly went busily about her work every morning and was finished by noon with all except Mr. Ross's apartment. But he never got up and went out before early afternoon, and Molly always had to wait before she could get in there and do her work. She used to stand or sit in a corner of the hallway near his door and kill time there. Sometimes Hedwig, the chambermaid, would stand there with her too. They would talk and make guesses about who these people could be. It was like the movies.

They weren't supposed to stand there in the corridor. Sometimes the housekeeper caught them and bawled them out. But usually they could hear her coming; hear the big bunch of keys clanking from her belt and so get out of sight.

It had been exciting when Mr. Ross was there. But Molly

had never thought it would come to anything like this. She sat here in the courtroom full of people and she was scared.

"THE MAN WITH THE BLACK NECKTIE"

Molly found herself looking at the gloomy, masklike face of Mr. Ross, whom she now knew as Luciano.

"Do you see anyone in the courtroom who was a guest at the Waldorf during the past year?"

"Yes," said Molly. "This man right here with the black necktie." And she pointed her finger straight at Charlie Lucky.

"Will you stand up now and see if you can point out anybody in the courtroom whom you saw going in and out of his apartment?" asked Dewey.

Molly looked around some more. There were a lot of men in a space inside a railing, all in chairs, crowded around some tables. Now she saw one she recognized.

"Yes," she said, "the fellow with the gray suit with the polka-dot tie."

"What is the color of the suit of the man next to him?" asked Dewey to clinch the identification.

"Green," said Molly.

"Indicating the defendant Wahrman," remarked Dewey for the record. "Have you seen him there on several occasions?"

"Oh, I can say about twenty."

"Who else do you see in the courtroom that you know?"

"This fellow here with the green suit and green tie and white shirt," said Molly. That was Little Davie.

"How often did you see him in Mr. Ross's apartment?"

"Oh, not many times. I would say about five."

"Whom else do you see? Stand up and look all around

and take your time. Do not be in any haste in answering."

Molly stood up, looked around, peering at faces uncertainly. She lifted her hand and started to point at George Morton Levy, Luciano's trial lawyer.

"Pointing to me?" asked Levy eagerly.

"No," said Molly, changing her mind. "I think that is about all," she said.

"Oh!" she exclaimed, pointing far over. "That man in the gray suit there." Molly had pointed out Meyer Berkman, assistant to Jesse Jacobs of the bonding office.

Molly said she could not recognize any more and Dewey turned her over to the cross-examiners, who set out to confuse her and break down the identification.

"A DARK STOCKY MAN"

The defense lawyers questioned Molly at length about her work, about her trips downtown to see Mr. Grimes and look at pictures. They made her turn her face away from the prisoners and try to describe them.

Soon confusion appeared in her story.

"You pointed to a second man here in the courtroom today," said Caesar Barra, Little Davie's lawyer. "Will you describe him to us?"

"The second man?" asked Molly. "He was short, stocky, dark. I saw him more than anyone else."

Dewey leaned forward eagerly. "What is the name?" he asked.

"I don't know their names," said Molly.

Mr. Barra proceeded with an apparent feeling of satisfaction. Little Davie was the second man. He was not tall, but he was neither stocky nor dark.

"He usually wore that green suit," said Molly.

Mr. Barra sat down. Other defense lawyers sought to resume their questions. They were having a lucky break and wanted to return and press the advantage. But it was Sam Siegel's turn to examine and he stepped up to question for the benefit of his client, Fredericks.

"May I ask one question," said he, endeavoring to clear up all the doubt. "You have looked at everybody, haven't you?"

"Yes," said Molly.

"And there is positively in your mind nobody else that you saw in the apartment of the man you have described as Ross, except this man here with the green suit and the man with the polka-dot tie?" asked Sam Siegel, pointing to Betillo and Wahrman.

"And the other man with the green suit," said Molly. "That short, dark fellow in the back there." And she was pointing straight at Jimmy Fredericks.

Somebody laughed. Then as everybody realized what had happened, the whole courtroom broke out into a roar. Siegel had brought out the identification of his own client.

The lawyer quickly changed the subject. He asked Molly all manner of questions about her work; how she went about cleaning bathrooms. But he had to come back to the identification. It was all clear now. When Molly had spoken of the green suit next to Little Abie, she had meant to identify Fredericks. There were two men with green suits and the short, dark, stocky man was the one who had been there twenty times.

After a while Dewey got another chance at his witness.

"Now will you step down off that witness chair, please," he said. "Come down here and just tell me which of these people you and I have been talking about. Now, we have agreed on Mr. Ross?"

"Yes," said Molly, stepping down from the witness chair into the crowded space within the rail, walking over toward the glowering defendants.

"Let her put her hand on them, will you, Mr. Dewey?" said Levy. "Put the hand, instead of pointing."

So there, before the burning eyes of the toughest gangsters in New York, little Molly walked over and put her hand on Abie Wahrman— "This one," she said. And then she turned to Fredericks and put her hand on him— "This one," she said. Molly walked over to Little Davie and tapped him too. "I cannot reach that man there," she said, pointing over to Berkman. Then she turned and walked back to Jimmy Fredericks. "I have seen this one more than any of the others," said Molly.

A CRASHING BLOW

Since Lucky had already entered his denial that he knew these men, Molly's appearance had dealt the defense a crashing blow, even the unofficial defense that was passed around the town's bar rooms and sporting places. For the wise boys along Broadway were saying that of course Lucky was a racketeer; of course Lucky was a big shot; that he was in just about everything; but not in prostitution.

It would not have been entirely inconsistent with that theory of the case for Lucky to have been associated with Tommy Bull, Little Abie, Little Davie, or many of the others, for they were in other rackets as well as prostitution. But Fredericks was different. He was, you might say, a prostitution man, pure and simple. And Molly said he had been to see Lucky more than any of the others.

There were to be many postmortems, arguments, and discussions about the Luciano case long after it was over, and always, if those discussing it knew anything about it, somebody made the point: you can't get around the little bathmaid.

XVIII. COUNTERATTACK

WAVERING WITNESSES

A big criminal trial is something like a football game, with both sides lined up, plunging at each other in a battle of wits, each momentarily taking the advantage, fighting back and forth. The prosecution takes the ball on the kickoff, and the defense takes it on cross-examination, trying to smash down the credibility and character of the accusing witnesses.

Ordinarily it is a very successful thing for a defense lawyer to prove that a state witness is a criminal or a person of disreputable character. In this case there was plenty of opportunity for that.

Out of Dewey's sixty-eight witnesses in the trial, forty were prostitutes and madams who told frankly about their disreputable careers. A dozen more were bookers, lobbygows, and male madams.

Joe Bendix, of course, was about as complete a thief as could be found, a thoroughly low character. His career and methods were examined minutely by his cross-examiners. In addition, Bendix's testimony received a damaging blow when it developed that he had written a letter to his wife, a night club girl, urging her to corroborate his story that she was at the Villanova Restaurant with him when he talked to Charlie Lucky. In the letter he had suggested that she tell a "clever" story at the Dewey office, because it was very important to him. Bendix had made the careless error of putting this let-

ter to his wife into an envelope which he had addressed to an
assistant district attorney, Morris H. Panger, with whom
he was dickering at the time for a lighter sentence. Only
after Bendix had appeared on the witness stand did the District Attorney's office bother to send this letter to Dewey.
Bendix's testimony took a pretty thorough kicking around.

Dewey did have several witnesses of good character in addition to the bathmaid, however,—the chambermaid, some
hotel managers, bellhops and waiters from the Barbizon
Plaza and the Waldorf. One after another they identified
various defendants as having been seen in Lucky's hotel
rooms. Some of these witnesses blew up. The manager of the
Waldorf Tower said he thought he had seen Abie Wahrman
in the hotel and then he picked out Lucky's lawyer, Moe
Polakoff, as the man he was identifying. The assistant manager of the Barbizon Plaza, shown a batch of about twenty
pictures, picked out two or three as men he had had a drink
with in Luciano's room. But when he got to court he said he
couldn't be sure.

But a bellhop who no longer worked in the hotel, whose
testimony was plainly a surprise to the defense, recognized
Little Davie and Tommy Bull without hesitation.

Another bellhop said he had seen Jimmy Fredericks playing cards with Charlie Lucky and that Lucky had addressed
Jimmy as "Joe." That seemed inconclusive, but evidence developed that Fredericks had on occasion used the name Joe
Marino. This bellhop, however, blew up his own testimony by
passing over the swarthy black-haired Italian Fredericks
and picking out in the courtroom the fat, baldish, Jewish
Jack Eller, who looked nothing like Jimmy. A day before
this the bellhop had picked out Fredericks without hesitation
when he had taken a look at him at the courthouse. Sur-

prised by the switch, Dewey sat down and waited for cross-examination.

At this point, as though by some uncanny mind reading, the defense asked for the statement the bellhop had made the day before, thereby dramatically revealing the switch in identification. Dewey was to make capital out of that later, pointing out that this was the only statement of the sort the defense had asked for from these hotel witnesses. He was to cite it in his summation as evidence of the fear, the terror, which had existed in the background outside the court. He was to charge that something had happened to this witness, to make him switch, and the defense knew about it.

Other witnesses stuck by their identifications and were the clinching part of the case.

The defendants made a great play by trying to trick the identification witnesses. Ralph Liguori wore horn-rimmed glasses to court. Others changed the way they parted their hair. During a recess they exchanged neckties.

COLLAPSE

The girls were in for a frightful ordeal. Nancy Presser, having told of her visits to Lucky at the Barbizon Plaza and the Waldorf, had to try to remember each tiny detail of all those occasions. Lucky's lawyer made great fun of her story that she had been given $50 on her first visit to the Barbizon, even though she and Lucky did not transact any business. Nancy retorted that she had gone there intending to practice her trade but had refused to do it when she found there was something wrong with Lucky.

Nancy, like the others, had to go through all the details of her drug habit, how she had acquired it and how she had taken the cure.

Finally, questions came down to the matter of describing the physical appearance of Lucky's hotel rooms. Nancy said that the apartment in the Barbizon Plaza was a parlor, bedroom, and bath. At the prosecution table this was startling. Queries were sent out to the Dewey office. Up to now it had always been assumed that Lucky just had a room at the hotel. Hotel registry sheets gave only single room numbers to the places he had occupied. The assistant manager of the hotel was asked to describe Lucky's apartment. He said it was a parlor, bedroom, and bath. The prosecution breathed more easily.

George Morton Levy, continuing his cross-examination of Nancy, asked her to describe how she got into the Waldorf to go into Lucky's suite in the tower.

When you enter the Waldorf from Park Avenue you go up a gradual flight of stairs between the terraces of the Sert Room and the Empire Room, then across the open space known as Peacock Alley and past a bank of elevators, before entering the central lobby of the hotel. To go to the tower elevator you turn left into Peacock Alley about fifty feet. The tower elevators are not conspicuous and are one of the most difficult things about a hotel in which it is easy to get lost.

Nancy wasn't able to be very definite about the way she got into the tower. She said she took the elevator before she came to the lobby. She was pretty sure it was the ordinary elevator.

"I know I lost myself," said Nancy. "I know I got lost in the hotel. I went from one elevator to another. I always did get lost in big hotels."

Levy did not press this subject further. It was an adroit bit of examination. It gave the impression, certainly to the newspapers, that Nancy didn't know how she got into the place.

Examination of the record, however, shows that while she was hazy, her story was not inconsistent with the facts. It appeared later that if she took the ordinary elevator she would have to change at the twenty-eighth floor to get to the tower elevator.

Levy made a great deal out of her assertion that she had gone to apartment 39-C without being announced from the lobby. But it later appeared that while there were rigid restrictions on visitors on many floors of the tower, there had been no requirement that anyone be announced in going to the thirty-ninth floor, either night or day.

Nancy was obviously weakening under the strain of her examination. All her testimony had been given in the wan, faint voice of a semi-invalid. Most of the time the stenographer had been required to read her answers in a tone that could be heard by the court.

Levy asked her to describe Lucky's apartment. Were there twin beds or single beds? Was there a radio? A piano? Was there a pantry?

Nancy became more and more uncertain. She remembered you went in and turned to the left.

"Now you describe that bedroom as a woman would, having the feminine touch."

Nancy looked about at the judge a bit helplessly.

"Your Honor, I would like to ask for a ten-minute recess."

As the court and lawyers discussed the matter for a few minutes Nancy got up and beat it for the door.

"Come back here and sit down," said the judge.

Finally Nancy got out of the room, went downstairs and

vomited. She couldn't come back to the witness stand. She reported the next day that she had vomited all evening and all night. She had become very ill as Levy questioned her about opium. She said that ever since she had taken the narcotic cure it always made her sick to her stomach when anyone talked to her about narcotics.

Nancy was called back again the next evening, but Levy said he did not want to examine her any more. He was satisfied with her breakdown. But Dewey called her for a redirect examination. He succeeded in rehabilitating her a lot.

The cross-examination about opium had opened the door so that Dewey could bring out that her opium-smoking companions had been Waxey Gordon and his bootlegging mob. That indicated she was not merely a two-dollar girl.

As for Nancy's inability to describe the details of Lucky's hotel suite, Dewey asked her how many hotel rooms she had been likely to visit every week during the period when she was doing a call business.

"Sometimes twenty, twenty-five, or thirty times," said Nancy.

"That is all," said Dewey.

RALPH LEARNS SOMETHING

While Dewey tried to keep the testimony in the trial on an austere plane, with words and incidents that would hardly offend the most blue-nosed censor, the defense from the beginning sought to emphasize that this was all a very dirty business. While Dewey called his witnesses prostitutes, defense lawyers referred to them as whores. Mr. Levy, the chief defense counsel, elaborately washed his hands of most of the untactful utterances of his colleagues, especially those of Lorenzo C. Carlino, counsel to Nancy's boy friend,

Ralph Liguori. Mr. Carlino was frequently asking the girls about their operations and various details of physical disability.

"Did you get sick to your stomach when you were staying with all these men?" shouted Mr. Carlino at Nancy.

"No," she said.

"Very pleasurable to you, wasn't it?"

"No, I couldn't say that."

"You enjoyed it, didn't you? You enjoyed your depravity?"

"No," said Nancy.

"How many men have you stayed with in your lifetime?"

"I cannot answer that question. Can you answer me how many people you have seen in your lifetime?" exclaimed Nancy.

"And you worked in a $2 whorehouse, didn't you?" roared Mr. Carlino.

"Certainly," said Nancy, "because Ralph sent me there, that was why. It wasn't because I wanted to."

"You have been diseased for a number of years, haven't you?"

"I have not."

"Aren't you suffering from syphilis?"

"Yes. I believe I got that from Ralph."

Gradually, on the not over-intelligent face of the ape-like Liguori a faint light of understanding began to break. He called his lawyer over to confer with him. Shortly later Mr. Carlino, with a brave sure confidence, challenged the prosecution to have his client examined by a doctor. During a recess Liguori took the Wassermann test. Mr. Carlino did not bring the subject up again.

PAY DIRT

Mildred Harris was the last of the women to testify. She was on the stand for something like nine hours, and also was carried through a minute biography of herself as an opium smoker, morphine addict, and madam, and all through the story of her arrest and her denials and her decision to testify.

Nowhere did they shake Mildred's testimony.

Having rung the changes on the depravity of ordinary prostitutes, the defense lawyers called upon Mildred again and again to deny that she was a lesbian. Especially they professed to find the most decadent significance in the fact that when the police raided her hotel room on February 1, they found her occupying the place with one Phil Ryan, a female impersonator who entertained in night clubs.

Mildred said that Phil was a friend of the family; that her husband Pete knew all about their friendship and that Phil had taken them both not long before that to the annual Fairies' Ball in Harlem. They had enjoyed it very much. Mildred said Ryan didn't live with her but he had been suffering from an attack of influenza and she had been nursing him during his convalescence.

Mr. Levy wanted to know whether Mildred had twin beds in her room and how she and Phil managed to get undressed without seeing each other.

"You had no hesitancy in undressing in front of that fairy, did you?" he demanded.

"I never undressed in front of him," said Mildred indignantly. "There were two bathrooms in that hotel room."

All through the trial the defense had been filled with shock and moral indignation at the thought that the girls in custody had been allowed to drink liquor. All through the trial there had been insinuations that high jinks had been going on between the girls and the Dewey men. One girl after another had been asked whether she had been taken around to night clubs.

Now they got what they had been building for. They had struck pay dirt.

"Yes," said Mildred. She had been to Leon & Eddie's at two o'clock one morning with a police officer and Mr. Gelb. She had one or two drinks of brandy and Gelb paid for them.

"Did you dance?"

"No," said Mildred.

"Sure about that?"

"Positive."

The defense lawyers' eyebrows were lifted in high arches. They looked at the jury as if to say: Now! You see? They had loosed a scandal.

Mildred is a great, big, tall, buxom woman with henna hair. Gelb is a little fellow, hardly more than five feet four inches high. If they actually had danced together in Leon & Eddie's it would have been a sight worth seeing.

POLICE ESCORT

The defense was to follow up the Leon & Eddie story later by presenting Patrolman George A. Heidt, the cop who had been to Leon & Eddie's with Mildred and Sol Gelb, as a witness for the defense. With many protests of reluctance, the policeman related the story of the visit to Leon & Eddie's and described how tight Mildred was.

The spectacle of a policeman appearing thus as a defense witness for the gangsters did not escape his superiors in the police department. Some inquiry into his affairs later brought to light the fact that in the eight years from 1926 to 1933, on a patrolman's salary, he had banked $74,500. In the one year 1932, he had banked $22,288. He lived in a penthouse at Thirtieth Street and Fifth Avenue. Heidt later was thrown off the police force when his explanations of his prosperity seemed unsatisfactory.

In December, 1937, however, the Appellate Division of the Supreme Court reversed the decision whereby Heidt had been deprived of his job, which was protected by civil service. It held that no one had disproved his explanations that he had piled up his big bank totals by a series of withdrawals and deposits and by inheritance of money. Heidt went back on the police force.

XIX. DEFENSE

COPS TO THE RESCUE

Just in the nature of things, even assuming that Lucky was innocent of this prostitution charge, he would have had a hard time defending himself. That he was a gangster and a big one there never was any doubt. He could not call high grade witnesses to give him a respectable front. He did the only thing he could do, tried to prove that he was merely a gambler.

The defense started by attacking the veracity and character of the prosecution witnesses.

A county detective and two policemen from Pittsburgh were brought to court to testify about the bad character of Dave Miller, as if he had not demonstrated that fairly well himself. They proved that Dave had lied when he denied that he and his wife had run a disorderly house in Pittsburgh and Mrs. Miller had been convicted.

Two policemen also appeared from Philadelphia to testify that Pete Harris, prostitution man, had a bad reputation for veracity. They said they wouldn't believe a prostitution man no matter what he swore.

Captain George Paul Dutton, in charge of regulating night clubs for the New York State police, also appeared for the defense, suggesting that he might be the mysterious Captain Dutton to whom Joe Bendix referred. He didn't know Joe Bendix but he did happen to know Bendix's present wife and that might have given Bendix the idea of using the name.

A police chief from New Jersey came up to testify that he had arrested Little Davie for running a gambling boat, to that extent confirming Lucky's claim that he only knew Little Davie through Davie's attempt to interest him in this boat.

In other words, the defense was able to produce various policemen, even from outside the state, outside the jurisdiction of the court, to come in and give what sort of help they could to the defense of the overlord of the underworld.

Several gamblers and bookmakers appeared to testify that Charlie Lucky was known to them as a gambler, as a man who was at the race track practically every day; that he had run the Chicago Club in Saratoga; that he had an interest in a big wire house in the horse book business. All this was obviously true.

As the defense opened, Dewey was prepared for a parade of half-world witnesses. Over in the Woolworth Building office he had a collection of all the bookers and madams who had testified; several other madams who had not been called to the witness chair also were there as a sort of brain trust to give him information about surprise witnesses that were called. To question them he had a direct wire from the courtroom. And as the defense presented its case, Dewey was terrible in cross-examination. It was a bit uncanny how much this clean, busy, respectable young man seemed to know of nearly everybody in the underworld.

BOY FRIENDS

A small swarthy young man named Lorenzo Brescio, known as Chappie, who had stayed with Lucky a good deal of the time at the Barbizon Plaza, came before the court and testified that he had never heard of Nancy Presser; that Charlie Lucky's girl was Gay Orlova, both while he was living at the Barbizon and at the Waldorf.

Miss Orlova had been getting quite a lot of publicity in the newspapers. In the absence of any pictures of Dewey's witnesses, Gay's carefully posed photographs, together with her assertions that she was Charlie Lucky's girl, had been meat for the tabloids.

Brescio, who was president of a beer distributing company licensed by the A.B.C. Board, was able, on cross-examination, to give very little indication that he knew much about the beer business. Vast gaps appeared in his memory of how he had been making a living for many years. For some time, however, he had had a pistol permit because he had found it necessary in collecting rents and insurance premiums in his business. He had to admit that he had been connected with a real estate outfit for only the briefest period. Brescio, whom Lucky called his "boy friend," was transparently a gangster.

(As this is written, in 1939, Brescio is one of the men mixed up in the prosecution of the taxicab racket which was one of Charlie Lucky's subsidiary interests.)

Gus Franco, Mildred Harris's old opium-smoking boy friend, took the stand to deny that he had ever threatened Mildred or that he had ever introduced her to Little Davie and Tommy Bull. He said he didn't even know them. Franco said he lived with Mildred until he found out she was running a house of prostitution and that he was so shocked he broke up with her.

Under Dewey's slashing cross-examination Franco made a very sad appearance. He was no worse a character than many of Dewey's witnesses had been. But he was trying to give himself a good character and he was so obviously lying.

It was pretty tough for Lucky if he couldn't produce better witnesses than these.

Ralph Liguori took the witness stand in his own defense. He tried to represent himself as someone who was shocked, after Nancy Presser's arrest, to discover that he had been living with a prostitute.

Liguori was ripped limb from limb on cross-examination. All the stuff about Gashouse Lil came out and he was unable to give any account of his doings except that he had been making a living shooting craps.

The burden of his testimony was a charge that he had been framed because he would not give perjured testimony against Lucky and the others, telling of his arrest long after the original raid and attempts made to persuade him to turn state's evidence. He told of dramatic scenes in the Dewey office in which he said photographs of the defendants had been pushed at him one by one and the demand made that he identify them and tell certain things about them. He made Harry Cole the main villain in this story and said that Nancy Presser and Thelma Jordan had been supplied with photographs of Lucky which they kept in handbags to help them memorize his face so that they could identify him in court. Liguori said that Cole promised him that he could go on living in an apartment with Nancy Presser while waiting for the trial if he would just testify as Dewey's office wanted him to.

"He told me if I would co-operate with the office he would send me to Europe with my girl for six months and they would give me plenty of protection," said Liguori. "He told me that Mr. Dewey was going to become a Governor and would give me all the protection I would want."

Liguori's mother and sister came to court to say he had told them that the Dewey office wanted him to commit perjury and save himself, but he had refused. Perjury was something he would not commit.

Obviously Liguori was a pimp, a robber, and a liar. Obviously also the heat had been turned on him in hopes of making him a witness. Why he had not taken a chance to open up and get off more easily is a matter for conjecture. That he should have gone on the witness stand at all was even more surprising, from the standpoint of self-interest.

Doing himself no good at all, Liguori was a perfect picture of an underling sacrificing himself for the boss.

FACE TO FACE

Charlie Lucky took the witness stand in his own defense and denied all the charges in bold broad strokes.

Lucky said he did not know any of the other defendants except Betillo who he thought had visited him once at the Waldorf. He denied that he had ever met Nancy Presser, Mildred Harris, Flo Brown, or Joe Bendix. He denied utterly that he ever had anything to do with prostitution business.

"Did you ever take a dollar proceeds from any whore or prostitute, directly or indirectly, in your life?" asked his lawyer.

"I always gave," said Lucky. "I never took."

Lucky said that he had been a gambler ever since he had quit a $5-a-week job as a shipping clerk when he was a young boy. He had hung around crap games and then had come up to the point where he was running crap games and booking horses himself. He had been in partnership with Fred Bachmann in the gambling business and the season before that had run the Chicago Club, one of the biggest gambling joints in Saratoga.

His criminal record, Lucky testified, consisted of a conviction for selling narcotics when he had been eighteen years old, twenty years before; and a conviction for maintaining a gambling house for which he was fined $1,000 in Miami in 1930.

Dewey rose to cross-examine. For the first time he was speaking to the man he had tracked down.

"Have you told us the whole truth about that little incident in Miami in 1930?" he demanded.

"The whole truth," said Lucky. "Yes, sir."

"How about the gun?"

"Mr. Levy didn't mention no gun," said Lucky, defensively.

"As a matter of fact," said Dewey, "you were also convicted of carrying a gun on the same occasion, weren't you?"

"Yes, sir," said Lucky, "but there is no charge against a gun in Miami."

In his first minute of cross-examination, Dewey had already caught him in a concealment. Tom Dewey has done many spectacular things in his career, but this examination was as dramatic as any. There was no point in asking Lucky about the prostitution business because Lucky had denied knowing anything about it. The only thing to do was to impeach his character, to show him up before the jury as the gangster that he was.

Like all of Dewey's accomplishments, the whole thing was based on the most energetic, painstaking preparation. For weeks, months, Dewey had had his men digging up material just because it was possible that Lucky might take the stand.

After Lucky's arrest, Dewey's office had sent to the Police Department for any information they had about him. After a considerable wait the police had sent back one sheet of paper—a mere police record—a list of Lucky's contacts with the law. That was all the police seemed to know about the man who was commonly considered to be Public Enemy No. 1.

Then the Dewey office went into action. The files of the Police Department were combed. Every time a man is arrested by a detective, the detective makes a report. One by one these reports were dug out, on each of the times that Lucky had been arrested and discharged.

Lucky had had pistol permits. An upstate county judge and court clerk spent nearly a whole week-end digging through dusty files in the courthouse cellar and finally came out with Lucky's application for a pistol permit. Dewey has a way of making people work for him. Lucky had had automobile licenses, driver's licenses. There was that time when he had testified before the Grand Jury at Staten Island after he was kidnapped. Now, as he faced the defendant, Dewey was loaded with documentary material.

Dewey started asking him about his arrest for selling narcotics. Lucky couldn't remember whom he had been buying from nor whom he was selling to. He knew he had only three transactions before he got arrested; went to the reformatory for six months; then reformed. He had never sold any more dope.

Lucky had a frightful time remembering any legitimate business he had ever been interested in. In this he was like Brescio, Franco, Liguori. After some hesitation he did remember that he had had a real estate office as a front at Center and White Streets, with a man named Manfrede, in 1926; they ran a bootlegging business selling alcohol. He could not remember who they bought from or who they sold it to. Finally he did remember that he once had a piece of a restaurant at Fifty-second Street. He couldn't remember his partner's name.

Nearly all Dewey's witnesses had been people of bad character. But under cross-examination they had talked with an amazing show of frankness, telling details of their lives with apparent lack of hesitation.

Now with Luciano, it was different. He was obviously concealing.

"And right up until the present minute, the only legitimate or pretense of legitimate occupation you have had or made in the last eighteen years is that you had a piece of a restaurant for six months?" said Dewey.

"That is right," said Luciano.

Bit by bit Dewey progressed, methodically, in a low tone of voice, tripping the witness in little lies. His questions seemed inconsequential.

Lucky denied that on August 28, 1922, he had told Patrolman Clay of the New York police force that he was married. He couldn't remember what business he told Patrolman Clay he was in. He couldn't remember other things which it was suggested he had told the police.

Dewey picked up from his table a sheaf of blue and yellow documents, handed them to a court attendant.

"Now," he said, "will you spread those before the witness; separate them in separate sheets."

Lucky, startled, puzzled, looked at the papers before him.

Dewey asked, "Now do any of those documents refresh your recollection?"

A competent newspaper reporter, in his account of this examination, relates that Luciano exclaimed: "Where did you get those?" The record shows no such remark. It seems clear that Luciano did not say it. But his face, his expression, his whole demeanor, shouted it.

Dewey had put before him all the collateral records and reports of the various arrests in his criminal career.

These things were not admissible as evidence in court. Lucky's arrests were not evidence against him for they were not convictions. But under the rules the papers might be shown him to refresh his recollection, and Dewey proceeded now to question him, not about the charges on which he had been held, but the things which he had told the policemen about himself on these various arrests.

He had Lucky denying that he had told one policeman after another that he was a married man; denying that he had told this policeman on that date and another policeman on another date that he was born in Italy. He admitted that he might have told the cops that he was a chauffeur. He admitted that he had known Joe the Boss. But no, he had not been Joe's chauffeur or his bodyguard.

The examination went on and on, not about Lucky's crimes or the crimes that had been charged against him, but his personal relationships with one policeman after another.

Having pretty well intimated that Lucky had lied on several occasions to policemen, Dewey began asking him his philosophy about truth telling.

"Now if you are under oath, you always tell the truth under every circumstance, is that it?" he asked.

"I am telling the truth now."

"But I am asking you: Do you tell the truth when you are under oath?" insisted Dewey.

"I says I am telling the truth now."

The witness was plainly in a great state of discomfiture. All those police records had been sprung upon him. How many bits of sworn testimony and affidavits might be before him in another minute!

"You do not want to answer that question, do you?" persisted Dewey. "Do you want some time to think it over?"

Dewey waited awhile and then ostentatiously sat down and waited for the answer. A full minute passed.

"We will just wait here until we get an answer," said Justice McCook. "There are three possible answers."

"I didn't say I told the truth all the time, but now I am telling the truth," said Lucky finally.

Soon Dewey had Lucky admitting that he had been lying under oath in order to get pistol permits. Soon he was refreshing Lucky's recollection about the incident in 1926 when Lucky was arrested in a car on Fifth Avenue in company with one Joe Scalise (a brother of the notorious Chicago assassin).

"And did you have two guns and a shotgun and forty-five rounds of ammunition in the car between you?"

"I just come back from the country, and I had a hunting outfit in there," said Lucky.

"You had two revolvers?"

"Yes."

"And a shotgun?"

"Yes."

"And forty-five rounds of ammunition?"

"And a couple of boxes of cartridges," said Lucky.

"What had you been doing in the country that day?"

"Shooting."

"Shooting what?"

"Birds."

"What kind of birds?"

"Peasants," said Lucky.

"Shooting *pheasants* in the middle of July?" said Dewey, correcting the pronunciation.

"Yes, that is right."

"Do you shoot pheasants with a pistol?"

"No."

"What were the pistols along for?"

"I had a permit for a pistol."

"Yes. What did you have it along for?"

"I carried it."

For four hours the examination ground along. It appeared that his bootlegging partner Manfrede had been arrested and convicted of receiving stolen goods, that Lucky had been held as a material witness at the time. Lucky said he did not know Manfrede was a fence.

"Isn't it a fact that you have been buying Bendix's stolen jewels for ten years?"

"I never met Bendix in my life."

What about Moe Ducore's drugstore at Forty-ninth Street and Seventh Avenue? Hadn't he hung out there? Hadn't he met Bendix there? Didn't he have a half interest in that store? No, said Lucky, he just had a passing acquaintance with Ducore.[1]

Dewey produced a telephone record showing that Ducore's drugstore had been called from Lucky's suite in the Waldorf. Lucky said he had never telephoned to Mr. Ducore.

---

[1] Ducore, long suspected, was convicted on March 2, 1939, as a receiver of stolen goods.

He was probably telephoning there to Georgie Burns, a boy that hung around the drugstore.

"Georgie Burns?" said Dewey. "He has been a dope peddler for twenty years, hasn't he?"

"I don't know," said Lucky. "Don't ask me."

"Isn't it a fact that he dishes out the dope for you?"

"For me? I don't handle dope."

"But you do not know whether Mr. Burns is a professional dope peddler or not?"

"No, sir."

"You claim that after you were convicted of dope peddling you never sold any more at all?"

"That is right."

"Do you recall a little incident on June 6, 1923?" asked Dewey.

"I don't remember what you mean."

"All right. Do you remember first on June 2, 1923, selling a two-ounce box of narcotics known as deacetyl morphine hydrochloride to John Lyons, an informer for the Federal Secret Service?"

"I was arrested but I never sold anything like that."

"Isn't it a fact that three days later, on June 5, 1923, you again sold one ounce of heroin to informer John Lyons of the Secret Service?"

"No, sir."

"Isn't it a fact that at 133 East Fourteenth Street in the City of New York on June 5 Narcotic Agent Coyle saw you sell narcotics to John Lyons?"

"That is objected to," said Mr. Levy.

"Sustained," said the court.

"Isn't it a fact that on that day your apartment was searched?"

"It might have been."

"Isn't it a fact that in your apartment were found two one-half ounce packages of morphine and two ounces of heroin and some opium?"

"No, sir."

"Isn't it a fact that thereafter you gave to Joseph Van Bransky, narcotic agent in charge in New York City, a statement that at 163 Mulberry Street they would find a whole trunk of narcotics?"

"Yes, I did."

"And isn't it a fact that thereafter a whole trunk of narcotics was found by the Secret Service at 163 Mulberry Street, New York City?"

"Yes, sir."

"And you still say you were not engaged in the business of narcotics in the year 1923?"

"I was picked up for it, but I was not—I didn't sell them."

"And you still testify under oath before this court and jury that you have not dealt in narcotics since the year 1919?"

"That is right."

"What were you—a stool pigeon?"

"I told him what I knew," said Lucky.

For weeks the defense lawyers had been pounding away at Dewey's witnesses, holding them up in contempt, picturing them as perjurers because they had done just the same thing. But now it seemed that the highest of the gangsters had himself turned informer when he ran up against the law. It was a frightful, humiliating admission for such a man as Lucky.

One witness after another had testified that Tommy Bull,

Little Davie, and Abie Wahrman hung out in Celano's Gardens on Kenmare Street.

Lucky admitted that he used to go there and eat once in a while. Celano was a friend of his. His friend Chappie Brescio often went there too.

Dewey played his trump card—a whole bundle of telephone slips showing calls being made from Lucky's room, morning, afternoon and evening, to Celano's Gardens.

Lucky would not deny the calls to Celano's, but he was sure he had never seen any of the other defendants there. Despite all the testimony, he insisted they had not hung out in that place.

There were more telephone calls, calls to Dave's Blue Room where Nancy Presser had told of seeing Lucky. There were two telephone calls to a garage on Delancey Street, tending to corroborate Flo Brown's story about the garage. There were calls to the Villanova Restaurant where Mildred Harris and Joe Bendix had reported seeing Lucky. There were calls to private unlisted telephone numbers of the great gangster Lepke, and Ciro Terranova, the Artichoke King.

Lucky had been under cross-examination for four hours. He had started out self-confident, a figure of a persecuted sporting man, but had become more and more hesitant and confused.

Now Dewey pulled out income tax reports. It appeared that in July, 1935, two weeks after the Dewey investigation had started, at the time when Dutch Schultz was being first tried for his income tax charges, Lucky had filed a delinquent return for six years with the federal government, six years being the extent of the statute of limitations.

Lucky had fixed his income at $15,000 for 1929, gradually increasing to $25,000 for the last year. Those figures were just estimates. He said he paid the government more than he owed it.

"You have not paid a dime to the state government yet, is that right?"

"That is right," said Lucky.

"And that is because the federal government prosecutes big gangsters and the state does not, by income tax; isn't that so?"

"I don't know," said Charlie Lucky.

XX. THE JURY'S ANSWER

REST FOR THE WEARY

It was 9:30 o'clock before the judge finished his charge and everybody went out to dinner. It was going to be a strenuous night. The jury had to get itself something to eat and then settle down to its deliberations before the passage of midnight had made it Sunday.

As midnight came and went, the crowd, which for a month had strained about the courtroom, had dwindled away almost to nothing. It would be a long time before the verdict came in. The jury might be out all night.

The evening newspaper men had long since finished their night's work and had gone. The morning newspaper men had written their stories and knocked off for the night. District reporters from police headquarters had come down to take over the vigil in case the verdict were brought in before the last edition of the papers.

There were a few who gathered in little knots around the courtroom: the defense lawyers and their friends who gathered around keeping up a great show of confidence; a few men of Dewey's office; a few reporters; trial fans, tensely talking about the case, hashing it over and over again. A lot of them were betting that Luciano would be acquitted.

Out in the corridor were wives of some defendants. They had been kept out of the courtroom during the trial. Now they stood there in little groups, just waiting. No one waited more tensely than they.

There is a weak, helpless feeling that comes at a time like this. Suspense is there, and tension, but the whole thing is out of the hands of everybody except the jury. For weeks there had been a struggle, a clash of words and wits, fierce bludgeoning of facts. But now there was nothing to do but wait.

The defendants were under guard in their room behind the trial chamber. Judge McCook had gone to his chambers. Dave Siegel, Little Abie's lawyer, was entertaining a group of friends at the restaurant across the square. They were all congratulating him on the acquittal which was sure to come.

Waiting in the courtroom, Dewey suddenly felt let down. For a month he had been keyed-up, on edge, battling night and day. On four hours' sleep he had talked all day, and for two hours more he had followed the judge's charge and the haggling of counsel over it. Now his whole year's work, the whole success of his job, hung in the balance. But there was nothing more he could do. He went upstairs alone to the top of the courthouse. There, in a little private room, he lay down on a couch and went to sleep.

NIGHT OF WAITING

A man waiting for the verdict made a lot of trips across the square. The restaurant there stayed open all night. At a time like this a man can drink a lot of brandy or a lot of Scotch and somehow not feel it at all.

A crowd gathered in the little park adjoining Foley Square facing the courthouse. They were Italian people, men, women, and small children. At three o'clock a squad of policemen came along, frisked the men for guns, told the women to take their babies home to bed. Still the crowd remained, waiting for the fate of the big shots.

The austere dignity of the court had vanished now. There were newspapers here and there scattered about the chamber. Three men sat at the corner of a big table playing pinochle. Somebody's office boy climbed into the witness chair, pretending he was Mildred Harris, while another youngster threw cross-examiners' questions at him. There were roars of laughter in the court. It was undignified, but it was harmless. People can stand just so much tension and suspense and then they have to be a little bit silly.

Up and down out on the courthouse steps by the colonnade of great pillars paced Lorenzo C. Carlino, Ralph Liguori's lawyer, the man who had most flamboyantly denounced the iniquities of the prosecution. He was standing there and walking back and forth talking to anybody who would listen, about how certain the jury was to bring in an acquittal. His voice boomed with assertive confidence. Then, in a pause between his words, could be heard a twittering of birds high in the courthouse portico.

It grew harder and harder to keep awake. A bit of sleep—any kind of uncomfortable, impromptu sleep—was the only thing a man wanted. A man could lie down upon a press table in the courtroom and get forty winks maybe. But hardly had he dozed before there came a rustle and a scurrying in the chamber. The court attendant was fussing around on the judge's bench, straightening it out. Another court attendant went around picking up newspapers. Vaguely it was realized that the judge was coming in and that the jury was coming in.

It was after five o'clock. The gray light of dawn was

creeping through the windows. Somebody went hunting for Dewey. He had to be there.

THE VERDICT

A little after five o'clock Dewey woke up. He arose, rubbed the sleep from his eyes, straightened his necktie and started downstairs.

At the elevator he met a court attendant coming for him.

"The jury is coming in," the officer said.

From somewhere a crowd had appeared, nearly filling the courtroom benches. Judge McCook came to the bench. Somberly the jury filed into its box. From the door at the back of the courtroom, flanked by detectives, filed in the prisoners, led by Charlie Lucky in gray flannel suit, black necktie, and pasty gray-granite face.

The defendants were all present. The lawyers were all present. The tall, gray Court Clerk McNamara rose and polled the names of the jury. All were present.

"Gentlemen of the jury, have you agreed upon a verdict?" intoned the clerk.

"We have," said Edwin Aderer, the foreman.

"How say you, gentlemen of the jury," asked the clerk, "do you find the defendant Luciano guilty or not guilty on Count No. 1?"

"Guilty," said the foreman.

"How say you as to the defendant Luciano? Is he guilty or not guilty on Count No. 2?"

"Guilty."

"Third Count?"

"Guilty."

"Fourth?"

"Guilty."

"Fifth?"

"Guilty."

"Sixth?"

"Guilty."

"Seventh?"

"Guilty."

Luciano stood there facing the jury with his somber mask as the words beat down upon him like a whip. Guilty! Guilty! Guilty! Guilty! Guilty!

Something was happening which never had happened in New York courts before. The verdict of guilty was being pronounced over one man sixty-one separate times; each time a felony; good for years in prison.

"The next defendant, Thomas Pennochio. Gentlemen of the jury, have you agreed upon a verdict? How say you, gentlemen of the jury, do you find the defendant guilty or not guilty on Count No. 1?"

"Guilty."

"Guilty."

"Guilty."

"Guilty."

"Guilty."

The clock at the back of the room was turning. The gray light grew stronger through the windows by the minute. But still the beating refrain went on. Guilty! Guilty! Guilty!

There outside the courtroom came a strange unearthly sound, muffled by the closed doors. The wives of the defendants were still there. Now they were moaning, screaming in the echoing rotunda of the courthouse.

A church around the corner was calling its people to early mass. The bell tolled, Guilty! Guilty! Guilty!

Guilty! Guilty! Guilty! Guilty! Guilty! In thirty minutes, upon nine defendants, the word guilty was pronounced 549 times.

As Dewey sat there in somber triumph, detectives noticed not far behind him a small, dark, sharp-faced man straining forward in his chair. His eyes bulged with a glaze almost of madness. His right hand was held tensely inside his coat. A detective motioned to his partner. Silently and swiftly they moved toward him. They calmly pinned his arms to his body and with quiet compulsion removed him quickly from the room. The man moved without resistance and spoke no word as they stopped outside the courtroom. There a policeman reached firmly inside the man's coat, grabbed his right hand and drew it forth.

In his white-knuckled fist was clenched a silver crucifix.

XXI. SENTENCE

A GLOOMY DAY

"Jack Eller," said Judge McCook, "your flabbiness of body and soul and your associations caused you for a time to take over the business of Nick Montana. You pleaded guilty here but too late to deserve much consideration."

The rain was pouring down; the lights were on in the courtroom to dispel a little of the gloom. Judge McCook sat on the bench like the wrath of Jehovah while before him stood the fat, perspiring Eller, and behind Eller sat the pale row of convicts awaiting sentence. Eller drew a sentence of four to eight years in prison. But out of consideration of their help to the state by turning state's evidence, the other three bookers—Harris, Weiner, and Miller—were let off with terms of only two to four years in prison.

"You are a silly imitator of the racketeers you admire," the judge told Ralph Liguori, Nancy Presser's man, and gave him a term of seven and one-half to fifteen years. Little Abie Wahrman's lawyer pleaded for mercy on grounds of his youth, but the judge gave him a stretch of fifteen to thirty years.

Jimmy Fredericks and Tommy Bull (Pennochio), were in a different category. Each had been convicted of a felony for the third time. It was mandatory that they be given sentences not less than the longest term nor more than twice the longest term prescribed for a first conviction for their offenses. They drew twenty-five years apiece.

With Little Davie Betillo the judge was tough, even though he was a first offender so far as felony convictions went.

"As Luciano's chief and most ruthless aid, without record of legitimate occupation, you are regarded by observers as the most dangerous of the defendants, except one; an unprincipled and aggressive egoist," said Justice McCook to Little Davie. "The prosecutor points out that four years of your life remain unaccounted for in the probation report, which roughly correspond to the period when, I believe, you were in Chicago. I am therefore unable to regard as important to my problem with you, the absence of a prior conviction."

On various counts of the indictment Justice McCook gave Little Davie three sentences to run consecutively, adding up to a term of from twenty-five to forty years.

Luciano, called to the bar, faced something worse.

"What have you got to say why judgment should not be pronounced against you according to law?" intoned the court clerk.

"Your Honor," said Luciano, "I have nothing to say outside of—I want to say it again—that I am innocent."

"An intelligent, courageous, and discriminating jury have found you guilty of heading the conspiracy or combination to commit these crimes. It operated widely in New York and extended into neighboring counties," said the Court to Luciano.

"This makes you responsible in law and morals for every foul and cruel deed with accompanying elements of extortion performed by the band of co-defendants. I am not here to reproach you, but, since there appears no excuse for your conduct nor hope for your rehabilitation, to administer adequate punishment."

He thereupon pronounced upon Luciano a sentence to serve from thirty to fifty years.

Under the New York law, Luciano, if he behaves himself in prison, will be due to be considered for parole at the expiration of twenty years, but not sooner.

The Court told the defendants he was convinced by the evidence at the trial and information since received that they would be responsible for any injury which the People's witnesses might thereafter suffer by reason of their testimony. He told them that if any witness for the People should be injured or harassed, the Court would request the Parole Board to keep the prisoners for their maximum sentence.

THE LUCIANO SENTENCE

The severity of Luciano's sentence was plainly intended to be a warning to other racketeers. In consideration of Lucky's power and abilities, it was also plainly intended as a means of protecting society against the boss gangster's talents. Luciano got his sentence, not because he was more guilty or more despicable than his colleagues in the dock, but because he was more dangerous.

There is probably no better example of the modern tendency of the courts to make the sentence fit the criminal rather than to make the punishment fit the crime of which he has been convicted.

So far as strict construction of the law goes, every madam, booker, and every other member of the conspiracy was equally guilty with Charlie Lucky of the crime—compulsory prostitution—of which they had been convicted. But the madams, even some of the assistant bookers, who testified, were turned loose.

The Luciano prosecution was not an attempt to abolish prostitution or even to drive it from the city, for that is a social rather than a criminal problem. The prosecution was the means of putting some big gangsters out of business.

There is plainly a similarity between the long sentence of Luciano and the sentence which was meted out to Al Capone, who got the maximum on his conviction for income tax violation, a sentence much more severe than what is ordinarily meted out to tax evaders.

There is a lot of confusion in the public mind and also in the theory of law in such matters. The old idea was, of course, that punishment should always fit the crime and in the days when that idea held full sway, the usual punishment was hanging. It is basic in our law, of course, that a defendant may be convicted only of specific crimes. He cannot be convicted of being a bad man, of being a racketeer, or of being a menace to society. But to the extent that penalties are provided for the crimes of which a man has been convicted, the years of his liberty are forfeited to the State.

Elasticity enters the law when the time for sentence arrives. At that point a man's life is truly at the mercy of a judge. The judge may turn him loose on probation and temper justice with mercy. The judge may also hold him for a long term, tempering justice with severity. It is not a pretty thought when one imagines one's self facing a court. It is one of the reasons why we need to have wise judges.

Someday, perhaps, judges will no longer wield such power, and the power will be put in other hands. There is a tendency that way. In some states now the duration of a prisoner's confinement is dependent entirely on the judgment of the

Parole Board. Parole Boards are not supposed to be chosen for political reasons or learning in the law, as judges usually are, but they are supposed to be experts in human personality, human conduct. As a matter of fact, we have come to the point where we have a few Parole Boards in this country which are not political. Perhaps someday we shall also come to that stage of scientific wisdom in which personalities may be thoroughly analyzed, and Parole Boards may know rather than guess which men are dangerous. In the present state of human fallibility, many of our judges and many of our Parole Boards are doing a conscientious and reasonably successful job in distinguishing between dangerous criminals and those who may be given another chance without excessive danger to society.

XXII. INNOCENTS ABROAD

COMMENCEMENT

The trial was over. Lucky had gone to prison. The prosecution still had on its hands some seventy women whom it had snatched away from lives of vice, and nearly all of whom, with a great show of sincerity, were expressing the desire to go forth and sin no more. The spirit of repentance and reform is contagious, and the House of Detention was alive with good intentions.

It was really a serious problem what to do with them. Dewey and his men did not want just to turn the girls loose on the streets, for in the course of five months they had become very good friends of these silly, weak, unsubstantial girls.

But these were not the only circumstances. Throughout the trial the defense had neglected no opportunity to smear the prosecutors with insinuations. Obviously efforts would be made by the underworld to make the girls recant their testimony and persuade them to make scurrilous charges against their recent guardians. When a lawyer is dealing with this type of witness he can't be too careful.

Justice McCook undertook to handle both aspects of the situation. Before the girls were turned loose he had them brought in before him, one by one, put them under oath, and asked each of them whether she wanted to recant her testimony; whether she had any charges to make about being improperly treated. The girls all stood by their stories and

were fulsome in their denials of all insinuations that anything scandalous or improper had occurred during their
incarceration.

Justice McCook talked to each of them about her future,
and in adjoining rooms he had gathered social service workers from agencies interested in this type of girl. He encouraged each of the girls to accept the assistance and advice of
the appropriate religious or welfare group. Most of the girls
did this.

The day the girls were released and given their accumulated witness fees resembled nothing so much as graduation
day at a girls' seminary. Some of them, we may be sure, went
forth with sober resolve to lead new lives henceforth, and set
about getting jobs for themselves. A good many of the others went straight across the street to the nearest bar, got
themselves thoroughly ginned up and then went down to the
Woolworth Building to try to get the boys to go out on a
party. It was a tough job to get rid of them.

What has become of all the girls now nobody knows. It
would be a pleasure to report that they all turned over a new
leaf and became virtuous, useful members of the community.
Some of them may have succeeded in permanently reshaping
their lives, but not very many.

Bennie Spiller probably has as good information as anybody on what became of them.

After the trial Bennie, the combination's shylock, made
his peace with the prosecutor's office. During the trial Bennie had made overtures to try to make a deal. He did that
after Tommy Bull tipped him off that his hero, Little Davie,
had him marked for slaughter. He had been deterred from
going through with it when Davie got wind of his intention.

Bennie was kept in jail in New York City for two years

and finally was given a suspended sentence by Justice Mc-Cook. Before going west to start a new life in a new community, Bennie took a walk around town to see some of his old acquaintances.

"You know," said Bennie, "the girls are practically all back in the business. But they got wise to themselves. They are all madams now."

FEAR

The girls who had directly testified against Charlie Lucky had marked themselves out for possible revenge. They presented a special problem. All of them had been given repeated assurances of protection and of assistance in rehabilitating themselves.

When Nancy Presser and Thelma Jordan were brought in before Justice McCook to discuss the matter of their release, they were not at all in a hurry to be turned loose. They were being kept at the time under police guard in the Fifth Avenue Hotel.

"What are your plans, Nancy?" asked the judge.

"I don't know what I am going to do. I am going to try to get a position with dresses or something like that," said Nancy.

The judge suggested to Nancy that she talk things over with a priest, since she was a Catholic. She thought it might be a good idea.

"Are you anxious to get discharged or don't you care?" asked the judge.

"Well, there is one thing," said Nancy. "I am afraid."

"And the reason you don't seek immediate discharge is before you get discharged you want some arrangements made that will protect your safety?"

"That is it."

"And if that can be combined with getting you a job, that will be just what you want, is that it?"

"Yes," said Nancy.

And she agreed that it would be a good idea for her to talk with the lady from the Catholic Charities.

"All right," said the judge, "then I will say good-by to you, Nancy, and one of these days I will be signing your discharge. You have been of great service to the State and if you have nothing on your conscience I hope you will get back into a decent way of living. Do you want to?"

"I certainly do," said Nancy. "I want to get out of it."

One reason why Nancy was afraid was that a few days before this she and Thelma Jordan had received a telephone call from Red-haired Mary Morris, Thelma's former roommate. Red-haired Mary was the girl friend of Johnnie Roberts, a gunman who had been Ralph Liguori's partner, and Mary said she had been told that as soon as they were turned loose Nancy and Thelma were going to be knocked off.

The girls had reason to be scared. They said they would not be safe anywhere in America because Lucky's organization went everywhere.

Harry Cole talked it over with Dewey and got permission to get together some private funds to send the two girls to Europe until things cooled off. After all, he had persuaded them to stick their necks out, and he had to stand by them.

TOURISTS

Nancy and Thelma were shipped off to Europe on the S.S. *Samaria* about the middle of July. It is really a shame that we cannot give a play-by-play report of the two girls' travels.

Each of them had her ticket and $200 cash, from funds privately contributed. They landed in England and they went to stay at the Hands Crescent Hotel at Knightsbridge and at the end of five days had spent $70 apiece. Then they moved over to the Regent Palace Hotel in Piccadilly Circus where they had been supposed to stay. It was cheaper there. But in a few weeks they were broke.

Nancy and Thelma had decided that they would reform. They were pretty near on the water wagon. Of course, they encountered men. One Englishman, when they were broke, lent them £7, or $35. But then they were very much disappointed in him. They even suspected he was trying to take advantage of two young girls in an improper way and didn't appreciate how virtuous they were. After that they simply refused even to talk to him, except on the telephone.

They cabled for more money and Cole sent them some. But soon they were cabling for more.

About the middle of September Cole and Dewey decided that this thing might be getting a little bit out of hand. They cabled for the girls to come home; bought them tourist class tickets on the *Berengaria*.

Nancy was very mad about that. It was very funny, she said; they had been sent to Europe first class and now they were going back tourist class. They had been darlings before, said Nancy, but now—just look at how it was.

Nancy had been having a good time in England. She wrote a letter to her parents before she started home:

"I had a nice Birth day In Eng. received perfume. French by the way. I like It very much a few dozens of flowers and a nice birth day party plenty of wine and a few more gifts.

"Will tell you all about It when I see you and I hope It's soon.

"Yesterday I went to the Windsor Castle. Saw all the old Buildings Where Henry the 8th lived and where the new King and his mother Queen Mary lives and all the Royalty. Its very old and very beautiful have more pictures will show you when I come home.

"P.S. I hope you like these pictures of the Castle."

JOB HUNTING

Nancy and Thelma were flat broke when they got back to New York early in October. They took a taxicab to the Woolworth Building and Thelma sat in it while Nancy went upstairs and got somebody to come down and pay the fare. Harry Cole gave them $10 and they went out and got a room in a hotel. They stayed in the Belleclaire Hotel on Broadway and then at the Monterey and every day they went downtown and told Harry Cole they were broke again and needed money to eat.

These girls didn't have much sense about money. He wouldn't give them more than $10 at a time because he knew it would go very fast. But even so, it was his own money he was giving them and he didn't feel like undertaking the responsibility.

The girls said that they really wanted to get jobs and go to work. As a matter of fact, they seemed to be quite changed creatures from those who had been arrested months before. But plainly, the financial help had to stop. And plainly, something more had to be done to help these girls get their new start in life.

Dewey got in touch with James Madison Blackwell, treasurer and attorney to a church mission society, an organization specializing in assisting young women who are in trouble. Ordinarily it steers clear of prostitutes, but in this case it made an exception.

The girls had a long talk with Harriet P. Scott, case supervisor.

"Both girls stated to me that they were in great terror of gang reprisals as a result of their testimony given in the Luciano trial," recalled Miss Scott later. "Both said they were in fear of death or worse than that—torture, which they said they had seen demonstrated on other girls and they said that if they were caught by the gang and an attempt made to make them sign anything, they felt they would recant the testimony which they had given at the trial rather than undergo what they had seen other girls suffer. Both further stated that they had seen men whom they recognized as belonging to the gang hanging around their hotel, and that they feared bodily injury and murder if they did not recant. They reiterated that if they should fall into the hands of the old gang with whom they had previously associated, they would give in and sign anything lest they suffer the fate of other girls."

"Believe me, I'd sign anything if I was tortured," said Thelma to Marguerite Marsh, executive secretary of the mission.

The mission people sent the girls up to Kingston for a few days. It was hard to find a place to send the girls because, as they said, the racketeers had connections everywhere. Finally they agreed on Cincinnati and the girls went there.

The girls stayed in Cincinnati about a week, ran up a hotel bill, but didn't find any job which seemed to suit them. The mission people gave the girls day-coach tickets on the railroad back to New York. Doubtless Nancy didn't like that at all. Day-coach riding had never been her style.

When they got back they told Miss Scott that since they were in fear wherever they were sent, they believed New York City would be as safe as any place, especially since the cops in New York knew about them and probably would be more willing to protect them than the police elsewhere in case they needed protection.

Soon after this Red-haired Mary and Herman Liguori, brother of Ralph, got hold of the girls and started to talk to them. Dewey's office saw no more of them.

XXIII. WESTWARD HO!

A BID FROM HOLLYWOOD

Out of all the women in the Luciano case it seemed as if Cokey Flo Brown and Mildred Harris had the best chance to retrieve their lives. They had more brains than most of the other women.

After the trial Warner Brothers' motion picture firm was much interested in trying to get film material out of the Luciano trial. Dewey would not have anything to do with exploiting the case itself, but here seemed to be an opportunity for Flo and Mildred to make a start and an honest living. Out of their experiences they could probably supply material for gangster pictures. They could be expert advisers.

Warner Brothers had a tie-up with *Liberty* magazine and out of this grew an arrangement whereby *Liberty* undertook to get material out of these girls. Edward Doherty, a staff writer, was assigned to interview them and ghost some stories for them.

Flo and Mildred went to live together at New Rochelle and as an advance against the price of whatever might be purchased from them *Liberty* paid them $50 a week apiece for ten weeks. Out of this Doherty got material for a series of "Underworld Nights" that were printed in *Liberty* and there was hope that the movies might buy rights to the material.

FEAR ON THE STREETS

On July 16, the day after Mildred had dispensed with her police bodyguard, she went to the Dewey office and reported an experience. She said that she had been to the Paramount Theater that afternoon and on coming out had encountered one of Charlie Lucky's brothers. Leo or Tony his name was. He said he wanted to talk to her, Mildred reported, and took her into the Astor Hotel bar.

"He said his brother was not sore at me for what I had done but that they were working on the appeal for him, and they were going to see all the witnesses and get them to make statements that what they had said was untrue, and he asked me if I would make such a statement, and I said I couldn't very well do that," reported Mildred.

"I was afraid to say no. I was in a queer position there. I told him I was leaving town; I was going out to Chicago for a couple of months and I would think it over. He said if I decided in their favor I should get in touch with Chappie. He said they would make it worth my while.

"I was frightened. After all, it is the first time I have been on Broadway alone. You know what I mean. And to run into somebody like that—I didn't know whether it was just a stall, whether it was just cover to keep me sitting there to show me to somebody or what it was. You know what I mean."

"You mean you don't know whether you were being fingered or pointed out to somebody?"

"Yes," said Mildred. "After all, I was scared. I had been walking around with protection so long, it is hard to be out on my own."

"Did you then say good-by to him?"

"Yes. I got up, jumped into a taxi and I must have run around half New York looking behind me," said Mildred.

"Was all of the testimony you gave at the trial true?"

"Yes," said Mildred.

And after a stenographer had typed up what she had said, Mildred signed and swore to it.

ESCAPE

On October 9, there appeared in the New York *Daily News* a story under the headline: "100 GRAND AT WORK FOR LUCKY."

The story related that a campaign was on to supply witnesses in the Lucky case with narcotics in order to get them to recant their testimony.

Barent Ten Eyck showed this to Cokey Flo, with whom he was still in touch, and got her to make a new sworn statement still asserting that the testimony she had given at the trial was true. It is clear now that during this period investigators for Luciano were in touch with Cokey Flo and Mildred.

Soon after this, *Liberty* magazine paid the girls off with a final payment of $500 apiece. Flo also had some money from the bail bond she had forfeited the winter before. Ten Eyck had persuaded the court to return this money to her.

Flo bought herself a car and one night suddenly put her cat and Mildred in it and started driving West. As she later put it, they "sneaked out of New York like thieves in the night."

Flo wrote to Ten Eyck from the Arlington Hotel at Hot Springs:

"We figured we would stop over for a day or two and look over the place that put up such a good fight for our friend

Charlie. This was the beginning of the end for him. Ha! Ha! on him, eh?

"Mildred promised me faithfully that she wouldn't try to get in touch with Pete or anybody else back east. So I told her if I ever caught her sneaking a word to him or receiving word from him or anyone else I would throw her out of the car and if we were settled anywhere she would have to get out. She promised so we will see what is what.

"Please don't tell anyone where we are even though we aren't going to stay here as we don't want anyone to know the direction we are going in. The last few days we were in New York we told everyone we were going to New Orleans.

"How is Livvy? Give him our best regards. Give Mr. Hogan our best also tell him we hope he has a happy honeymoon. Regards to Sol Gelb and everyone else. Regards to Mr. Dewey too."

Flo, using the name of Gloria Moore, and Mildred, using the name Norma Gordon, went to Pomona, California, and there Flo bought a filling station. They liked California a lot and Flo picked and ate so many oranges as she passed the groves that she said oranges were practically coming out of her ears.

Ten Eyck wrote Flo that her former maid, Addie, wanted to send Flo her fur coat. Flo warned him not to give Addie her address:

"I think her wanting to give me my coat is just a 'bluff,' because she had all the time in the world, to give it to me, when I was in N. Y. They tried to contact me through her once before, you know. And if Dorothy Russell calls to find out where I am don't tell her either, because they talked to her too, I found out. I knew that before I left N. Y. She must of got hold of Addie, and they must of cooked up this

idea of getting my address, because Dorothy knew I used to
trust Addie to the limit. But I don't trust anyone now.

"It certainly is wonderful news, about them buying the
title at least. It would mean an awful lot to us. We are going
along fine. I am enclosing my business card. I had them
printed, as I go around soliciting business. But I solicit legit
business now! How do you like my card? The reason I named
the station 'The Rooster,' is because the Hot Dog Stand
next to us is a building in the shape of a huge hen, a chicken.
So we have a rooster painted on our station, and they call
their place 'The White Hen,' we call ours, 'The Rooster,'
see? Cute?

"Please tell Doherty and Mr. Oursler, we thank them very
much for being so good and kind, about splitting the money.
We appreciate it very much. We sure could use it. We could
buy a little more stock, and maybe buy out the 'White Hen.'
Everyone says we are doing fine for a beginning. We are
selling more gas, already, than the other two stations near
us. And they have been there a long time. Besides, everyone
tells us, this is the very slowest time of the year. After the
middle of Feb. we should do a lot better. It's a hard struggle,
believe me. It's no bed of roses. But we don't care. We are
willing to work hard. And we are very happy too. It's a new
life, and for all the hard work and everything, I wouldn't
give it up, to go back to the old way of living. No sir! Never!
I like this. We are poor, but we like the work, and are in the
open air, its healthy, and work never killed anyone. You
should see us giving service to a car! Oh, boy! Mil gives the
gas, while I pull up the hood of the car and measure to see if
they need oil. Then I look at the water. Then we clean their
windshield. Naturally, a lot of people are surprised to see

two girls run a gas station. So we give them the line, about how we just started, and we want to make a go of it, and we would appreciate it, if they would buy their gas from us, and help us to get started. We have made a lot of steady customers, already, really!

"Gee, I sure wish you could see our place. We keep it nice and clean too. I rake the gravel every morning. It makes my back feel like its broken in two, but it makes the place look very neat. You sure would be proud of us, if you saw the place. Gee, its getting late. I have to get up at five o'clock, to open up.

"And as far as you are concerned, Mr. Ten Eyck, I can never thank you enough, for what you have done for me. I'll probably never be in a position to repay you, but I'll always think of you, and pray for all good things to come to you and yours. Thats all I can say, and it comes from the bottom of my heart. Some day you'll feel real proud of us, I know, because we are going to make good, and make good in a big way too.

"Well, I hope to get the money soon, so we can take over the 'White Hen,' Oh boy, I haven't been drunk since I've been out here, haven't had time, but if we get the place next door, I'll have to celebrate!

"Yours as ever,

"F. B."

MYSTERIOUS STRANGERS

Three days before Christmas Ten Eyck received a telegram from Mildred Harris which she had sent collect in the late evening of December 21. It said:

AM COMPLETELY WITHOUT FUNDS HAD NO MONEY TO INVEST WITH FLO SO THE ARRANGEMENT IS NOT WORKING OUT SO WELL TRY TO GET MONEY FROM

MOVIE COMPANY AT ONCE MUST HAVE HELP AT ONCE
LETTER FOLLOWS

NORMA GORDON
WHITES AUTO CAMP

Ten Eyck was naturally upset by this. He wrote Mildred a non-committal letter asking her for further information and giving her the discouraging news that a motion picture company which had been considering parts of the *Liberty* articles had backed out of the deal. No more money was in sight.

He wrote to Flo also, asking her what the trouble was and hoping she and Mildred would get along all right.

The day after Christmas he received an apologetic letter from Mildred written two days after her telegram:

"You know doubt think I have a lot of nerve to send a collect telegram to the office but I am desperate. I have know one in the world to turn to. Of course I haven't any right to ask you for help but I don't know what to do.

"I am a stranger in a strange land. Don't know a soul out here. I had hoped that we could stick together. I know she is worried to. She put nearly all her money in this place but of course it is a slow turn over. It takes time to build up.

"I wish you would write to her. She takes your advice. Tell her that we should stick together. To give me a chance to pay her by hard work. I am sure a word from you would go a long way.

"I am worried to death about those people to. You are allowed to have a gun out here in your home and your place of business. So today she said she was going to buy one."

In the same mail Ten Eyck received a letter from Flo which indicated why she was going to get herself a gun. She wrote:

"Pomona, Calif.
"Dec. 23, 1936

"My dear Friend Mr. Ten Eyck:

"Well in a couple of days it will be Christmas, but it sure doesn't seem like it out here. It seems more like the Fourth of July, the sun is so hot.

"I hope you have a very Merry Christmas, and a Happy New Year!

"And now, for the real reason of this letter.

"Did you or anyone in the office send anyone out here to investigate us? I don't think it was you, on account of the way they are going about it. Someone in your office must have given them my address. Whoever receives your mail, or whoever mails your letters. There is a leak somewhere. Here is the whole thing, and you can figure it out, yourself.

"This morning a truck driver came over from the White Hen, the Hamburger stand next door and talked to Mildred. I was at home sorting out our dirty underwear we are going to wash today. He said to her, 'Do you have another girl for a partner here?' Mil answered, 'Yes, I do, why?' He said, 'Well, I didn't know whether to tell you this or not. I was afraid you might tell me to mind my own business, but then I didn't want to see two women alone out here get into any trouble, if I could be of any help.'

"Norma said, 'Why, what are you talking about, what do you mean?' So he explained, saying, 'I was in a gas station, a Texaco gas station further down, and I heard two men talking. One was a guy from out of town, he must of been from out of town, because he had a white license plate on his car. (Calif. license plates are orange, with black numbers.) He was talking to the attendant of the station. He said to him, do you know a couple of girls that have a Service Station here? One goes by the name of Gloria Moore, the other one, I don't know what name she goes by. They came out here a short time ago from back East, and they are trying to go straight and I was sent out here to check up on them. I'm on my way to the Police Station now.'

"The attendant answered that he didn't know who he meant. He didn't know the name, or the people.

" 'So when I heard that,' the driver said, 'I thought I'd come over and tell you girls. I didn't know whether you did anything or not, but I figured I'd better warn you.'

"Mildred thanked him, and told him, the man couldn't mean us, as we had done nothing wrong in our lives to be going straight, for.

"This afternoon, when Mildred went home, the landlord told her there was a call from the Western Union for Miss Gordon. So Mildred called the Western Union and they said there was no telegram for her, and they had not called. No one could have sent us a wire, or even a letter to where we live, because we have given no one that address, or phone number. We don't even know the address or phone number of where we live, ourselves! Of course there are a few people in the town that know where we live, but no one, anywhere else. They know we live in Whites Auto Camp, thats all.

"Please check up on your end, and let me know if anyone in the office looks over, or can look over, the envelopes, of your mail, before its laid on your desk. A couple of times I put the return address on. And I used the name Gloria Moore, back east, and G. Moore was on my return address on the letters to you. Could any of the cops around the office, of seen that G. Moore on the back of the envelope, in the mornings, before you got the mail. I think Daley at the desk sorts out mail, doesn't he? Maybe, while he was sorting out the mail at his desk in the hall, someone could watch over his shoulder and see the G. Moore, Pomona, Calif. See what I mean?

"Yours,

"F. B.

"P.S.

"I'm sure he didn't go to the police station, if he did, he wouldn't have had to fish around, asking people. Because this is a small town, all the cops know us. They stop in and say Hello, lots of times."

Long later it was revealed that at 1:10 A.M. on December 22, three hours after she had sent her telegram to Ten Eyck, Mildred had sent another telegram. It read:

```
                              1936 DEC 22 AM 1 10
SB387 21 PM 3 EXTRA XC—POMONA CALIF 21
  JOE WEINTRAUB—
539 ROCKAWAY PARKWAY BROOKLYN NY—WIRE DUNNS
ADDRESS AT ONCE ANXIOUS TO GET IN TOUCH WITH
HIM ALSO JEAN ERWINS ADDRESS LETTER FOLLOWS—
                        NORMA GORDON
                        WHITES AUTO CAMP
```

Jo Jo Weintraub, who had been given immunity as a witness in the Luciano case when he testified about his activities as Pete Harris's assistant, had tried all summer to get a job, without success. In the autumn he had been taken on to assist in digging up material for Luciano's appeal. He had seen Mildred before she left New York. Dunn was the investigator for whom he was working.

The mysterious men who inquired about the two girls had turned up in Pomona the day after Mildred had sent her telegram to Jo Jo.

After the letters written by the girls that day, Ten Eyck did not hear from them any more. The underworld had caught up to them.

XXIV. APPEAL

REPUDIATION

One day in the middle of March, 1937, as Dewey was approaching the end of the trial of the restaurant racketeers, startling news was brought to him. Luciano had filed a motion for a new trial, backed up with affidavits from three of Dewey's star witnesses—Nancy Presser, Mildred Harris, and Cokey Flo Brown—in which they repudiated their testimony.

Back with their old associates in the underworld, the girls had struck a blow at the Luciano case which well might smash it down. Nancy Presser said that everything she had told was false.

"I did not know, and except for a couple of times that I saw the defendant Lucky from a distance in Dave's Blue Room, I have never seen the defendant, Charles Luciano," said Nancy.

Then she went on to deny everything in detail that she had said about him. She said she had never been to bed with Lucky. She said that during the recess of the trial she had been told that Lucky was diseased and that was how she came to know it and tell about it.

Judging from Nancy Presser's affidavit, she had spent most of her time in the Dewey office drinking liquor and listening to the plea, "We have got to have Charlie." She said that she had been threatened with prosecution on narcotics charges and for forging Gashouse Lil's check if she did not testify the way they desired. Of course, it had been Nancy who had told them about the narcotics and the forgery herself, after she had opened up and started talking; and there had never been any good narcotic case against her anyway. But the way she said it in her affidavit, it was a pretty violent blow at the men who had questioned her.

Mildred Harris did not go whole hog in her repudiation. In her first statement to Luciano's lawyers, she had merely withdrawn a number of points in her testimony so that in a legalistic sense it did not apply to the specific charges on which Luciano was being tried. As a matter of fact, she added a few details about her acquaintance with Luciano. But that statement had not been good enough and later she had made another, repudiating her testimony more thoroughly.

Cokey Flo Brown said that her testimony about Luciano had been entirely made up; that she had never known Luciano. She said that all the things she had told were put together out of stories which Jimmy Fredericks had told her about the prostitution racket and she had merely put Charlie Lucky into the stories in hope of getting herself out of trouble.

The repudiations did not come entirely without anticipation. The prosecutors had known that these girls would be under pressure to recant as soon as they were away from the immediate protection of the police and as soon as economic pressure was on them. Time and again the girls had made new statements and sworn to them, reiterating their testimony. Time and again they had told of their fears and threats of violence.

DISCOVERIES

It was a day or so after the appeal had been presented before anybody did anything about it. Dewey was going on with his restaurant racket trial which kept him busy night and day. Momentarily the men in the Dewey office were stunned. Then the assistants in the Luciano case, realizing that their characters had been attacked, went into action. They began again to collect affidavits, analyzing the facts set forth in the repudiations. Their answer was finally set forth in 382 printed pages, plus photostatic exhibits.

The internal evidence in Nancy's affidavit, such as the matters about the narcotics and forgery, clearly showed that it was loaded with perjury. The whole story of Flo's and Mildred's trip westward, told in their letters, did much to belie their present assertions. Ten Eyck dug out his original hasty notes on Cokey Flo's first interview to refute her present claim that the story had been dragged out of her over a period of a whole week. The inside story of the investigation was set forth in detail in the Dewey office's answer.

Jo Jo Weintraub, a State's witness who had been set free, and who had hunted all summer for a job, now bobbed up in the story again and again. It became clear that Jo Jo had gone to work for Luciano's lawyers in the autumn and had done the spade work of investigation and rounding up the witnesses for the former G-Men and lawyers who had finally obtained affidavits for appeal.

On February 25, 1937, it developed, Jo Jo had taken Mildred and Cokey Flo to Town's Hospital at 293 Central Park West, a sanitarium for drug addicts, and had paid their way there for a two weeks' cure. This was the master blow of counter-offensive against the recanting affidavits.

The repudiating statements made under oath by Mildred and Flo showed that under the guiding attention of Luciano's lawyers, they had both denied that they were taking narcotics at that time. It was clear now that when they went back on their stories they had been under the influence of drugs. A few days after making these recanting statements, they had entered the sanitarium. Immediately after leaving the sanitarium where they had taken the cure, they had gone downtown and made the affidavits which were to be presented to the court.

"A fraud upon the court!" cried Dewey before Judge McCook. He presented facts to support his charge.

The argument on the motion for a new trial was not entirely one-sided. Nancy Presser had been cross-examined during the trial about whether she had not been promised a trip to Europe. She had denied it and Dewey had ridiculed the idea. It developed now that she had been on a trip to Europe. Mildred Harris had, for some reason, denied the existence of her immunity letter and now it was produced. Yet in instance after instance, Dewey was able to produce evidence and affidavits from reputable persons contradicting or showing the untruth of assertions made in the recanting statements. He was able to support his charge that "the moving papers reek with perjury."

Luciano's lawyer, Moe Polakoff, insisted that he should be permitted to bring the girls in court again and put them on the stand to give a new line of testimony. Justice McCook denied that request and refused the motion for a new trial.

THE FINAL WORD

After reading the 7,000-page record, the five justices of the Appellate Division of the Supreme Court unanimously upheld Judge McCook's decision. The nine judges of the Court of Appeals, with one dissenting vote, also upheld the Luciano conviction. And the Supreme Court of the United States later refused to hear an appeal.

With that, the Luciano case was over. The fine points of argument as to truth, perjury, points of law, the errors which may or may not have been committed in the trial, could be argued and discussed through another volume. But it would serve no purpose. The courts have spoken.

Charlie Lucky, as this is written, has served hardly one-tenth of the absolute minimum his sentence provides. He will be in Dannemora a long time more. It is ironic when you think of it—the power he held, the gaudy extent of the criminal world—and there he is locked up for a blowsy, cheap, second-rate racket that his underling, Little Davie, started.

People told Lucky that Little Davie was no good. People told Lucky that Davie ought to be knocked off and tried to get the O.K. to do it. But Lucky knew him when he was a kid.